INTELLIGENT INFORMATION SYSTEMS:
Progress and Prospects

ELLIS HORWOOD SERIES IN ARTIFICIAL INTELLIGENCE

Series Editor: Professor JOHN CAMPBELL, Department of Computer Science, University College London

INTELLIGENT INFORMATION SYSTEMS:
Progress and Prospects

Editor:
R. DAVIES, B.Sc., ALA
The University Library, University of Exeter

ELLIS HORWOOD LIMITED
Publishers · Chichester

Halsted Press: a division of
JOHN WILEY & SONS
New York · Chichester · Brisbane · Toronto

First published in 1986 by
ELLIS HORWOOD LIMITED
Market Cross House, Cooper Street,
Chichester, West Sussex, PO19 1EB, England
The publisher's colophon is reproduced from James Gillison's drawing of the ancient Market Cross, Chichester.

Distributors:

Australia and New Zealand:
JACARANDA WILEY LIMITED
GPO Box 859, Brisbane, Queensland 4001, Australia

Canada:
JOHN WILEY & SONS CANADA LIMITED
22 Worcester Road, Rexdale, Ontario, Canada

Europe and Africa:
JOHN WILEY & SONS LIMITED
Baffins Lane, Chichester, West Sussex, England

North and South America and the rest of the world:
Halsted Press: a division of
JOHN WILEY & SONS
605 Third Avenue, New York, NY 10158, USA

Contents

Preface

> Some books are to be tasted, others to be swallowed, and some few to
> be chewed and digested.
>
> (Francis Bacon, Of studies)

Bacon's' aphorism came to mind when I was wondering how to explain to
the somewhat heterogeneous readership for whom this book is intended, the
best way of studying it. The book is intended to indicate to librarians and
information scientists why and how the techniques of artificial intelligence
and cognitive science are, or will be, relevant to their activities. At the same
time, it is hoped that computer scientists, particularly those with an interest
in the application of AI, will gain an appreciation of the scope for the
exercise of their talents in the library and information science field.

   The diet is not a bland one, and consequently librarians and computer
scientists will not find every morsel equally delectable. Nevertheless, if they
apply Bacon's approach to the parts of the different chapters, both groups
should find plenty of intellectural sustenance worth chewing upon, and
could simply taste or swallow those items requiring a fair level of prior
technical knowledge of the other discipline. In that way, they will learn to
recognise the flavour of topics they may return to later.

   The organization of the book is based on more of a heuristic than a
taxonomic principle. Some of the chapters could belong to more than one
section. In particular, the division between the first two parts is fairly
arbitrary though it has its pedagogic advantages. Information storage and
retrieval are two sides of the same coin, but it is difficult to view both sides
simultaneously. Therefore storage (database creation and cataloquing) is
considered first, followed by retrieval. Referral is based on information
retrieval, but may be greatly facilitated by taking into account factors which
are often neglected in the practice and study of retrieval, e.g. the individu-
ality of users. This leads on naturally to the discussion of cognitive science,
an area likely to have a decisive impact on the future of information science.
To round off the book, the concluding chapter puts current aspirations into
historical perspective, thereby serving as a remainder that the changes now
taking place should be of concern to humanists as well as technologists.

   Finally, I must express my thanks to certain individuals. Ajit Narayanan
of the Department of Computer Science, Exeter University, helped to get
me involved in this field in connection with a cataloguing project carried out

by Brian James. Masoud Yazdani, of the same department, suggested that a book on AI and librarianship/information science was needed. The advice of Professor John Campbell of the Department of Computer Science, University College London, proved invaluable. Above all, I learnt a lot from the authors of the different chapters and I hope readers will do so too.

University Library, Exeter   Roy Davies
April 1986

ACKNOWLEDGEMENT

Chapter 7 by Elaine Rich originally appeared in the *International Journal of Man–Machine Studies*, 1983, vol. 18, pp. 199–214, and is reprinted here by permission of Academic Press Inc. (London) Ltd.

Introduction: Artificial intelligence and librarianship

It is a commonplace to suggest that the nations of the world are moving, at varying rates, into the era of the Information Society. This is a more accurate term than the designation 'post-industrial' which is sometimes used. Agriculture is as essential to us all now as it was before the dawn of the industrial era, and likewise, industry will still be vital in the coming era even if it employs a declining proportion of the population. Among the first and foremost of those to study the production and distribution of knowledge from an economic point of view was Fritz Machlup (1962), who proposed the following taxonomy:

(1) Practical knowledge
  (a) professional knowledge
  (b) business knowledge
  (c) workman's knowledge
  (d) political knowledge
  (e) household knowledge
  (f) other practical knowledge
(2) Intellectual knowledge
(3) Small-talk and pastime knowledge
(4) Spiritual knowledge
(5) Unwanted knowledge (outside the individual's interests, usually accidentally acquired and aimlessly retained).

Much information is of a fleeting, ephemeral nature, but some is relatively long-lived and augments mankind's stock of knowledge. Anything accelerating the growth of this stock of knowledge, in categories 1, 2 and 4 at least, should be regarded as beneficial but all too often the information explosion is regarded as a problem. This was so even in Old Testament times, as shown by the well-known complaint in Ecclesiastes (chapter 12, verse 12): 'of making many books there is no end; and much study is a weariness of the flesh.' In Roman times similar sentiments were expressed by Cicero (Tusculan Disputations II, ii, 6) who laid the blame squarely on the Greeks:

> But once these studies [of philosophy] are transferred to ourselves we shall have no need even of Greek libraries, in which there is an endless number of books due to the crowd of writers; for the same things are said by many since the day they crammed the world with books: and things will be the same here too if a larger stream of writers sets towards these studies.

Today the scale of the problem is vastly greater, but our ability to cope has also grown. For this, use of computers is increasingly responsible. Koenig (1982) has described this trend as an 'information controllability explosion', as the rate of growth in the capacity to store information easily outstrips the rate at which the number of publications is increasing. Nevertheless, if it became possible to store the entire contents of the Library of Congress on an optical disc we would have succeeded merely in making a bigger, more intricate maze in which to lose our way. The greater our ability to store information the more attention must be paid to the problems of organizing it. Many people are reluctant to venture into the relatively small mazes created by designers of existing information systems (Cooper 1978). This behavioural phenomenon is so widespread that it has been described as a law by Mooers (1960). Michie too has drawn attention to this problem and has prescribed a remedy:

> He [the scientist] will go to enormous lengths to get the information out of a 'question-answering machine made of meat', to paraphrase Minsky, rather than be driven to read it up for himself. What is more he is right. The scientist, like everybody else, is busy. He insists on his information being as much as possible *pre-digested*. The difficulty and inconvenience of retrieval from the raw state is such that scientists go out of their way to avoid it. In the long run the only technology which can break that barrier is artificial intelligence, the artificial librarian's assistant. The truly intelligent terminal for interrogating library catalogues could make the business insightful, as today the librarian does. (Michie 1980)

Before Michie's promised land is reached, considerable work of an exploratory character will be required. At present we have some very crude outline sketches of the entire territory plus some detailed plans of miniscule tracts, the precise locations of which are indeterminate. Both librarianship and artificial intelligence (AI) have made contributions to this process of mapping the terrain of knowledge. Librarianship is concerned not only with the positions of the continents but also the locations of different topographic features: at one extreme the upper reaches of classification schemes attempt to locate the different disciplines with respect to each other (the disagreements of the creators of these schemes show how crude these sketches are); at the other extreme the lower reaches of classification schemes and various indexing systems identifying precise topics. At these levels the cartographic work may be of a very sophisticated nature. A rather extreme example is provided by the category of 'syncategorematic nouns' in the PRECIS indexing system, best known for its use in the British National Bibliographer. Syncategorematic nouns are artificial constructs which are not true subspecies of their apparent classes, e.g. rubber ducks, glass eyes and toy bears (Curwen 1985). At this micro-level, the concerns of librarianship and artificial intelligence overlap. It is probably more than a coincidence that the inspiration of PRECIS and the AI theory of conceptual dependency (Schank 1975) should both be associated with linguistic theories of the case–grammar type.

In one respect the concerns of artificial intelligence are much narrower than those of librarianship: only the aspects of the topography of knowledge and not its counties or countries, let alone continents, have been surveyed so far. Yet the concerns are much deeper, as they include the geology as well as the topography of what we know. Much human knowledge has never been properly analysed or recorded. Samuel Butler, an arch-critic of the Darwinian view of evolution, believed that there was a strong connection between memory, instinct and heredity. Consequently, he stressed the importance of knowledge of which we are only partially conscious, or completely unconscious: 'the more the familiarity or knowledge of the art, the less is the consciousness of such knowledge ... On the other hand, we observe that the less the familiarity or knowledge, the greater the consciousness of whatever knowledge there is'. Furthermore, he added, 'consciousness of knowledge vanishes on the knowledge becoming perfect' (Butler 1910). The truth of Butler's assertion is demonstrated by the fact that AI researchers find it much harder to understand a skill which anybody can master, such as riding a bicycle, than something as difficult to learn as medical diagnosis.

Even in medicine and other professions, in business and administration, and in numerous aspects of daily life, much knowledge is of a tacit kind. According to the economist F. A. Hayek (1973, p. 11):

> Man is as much a rule-following animal as purpose-seeking one. And he is successful not because he knows why he ought to observe the rules which he does observe, or is even capable of stating those rules in words, but because his thinking and acting are governed by rules which have by a process of selection been evolved in the society in which he lives.

As Hayek explained, much of this tacit knowledge consists of rules which experience has shown to be reasonably reliable even if many of them are by no means infallible. 'Heuristics' is another term for these guidelines. One of the benefits of developing expert systems is that tacit knowledge may be elicited, elucidated and recorded, a process known as 'knowledge engineering'. This may be followed by 'knowledge refining', whereby the knowledge is made explicit in a form readily intelligible to people. Furthermore, certain AI programs, usually of a less utilitarian nature than those used in expert systems, may be regarded as possible models of mental processes. Hence the interest of cognitive phychologists in the field.

The methods commonly used in artificial intelligence for respresenting knowledge may be divided into two groups. The first consists simply of rules, e.g.:

IF a borrower is late in returning books THEN he/she is fined at a rate of x pence per book per day overdue.

A second example might be:

IF a patient has a runny nose and a raised temperature THEN he/she is suffering from a cold

The second rule differs from the first in that it would have to be qualified by a certainty factor or the probability of its being true, as various diseases may hve some symptoms in common. Both categorical and probabilistic rules are used in expert systems but the latter are particularly suitable for enabling reasonably reliable conclusions to be drawn on the basis of uncertain knowledge.

In any complex process of reasoning, a whole series or chain of rules may have to be considered, just as in the identification of a chemical compound by traditional, qualitative techniques a sequence of operations for successively narrowing down the possibilities would be performed. Though manual in nature, such a scheme of analysis is an example of 'forward chaining', so-called because the data is considered before the conclusions, which is the same order as used in writing the rules. However, that mode of reasoning can be rather time-consuming if you merely want to establish the truth or falsity of a single hypothesis. A chemist may suspect that a colourless, odourless gas is oxygen and could test this supposition very simply by seeing whether or not the gas re-ignited a glowing splint. Whenever we look for evidence to confirm an opinion, we are performing 'backward chaining'.

Rules have the advantage of being fairly easy to add, delete or modify without disrupting the rest of the knowledge base. With the sacrifice of some flexibility in favour of rigour, they may be translated into statements of first order logic when PROLOG or other logic programming language is used. The type of area in which rules are most appropriate is one which the knowledge consists of empirical associations (e.g. between symptoms and diseases) learnt through years of experience in solving problems in that area (Waterman 1986).

In contrast, where taxonomic knowledge is important, a carefully structured form of representation may be preferable to a somewhat amorphous set of relations. Such a situation exists in geology, where PROSPECTOR, an expert system for locating ore deposits, makes use of mineralogical and petrological classification. Methods of representing or imposing some form of structure include semantic nets, frames and scripts. Actually, a script is basically a frame used to represent what typically happens in routine events (e.g. visiting a restaurant), and frames do link concepts in a way similar to semantic nets. Therefore, only frames will be considered in this introduction. Waterman (1986) explained frames by showing how they could be used to represent the concept of a report. As that is a most apt illustration for a book on librarianship and artificial intelligence, the gist of his argument is repeated as shown in Fig. 1.

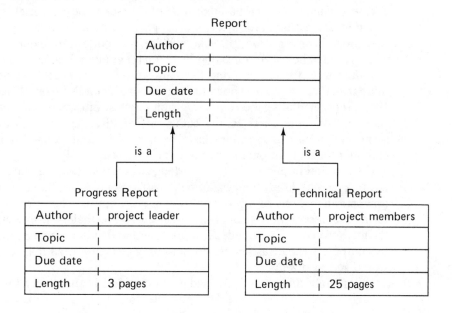

Fig. 1 — Frame representation of reports (adapted from Waterman 1986).

Below the level of progress reports and technical reports in Fig. 1, frames representing specific instances of those two types could be added. The slots in the diagrams define the attributes of a report, e.g. author, topic, etc. The data already in certain slots are the default values of the corresponding attributes. These entries would be overwritten when or if the actual data are input, but default provision is an important feature of frames as it helps to ensure that reasoning processes are not stymied by incomplete information. Various program procedures may be associated with certain slots. In the above example, when the author and date due slots are filled, a message informing the author of the deadline could be printed out. Thus factual knowledge and the reasoning knowledge for manipulating it co-exist in this form of representation.

It is impossible to get very far in any discussion of knowledge without considering semantics, and therefore aspects of linguistics are very relevant to artificial intelligence. In a language like German, the inflection of verbs, nouns and other parts of speech helps to clarify the meaning of the sentence. English relies on word order or the use of prepositions. The differences between these languages are an indication of the limitations of the traditional system of cases, e.g. nominative, accusative, genitive, dative, etc., which is based on Latin grammar. A more important drawback is that the connection between the traditional categories and semantics is rather loose. Merely changing the verb from the active to the passive voice alters the subject of a sentence even though the meaning remains the same.

Considerations such as these led Fillmore (1968) to formulate the theory of case grammar, which is based on a set of nine semantic categories: agent, experiencer, instrument, object, source, goal, location, time, and path. In reading and conversation, prior knowledge is important in understanding what is read or heard, as much may be taken for granted. Frames and scripts are often used for representing this background knowledge. The slots in these structures may correspond to the cases of Fillmore's theory (Charniak 1981), thus facilitating the comprehension process. Librarians will note the similarity of these cases to the categories of PRECIS and will not be surprised to learn that frames have been used in conjunction with case grammar for semi-automatic indexing (Nishida *et al.* 1984).

The different methods of knowledge representation all have their advantages and disadvantages. Some expert systems use different methods for separate aspects of a problem-solving task, but the choice of the best form of representation is not always clear-cut. Nevertheless, irrespective of the method chosen, knowledge is represented so that it can be manipulated by computers rather as people do, and only incidentally so that it can be stored and retrieved.

Ultimately this use of knowledge should include the ability to learn, though whether it will ever be possible for machines to exhibit true intelligence is still a subject of intense controversy. Consiseration of the related issue of generalization will shed light on the matter. Without the ability to generalize, our knowledge would consist of memories of specific happenings and would be applicable to future events only if the exact combination of circumstances were to arise again. Scientific laws are simply generalizations of an extremely accurate and reliable kind. Generalization, then, is an essential component of learning, but all that computers are capable of doing is manipulating symbols. How can that result in generalization?

Consideration of the ways in which librarians manipulate symbols will supply some answers. When using a classification scheme, e.g. Dewey, if anything is found at a specific class number the librarian will move up the hierarchy and examine books belonging to a broader class. That is a form a generalization. Similarly anyone with much experience of information retrieval will have broadened a search statement by dropping a term linked by the Boolean operator 'AND' or by adding alternatives linked by 'OR'. Climbing a hierarchy, dropping conditions and adding alternatives are just three of the range of generalization methods used in artificial intelligence (Winston 1984). Techniques of this nature are being used with some success in the branch of AI known as 'machine learning'.

Libraries are commonly pictured as storehouses of knowledge, preserving a kind of collective memory. But memory is only one of the powers of the mind, and over the years writers such as H. G. Wells (1938), Vannevar Bush

(1945), J. C. R. Licklider (1965), Manfred Kochen (1972) and Ted Nelson (1983) have argued that something more akin to a functioning brain than a passive memory is needed. By adding intelligence to memory that aim may be realized. This book charts some steps which, though the journey may be long, point us in the direction of that goal.

REFERENCES

Bush, V. (1945) As we may think. *Atlantic Monthly* **176** (1) 101–108.

Butler, S. (1910) *Life and habit*, 2nd edn. London, A. C. Fifield.

Charniak, E. (1981) The case-slot identity theory. *Cognitive Science* **5** (3) 285–292.

Cooper, W. S. (1978) The 'Why bother?' theory of information science. *Journal of Informatics* **2** (1) 2–5.

Curwen, A. G. (1985). A decade of PRECIS. 1974–84. *Journal of Librarianship* **17** (4) 244–267.

Fillmore, C. J. (1968) The case for case. In: Bach, E. and Harms, R. T. (eds) *Universals in linguistic theory*. New York, Holt, Rinehart & Winston, pp. 1–88.

Hayek, F. A. (1973) *Law, legislation and liberty*. Vol. 1, *Rules and order*. Chicago, University of Chicago Press.

Kochen, M. (1972). WISE: a world information sysnthesis and encyclopedia. *Journal of Documentation* **28** (4) 322–343.

Keonig, M. E. D. (1982) The information controllability explosion. *Library Journal* **107** (19) 2052–2054.

Licklider, J. C. R. (1965) *Libraries of the future*. Cambridge (Mass.), MIT Press.

Machlup, F. (1962) *The production and distribution of knowledge in the United States*. Princeton University Press.

Michie, D. (1980). The social aspects of artificial intelligence. In: Jones, T. (ed) *Microelectronics and society*. Milton Keynes, Open University Press, pp. 115–143.

Mooers, C. N. (1960). 'Mooers' Law', or why some retrieval systems are used and others are not. *American Documentation* **11** (3) ii.

Nelson, T. (1983). *Literary machines*. South Bend, the author.

Nishida, F., Takamatau, S. & Fujita, Y. (1984) Semiautomatic indexing of structured information of text. *Journal of Chemical Information and Computer Sciences* **24** (1) 15–20.

Schank, R. C. (1975) *Conceptual information processing*. Amsterdam, North Holland.

Waterman, D. A. (1986) *A guide to expert systems*. Reading (Mass.), Addison-Wesley.

Winston, P. H. (1984) *Artificial intelligence*, 2nd edn. Reading (Mass.), Addison-Wesley.

Wells, H. G. (1938) *World brain*. Garden City (N.Y.), Doubleday, Doran & Co.

Part 1

Database creation and cataloguing

According to Jacques Vallée, a French computer scientist:

> the prime fallacy of computer 'information retrieval' is found very simply
> in the term itself: you cannot 'retrieve' information from a computer for
> the simple reason that you cannot store information in a computer in the
> first place! All you can ever store in a computer is DATA, and the
> relationship between data and information is a fundamental mystery . . .
> data turns into information only when someone asks a question about it.
> Therefore the real information is in the question, not inside the
> computer. But then how can I, as a programmer, design an efficient
> information system unless I can absolutely predict all the questions that
> will be asked, and anticipate the process by which I will provide an
> answer? (Vallée 1982, pp. 45–46)

Although there is a lot of truth in Vallée's argument, like most polemi-
cists he overstates his case. To answer his criticisms we need to re-examine
the ways in which we store data. One fairly recent method of organizing data
is by means of frames, and an explanantion of this concept given by Minsky
(1975) could be used as a partial answer to Vallée's point about predicting
questions: 'A frame is a collection of questions to be used about a hypothetical situation; it specifies issues to be raised and methods to be used in dealing
with them'.

In the first chapter in this section, Sommerville and Wood discuss the use
of frames in organizing a catalogue of components of software. As programming is a costly, labour-intensive activity, it could become vulnerable
eventually to Baumol's disease, a condition discussed in the chapter by
Davies in this section. Software reuse on a large scale would prevent that
possibility, and therefore this topic could have considerable economic
significance. It is quite common to store information simply as character
strings with little concern for syntax. In some systems, syntactical considerations are important, but Sommerville and Wood go beyond this. Their use
of frames enables them to tackle semantic issues as well, in a way that is not
possible with classification schemes. Over the years, many faceted classification schemes have been developed for use in fairly specific areas. Perhaps
the use of frames may be feasible in some of those areas too.

Whereas Sommerville and Wood present an alternative to conventional classification, Coelho describes a new procedure for applying a hierarchical classification scheme. Nevertheless, one common feature is the use of the logic programming language PROLOG, which has been found to be eminently suitable for creating and interrogating databases. Computer scientists can treat this chapter as a case study in the development of a natural language interface TUGA, which has subsequently been used in other areas beside classification (Coelho 1985). As most librarians are much less familiar with such interfaces than with menu selection and command languages, the account of TUGA's capabilities should prove informative. The technique of classification by means of comparison with materials already in the database also deserves consideration. Although in cases of doubt librarians often check the shelves or catalogue, classification is usually taught as if it should be done purely by reference to an abstract scheme. Coelho's method would help to ensure consistency.

The structure of the frames in the first chapter and the nature of the logical assertations in the second dictate the type of questions that can be answered. The traditional author/title catalogue also has a structure designed for the purpose of enabling the answering of certain types of question. This is discussed in the first part of the chapter by Davies. Cataloguing is a process governed by a large body of rules concerned to a large extent with onomatological relations (i.e. those involving variant forms of personal, corporate and geographic names) and textual relations (e.g. between different editions, or between original works and translations, adaptations, concordances and commentaries). The original task of codification can be compared with knowledge engineering in other domains in terms of difficulty. Panizzi wrote:

> When we drew up these rules, easy as it may seem, my assistants and myself worked all the day long for weeks; we never went out of the library from morning to night. We worked the whole day, and at night too, and on Sundays besides ... (quoted in Cowtan 1872, p. 282)

This chapter concentrates on the issue of the extent to which cataloguing is a suitable domain for an expert system and takes a brief look at some Swedish work on improving the codification of the rules by using techniques of knowledge engineering.

REFERENCES

Coelho, H. (1985) The paradigm of logic programming in a civil engineering environment. *Computers and Artificial Intelligence* 4 (2) 115–124.

Cowtan, R. (1872) *Memories of the British Museum*. London, Bentley.

Minsky, M. (1975) A framework for representing knowledge. In: Winston, P. H. (ed.), *Psychology of computer vision*. New York, McGraw-Hill.

Vallée, J. (1982) *The network revolution*, Harmondsworth, Penguin.

1

A software components catalogue

Ian Sommerville, Department of Computing, University of Lancaster, UK, and
Murray Wood, Department of Computer Science, University of Strathclyde, UK

1. INTRODUCTION

The costs of developing an maintaining large and complex computer software systems are immense and make up an increasing part of the Gross National Product of the countries of North America and Western Europe. Although precise figures are difficult to come by, Lehman (1980) suggested that software costs made up about 3% of the US GNP in 1977, and it is reasonable to surmise that this figure has increased significantly since then. Indeed, Boehm (1979) points out that the growth in expenditure in software considerably exceeds overall economic growth, with the result that by 1990 software costs would constitute between 7% and 10% of the GNP of advanced nations.

Software engineering is the application of computer science and associated topics in the development of software systems, and it is now clear that effective software engineering practices are of critical importance if software is to be developed on time, within budget and to specification. At the time of writing, the USA, Japan and most West European nations have established special research programmes in software engineering. The aim of these programmes is to develop techniques which will increase the productivity of software developers and decrease the costs of software development and maintenance.

In the UK, the Alvey report (1982) identified the need for a programme of software engineering research, and the main thrust of this programme is the development of so-called Integrated Project Support Environments (IPSE). An IPSE is an integrated set of software tools (programs which assist software development) which support the development and maintenance of computer systems from initial conception through to operation and maintenance. They differ from programming support environments like Unix[TM]† (Ritchie & Thomson 1978) in that they support development activities such as requirements specification and design as well as implementation activities such as programming and system testing.

---

† Unix is a trademark of Bell Laboratories.

The work described in this chapter is being carried out in the context of the ECLIPSE IPSE (Alderson *et al*. 1985) which is being developed by a consortium of UK companies and universities. Part of the ECLIPSE project is explicitly concerned with developing methods and tools to support the reuse of existing software, and our work on the development of a software components catalogue is part of this project. This catalogue is not simply a keyword-based system but incorporates knowledge-based techniques which we believe enhance its utility and will improve its performance in practical use.

In the remainder of the chapter, we discuss software reuse in general and identify different classes of reusable software components. We then go on to discuss the requirements for our system, identify problems which arise with keyword-based approaches, describe the notion of conceptual dependency and then describe the prototype implementation of our components catalogue. Finally, we identify further developments in this area which we intend to pursue in the near future.

2.   SOFTWARE REUSE

The reuse of software components which have been developed in previous projects is one of those motherhood principles which is generally espoused but little practised, except in very specific areas of software development. There are powerful economic arguments for reusing an existing component rather than reinventing that component anew, and Boehm *et al*. (1984) have suggested that we will only see very significant improvements in software productivity when software reuse is widely practised. Not only does reusing an existing component reduce the development cost of a software system, it should also reduce the testing costs as, presumably, that component has already been tested in some other system.

Given, therefore, that reuse is widely accepted as a 'good thing' and that it has a clear economic benefit, why then is it not more widely preactised, particularly in the development of large and complex software systems? The reasons why software reuse is the exception rather than the rule are partly technical, partly human and partly a consequence of the way in which software is produced. Our work is aimed at some of the technical problems and space does not permit a full discussion of the non-technical factors which influence the reuse or otherwise of software. In summary, the human problems are a result of the fact that software development is seen as a highly skilled activity and reuse implies some kind of deskilling; the economic problems are a result of the difficulties of deciding who owns an intangible object like a softwarer component when the component is developed by X for Y.

Leaving aside these problems which present difficulties all of their own, the technical problems of reusing software may be summarized as follows:

(1) It is more expensive and difficult to develop a generalized component for potential reuse than it is to develop a specific component for a

specific system. Indeed, as relatively little software reuse is practised, we are not really at all sure what characteristics of a software component lead to or militate against future reuse of that component.

(2) There are no effective catalogues of existing software components apart from ad hoc lists provided with specific systems such as Unix. Where such lists exist, only very simple keyword-based retrieval systems are provided to assist the user in finding the required component.

(3) The nature of software components and system requirements is such that in many cases a software component is almost, but not ideally, suited for a particular task. Whether or not that component can be reused depends largely on the difficulty of modifying that component.

The ECLIPSE reuse project is tackling all of these technical problems associated with software reuse, and we are particularly concerned with the development of a software components catalogue. This is not simply a classified list of software components; it is an integrated component classification and retrieval system which is based on the semantics of a natural language description of the function of software components.

3. REUSABLE SOFTWARE COMPONENTS

The first thing that we have to do in setting up a software components catalogue is to decide what we mean by a reusable component. It seems to us that there are three classes of software component which might usefully appear in such a catalogue:

(a) General-purpose software systems which might be used, *without change*, in a variety of different applications. Typically, such components are large software systems in their own right — a database management system is perhaps an archetypal example of such a component. Other examples are word processing systems, editors, etc. It is useful to have such components in binary form only, and it is useful to have entries for such components in the catalogue even if the component itself is not held in the component database.

(b) Primitive software components such as functions or abstract data types (an abstract data type is a data type where the implementation details are concealed and access is limited to a number of pre-defined functions). Again these would probably be incorporated in a software system without change although, on some occasions, it may be useful to have these in source code form so that they could be adapted and optimized for use in a particular software system. Examples of such components include mathematical functions such as those provided in the NAG (Numerical Algorithms Group) library and some (but not all) Unix command processes (deroff, which removes text formatting commands, for example). The characteristic of components in this class is that they do one thing and one thing only and that it is possible to define what the component does in a precise and (perhaps) in a formal way.

(c) Software sub-systems which are essentially large chunks of code which carry out a set of related tasks. In general, these will only be useful if they are available in source code form, as it is unlikely that they will do exactly what is required for a particular software system. They provide a general capability, but it may be necessary to adjust their interface in order to make use of them is particular circumstances. Examples of such components might be the lexical analysis part of a compiler (a generalized component which produces tokens from an input stream of characters), a navigation sub-system, and a graphics sub-system to provide graphical I/O on a bit-mapped workstation.

Components from class (a) above are generally very large and software systems tend to be developed around them rather than simply to include them. We have not considered the problems of including such components in our catalogue but, intuitively, it seems that a simple retrieval mechanism is all that is required to find such components.

Initially at least, we have concentrated on building a catalogue of primitive components, class (b), and on establishing a retrieval mechanism for such components. Although the economic benefits of reusing larger-scale components such as those from class (c) are obvious, there are great problems in classifying and retrieving such components.

For example, say a user requests a 'tokenizer', ideally the components catalogue would know that this is more or less what the lexical analysis phase of a compiler does and that such a component would fulfil the user's requirement. Thus, the components catalogue must incorporate some semantic knowledge about how a component is used and about the component's logical function.

Furthermore, even if components in class (c) are not directly applicable to a particular requirement, it may be the case that within that component there are single functions or sets of functions which might be reused. These may not be primitive components in their own right as they may depend on particular sub-system data structures, but they may be sufficiently adaptable to be modified; or it may be possible to reuse the data structure. It would be very useful indeed if (somehow) the components catalogue could incorporate the knowledge that a particular sub-system made use of other operations and that these *semi-primitive* functions are potentially reusable.

4.   REQUIREMENTS FOR A COMPONENTS CATALOGUE

The primary requirement of the component catalogue is the ability to match users' requests for software components onto descriptions of software components which satisfy these requests. Since software components have the property that they are flexible (their code or designs may be adjusted) the system must also have the capacity to match requests onto components which only partially satisfy the requirements ('fuzzy matching') and which, with alteration, may be of use. In order to perform such matching, the system is dependent on a representation scheme for component requests and component descriptions which captures the relevant information from both, yet is simple enough to be manipulated by computer.

A second requirement is that the system should be usable with the minimum of training effort by any user/developer of computer software. If a large amount of effort is spent in training then the benefits from reuse are reduced. This requirement rules out formal specification as a method of software component description and request specification. (Formal specification also seems inappropriate for performing fuzzy matching). Ideally the system would have natural language interfaces whereby software component descriptions or requests for software are analysed, producing corresponding internal representations. Since developing such an interface is a research project in itself, we have limited our requirements for interfaces so that the analysis of component descriptions is done by an expert human cataloguer and the request interface is a standard form which takes keyword or simple phrase responses to system prompts.

A third requirement of the system is the ability to build knowledge of software components into the matching process. There are a number of areas where knowledge is required. Knowledge is required to recognize that, although requests/descriptions of software in natural language are syntactically different, they are semantically similar. Knowledge is required to determine when a component, although not wholly satisfying a request, is close enough to be of interest. Also, it may be useful to utlize knowledge that components are contructed from sub-components which perform distinct tasks, therefore extending the range of requirements that the 'super' component may satisfy. Most of software component knowledge does not consist of concrete rules; rather it is of the form of heuristics.

The final requirement of the component catalogue is that the system should be extensible. Since the software development process covers a very wide range of application areas, it is impossible to construct a demonstrable system that utilizes software components from all areas. The methods used should be such that they can be applied to software components regardless of the application type.

5.   KEYWORD CLASSIFICATION APPROACH

In this section we briefly decribe an initial approach to the problem and assess how it meets our requirements. The approach was based around a classification of software and an association of keywords with each of the recognized classes. Using the software components available with the Unix operating system as our source of components, we constructed a hierarchical classification of Unix software. Each classification was analysed and a representative set of keywords for each class selected. The classification was based on a one or two line summary of the component extracted from the Unix operating system manual. The software components were manually classified into the respective classes, no limitation being placed on the number of classes a component could belong to. Retrieval consisted of requesting keywords from the user and returning the components in the class(es) associated with the keyword. If the class was considered too large to return for user analysis, then a straight keyword search would be applied to the descriptions in the class and only those containing the keyword were returned. A thesaurus facility was incorporated into the system by including not only keywords but words similar in meaning and semantic derivatives as representatives of each class.

Although this approach is quite straightforward and performed reasonably well for the small library of software components we had (~700 components), we identified a number of weaknesses. Classes of components tended to be too large to form manageable responses to the user. Even in our small catalogue, the 'communication' class of software component had almost 100 components. This could be partially solved by splitting the class into sub-classes, but it then becomes difficult to identify appropriate keywords for each class. When a request results in a large number of components, applying a keyword search is unsatisfactory, as keywords alone do not adequately describe components. This causes problems ranging from null repsonse, because the user specifies an unused keyword, to an overwhelming response because the keyword is too general. These problems are caused by attempting to describe software components in terms of single keywords and they arise in most keyword-based retrieval systems. What is required is a description that is more representative of software components.

A second problem of this approach is that the classification scheme is too rigid. It is constructed by analysing the subject area and deriving classes that seem appropriate. Therefore, components either fit into a class or do not. If a component does not fit a class, it is not possible to denote this and there is no easy way of adding new classes. In classification terminology, a scheme that uses predefined classes is termed enumerative, and there are acknowledged weaknesses in their use. Prieto-Diaz (1985) concludes in a survey of classification methods that in areas where flexibility is required, 'An enumerative scheme is not practical beyond small collections ... Enumerative schemes are usually avoided for document retrieval, index construction or classification of document abstracts.' He argues for the use of faceted classification. Such as classification allows the creation or synthesis of specific categories by combining terms from different classes or 'facets'. This approach is more flexible than an enumerative scheme but is still dependent on keywords.

Finally, the approach partially satisfies our requirement to build knowledge into the system, in the sense that the classification approach using a thesaurus does cope with semantically similar keywords, but we argue that keywords do not adequately describe the semantics of software components and so this is of little consequence. Building knowledge about software components into the system is also difficult since knowledge has to be associated with a complete class of software components or with a single keyword.

In conclusion we felt that keywords in themselves do not sufficiently describe software components nor requests for software components and that an enumerative type of classification scheme does not provide the required flexibility.

6. CONCEPTUAL DEPENDENCY

We felt that is was necessary to look for an internal system represenation for software components other than that of keywords. Natural language understanding/question-answering systems provide a mechanism for representation of natural language concepts, known as conceptual dependency. As we will show, is seems that the basic idea behind conceptual dependency may be applied in a simplified way to the representation of software component descriptions and software component requests.

'Conceptual Dependency is a representational system that encodes the meaning of sentences by decomposition into a small set of primitive actions' (Lehnert 1978). The core of such an approach is a number of fundamental **concepts** which are sufficient to capture the semantics of any domain of interest. Schank (1972) lists three types of concept — nominals, actions, and modifiers. Nominals are considered to be things that can be thought of by themselves without the need of relating them to some other concept, e.g. duck, book, New York, file, bit, etc. An action is that which a nominal can be said to be doing. There are certain basic actions which are the core of most verbs in a language. A modifier is a descriptor of the nominal or action to which it relates, and serves to specify an attribute of that nominal or action, e.g. adverbs and adjectives. Each of these conceptual categories can relate in specified ways to each other. These relations are called **dependencies**.

These ideas are implemented in a natural language database system (Waltz *et al.* 1977) in a form known as Concept case Frames. Each concept case frame consists of the **act** (typically related to the verb) and a list of noun phrases which can meaningfully occur with the act. Each act covers a number of related verbs. These frames are used as tools to build a query to the database by filling in the slots of the template with information extracted from the current request, earlier requests, world knowledge and default values.

A practical realization of this approach involves an analysis of the problem domain, resulting in the distinct conceptual actions that can occur, the distinct conceptual objects that are acted on and the modifiers which describe these actions and objects. These are then related in the form of conceptual case frames for each action, which have slots which specify objects that are meaningfully manipulated by the action in the domain of interest. A natural language parser maps the verbs in textual input onto the conceptual actions, and nouns onto the object slots.

An example is the conceptual action PTRANS which represents the transfer of physical location. PTRANS has object slots requiring an actor, an object, an origin and a destination. The sentence 'John gave Mary the book' would map onto a concept case frame representing the PTRANS action as follows:

John

| *source*

John — PTRANS — Book

actor | *destination*   *object*

Mary

This would form the system's internal representation of the sentence, capturing the semantics of the act to give.

As we stated in the assessment of the keyword classification approach, keywords alone do not satisfactorily describe software components. It seems that a system which is based around the concepts of software components, relating these concepts in the form of frames, provides a more complete picture of a software component.

Within the restricted natural language domain of software component descriptions there are only a limited number of basic concepts. Following Schank we can separate three fundamental types of concept — action, nominal and modifier. Actions correspond to the basic, fundamental **functions** that software components perform. Nominals correspond to the objects that perform the function (the software component itself), objects that the function manipulates and objects produced as a result of the function. Modifiers describe actions and nominals. Corresponding to dependency relations or conceptual case frames we have our own frames, 'Software Function Frames'. There is a software function frame for each basic function that software performs, based around the action, with slots for the objects manipulated by the component. Since, in general, software components perform a function and furthermore it is the function which characterises the software component, a representation scheme which captures the function provides a sound foundation for the description of software components, the description of software component requirements and the matching of the two.

This is confirmed by the work of Prieto-Diaz (1985) in his classification scheme for software. When considering descriptors for software components after a study of software descriptions, he concludes, 'Program listings are characterized by describing the function performed by the program . . .'. He then goes on to use the function and the objects that are manipulated by the function as a basis for a software classification scheme.

A component catalogue based on these ideas requires an analysis of the software component domain resulting in a set of basic functions for software. There is a direct relationship between verbs in software descriptions and the basic functions of software components. There should be one basic function for each 'classification' of conceptually similar verbs, that is, verbs that describe semantically similar software functions. An example of conceptually similar verbs might be search, look and find. Also required is a classification of the objects manipulated by software components into classes or 'nominals' that represent conceptually similar objects. An example of a nonimal might be 'file_bit', that is, objects that are parts of a file; typical members of this nominal classification are line, word, pattern, etc.

Having decided on the basic functions of the software component domain it is necessary to develop a set of software function frames. For each recognised basic function of software there is such a frame which relates the objects to the function. Each frame has a variable number of slots, the number being dependent on the meaning of the function. In our current domain the number of slots ranges from one to three. An example of each is:

— control function has one slot, for the object that is controlled.
— print function has two slots, the object that is printed and the object that is the destination for the print (e.g. a terminal or a line printer).
— the communication function has three slots, the object that is communicated, an object that is the source of what is being communicated and an object that is the destination for what is being communicated.

For any software component function all, some or none of the slots may be filled. Currently these slots are unrestricted, that is, any object can fill the slot. In later versions we shall consider restricting the objects that can fill a slot to those that can be meaningfully associated with an action. Rules defining such restrictions would be useful in automatic analysis of limited natural language requests or descriptions.

As an example of a software function frame, the conceptual action of 'searching' might have three slots — one for the actor carrying out the search, the software component itself, one for the object that is being searched and one for any object that is being searched for. A completed software function frame that captures the function of the Unix software component 'grep', which can be described by the phrase 'searches a file for a specified pattern', might be:

pattern

| *object that is searched for*

'grep' — search — file

actor   *object that is searched*

Thus the actor is the software component called 'grep', the object being searched is a 'file', and the object being searched for is a 'pattern'.

While there are other properties of software components such as operating system, implementation language, host machine, etc. which require consideration before a software component may be reused, we feel that they offer little as far as retrieval is concerned. If there are a number of components which perform the same function on the same objects then these environmental considerations can be used either by the user or the system to distinguish them.

In conclusion we would argue that software components, unlike more conventional objects of information retrieval, have a special characteristic which allows them to be described in more detail than is possible with independent keywords. This special characteristic is the function that the software component performs. We suggest that a suitable representation for software component descriptions and software component requests is a software function frame which relates the software function to the objects.

7.   INITIAL RESULTS

We have implemented a prototype component catalogue based on the ideas outlined above, using the programming language Prolog and a set of software components from the Unix Operating System. There are four main areas to the work: the construction of a dictionary of software component terminology; construction of a library of software components represented by software function frames; construction of a sub-system that interacts with the user building a software function frame representing the request; and construction of a matching sub-system which attempts to find a best match for the user's request within the library of software component representations.

Through experimentation with different versions of our ideas we have found that the classification of any items, be they verbs as conceptual actions or nouns as nominals, or the construction of software function frames to represent components should be as wide-ranging as possible. That is, if an item could possibly belong to a multiplicity of classes then it should be entered in all those classes rather than try and tie items down to one specific class. This approach copes to some extent with the problem of different classifiers having different views of how a software component should be described. Thereafter the matching process is strictly constrained, relaxing gradually if no match is found. This rule resulted from classifying words in one particular class or components as being of a particular function. In experimentation with users we discovered that they legitimately viewed components as being described by a different function which, because of the strict classification, caused a failure to match. Initiating the search process by first looking for strict matches and gradually relaxing the criteria for a match until one is made, the system funds the components(s) that best fit the users requirements.

We now give a brief overview of the constituent sub-systems.

7.1   Construction of the dictionary

From previous work on the analysis of software component descriptions we had built a dictionary of about 300 verbs and nouns relevant to the function of Unix software components. (This dictionary is continually updated as the system registers unknown words which are then added to the dictionary by the human cataloguer). The verbs and nouns were manually classified into

classes which were thought to represent the basic actions and basic objects of
software components. This was an iterative process — as the system was
developed and tested and new words were discovered, classes were merged
and split until it reached its current state. Some examples of dictionary
entries are:

        verb(locate,action_search).
        verb(terminate,action_control).
        verb(display,[action,_print,action_inform]).
        noun(directory,nom_file).
        noun(expression,[nom_maths,nom_filebit]).

These are in the form of Prolog facts. A fact has the form

        functor(Arg1,Arg2,...).

In the example dictionary entries above, there are only two arguments. The
functor or name of the clause is either verb or noun, depending on whether
the word is a verb or noun. The arguments are the word itself (1st arg.) and
its conceptual classification (2nd arg.). If the word could belong to a number
fo classes then the classification is a list (denoted by the '[]' brackets in
Prolog) of alternatives. Therefore the above facts denote that:

— locate is a verb classified as an action of type *search*.
— terminate is a verb classified as an action of type *control*.
— display is a verb classified as an action of type *print* and an action of type
   inform.
— directory is a noun classified as a nominal of type *file*.
— expression is a noun classified as a nominal of type *maths* and a nominal
   of type *filebit*.

Obviously many of the words do not strictly fit into one class only. Display,
for example, can mean 'print' or it can mean 'provide information'. In
Keeping with the 'loose classification' philosophy such words are entered in
all the classes they could meaningfully occur in.
   In some contexts, actions such as 'provide information' and 'print' are
closely related. For example, the action associated with the phrase 'report
an error' could belong to either class. It is often worthwhile, if a search is
exhausted using one action, to search using an alternative, closely related
action. To provide this facility we have a second classification of actions
whereby a limited number of actions are denoted as being possible alternatives for each other — a thesaurus of actions.

7.2   Construction of the library of components
As we have stated earlier, we used part of the library of components
available with the Unix operating system as our source of software components. Although Unix software components are intended for software

development they are a realistic example of reusable software components. It was one of our original aims that the system should analyse natural language descriptions components, itself building the corresponding 'software function frame'. Since the aim of this prototype version was to test the capability of our representation as the basis for the matching of requests against descriptions, the natural language analysis part of the system (which is ambitious anyway) was carried out manually. The Unix manual entries for the 300 or so components we selected to use were studied, extracting the information which described the function of the component. For each function a software function frame was constructed. Again, the maxim of 'loose classification' was applied, resulting in components being described under all appropriate functions.

7.3   The user interface
Our requirements were that the system should be usable without special training effort or learning of query languages. In this prototype system the user's input takes the form of keyword responses to prompts from the system. The system builds a software function frame representing the user's request by prompting the user, either for a verb describing the action the component performs, or a noun representing objects manipulated by the component. If the user inputs a verb, the system finds a skeleton frame corresponding to the action which conceptualizes the verb. For each frame slot there is a corresponding prompt which the system displays to the user in search of objects that are manipulated by the component. If the request is initiated with an object, the user is then prompted for a verb which describes the way in which the object is manipulated. During the request-building process the system can be asked for help regarding appropriate responses. The system uses partially completed frames to search the database, collecting together all the known values for 'slots' yet to be filled. These are then displayed to the user for use in responding to the remaining prompts.

An example of the request-building process plus responses is shown in Fig. 1. The components retrieved are from the utility program section of the Unix manual. The emphasis in this prototype system has been in developing a representation for component descriptions and therefore the interface has been kept relatively simple. In later version we aim to make use of the windowing facilities of the SUN workstation to improve the user interface to the components catalogue. (In the example, the system prompts are in normal typeface, user responses in bold typeface and author's comments in italics.)

7.4   Matching of requests and descriptions
Since requests and decriptions have the same internal representation, namely software function frames, using Prolog's built-in control and search mechanisms (see later example) means the matching process is only depen-

Input a verb describing the ACTION the component performs:
compile
Verb: compile
compile is an action of type compile
By specifying objects the search is restricted — only complete relevant fields
Type ? for typical examples

Is thre a source language that is compiled: **pascal**
Is there a target language/machine: (*non specified*)

PC is a pascal compiler   (*component satisfying*
                                                  request)

Do you wish to continue
search ? **y**

                                             (*more components*
                                             satisfying request)
PX is a pascal interpreter
PIX is a pascal interpreter and executor
PMERGE assembles separate pascal programs into a single program
(*The search has been relaxed by replacing the verb 'compile' by the conceptual action 'compile'. Included in this classification of action are the verbs 'interpret' and 'assemble'. Therefore any components which 'interpret pascal' or 'assemble pascal' are found.*)

Do you wish to continue search ? **n**

Fig. 1. — Request formulation and system response.

dent on rules for the best match of the two. An exact match is required if possible. This is implemented by looking for components that are described using the same verb and nouns as the user specifies, thereafter a match is sought of actions instead of verbs, then nominals instead of nouns, then if multiple object slots are filled single object matches are sought and finally just matches of action or object alone.

As in all information retrieval systems, the notions of recall (the proportion of relevant material retrieved) and precision (the proportion of retrieved material that is relevant) are important considerations. By completely relaxing the search we can maximize recall but at the cost of poor precision. Crucial to the component catalogue is that recall should be maximized so that any relevant components are retrieved. At the same time there is no point in returning a large portion of irrelevant components to make sure all relevant components are returned. This is one of our criticisms of a keyword-based system. We argue that since our representation is more representative of a software component we have increased both recall and precision.

8.   SYSTEM IMPLEMENTATION

In choosing an implementation language for a system based on these ideas, there are a number of criteria to be considered. We have to be able to represent and manipulate large numbers of component representations. We have to be able to search through these representations matching on all, some or one of the fields in the representation. We would like be able to add 'heuristic' rules which aid the 'fuzzy' matching process and also, eventually, rules representing knowledge about software component functions.

As well as having the general properties of being easy to read, understand and being more 'high–level' than imperative programming languages such as Pascal or C, Prolog goes some way towards satisfying the above requirements. Firstly, since Prolog is designed to solve problems involving objects and the relationships between objects, it provides a natural representation for our software function frames. For example, the search function described earlier is represented by the Prolog clause:

search(Component,Where,What).

which is interpreted as 'Component' performs the 'search' function on the object 'Where' searching for objects of type 'What'. A realisation of this for the software component called 'grep' and described earlier as 'grep searches files for specified patterns' would be:

search(grep,file,pattern).

Central to our catalogue is a Prolog consisting of such 'facts' represeting the library of software components.

A second feature of Prolog is the built-in control and pattern-matching capabilities designed for search space traversing. These facilities are necessary when searching a large database of component representations and are highlighted in the following example based on the clauses shown in Fig. 2.

Clause (i) is a Prolog 'fact'. As we have said above, this represents the component 'grep' which 'searches files for specified patterns'. There would be at least one of such facts for each component in the database.

Clause (ii) is A Prolog 'rule'. This states that

IF
    component 'Comp' performs a search action on objects of type
    'Comp_Where' for objects of type 'What'
AND
    'Require_Where' is a noun of classification 'Nominal'
AND
    'Comp_Where' is also a noun of classification 'Nominal'
THEN

(i) search(grep,file,pattern).
(ii) search(Comp,Require_Where,What):–
        search(Comp,Comp_Where,What),
        noun(Require_Where,Nominal),
        noun(Comp_Where,Nominal).
(iii) search(Comp,Where,Require_What):–
        search(Comp,Where,Comp_What),
        noun(Require_What,Nominal),
        noun(Comp_What,Nominal).
(iv) noun(word,file_bit).
(v) noun(pattern,file_bit).

Notes:
1. Clauses (ii) and (iii) are presented in a simplified form. Since they are defined recursively the could in fact cause an infinite loop. The loop-checking mechanism has been omitted for the sake of clarity.
2. In Prolog, arguments starting with capital letters are variables, lower case constants.
3. Commas between clauses denote 'and'.
4. A match occurs in Prolog if two clauses have the same functor and for each argument constants match constants and variables match anything. If a variable matches a constant it becomes 'instantiated' to that constant.

Fig. 2 — A snapshot of a component catalogue on Prolog.

the component 'Comp' will also search objects of type 'Require_Where' for objects of type 'What'.

The rule basically says that, if a component searches for objects 'What' in objects of the class of nomional 'Comp_Where', and furthermore 'Require Where' and 'Comp Where' are classified as the same type of nominal, then a request for components searching through objects of type 'Require_Where' may be satisfied by a component that searches through objects of type 'Comp_Where'.

This rule is one of the ways in which the criteria for a match are relaxed. It replaces the requirement that requests should be matched against descriptions with objects matching objects by the less strict requirement that only the nominal classification of the objects need match.

Clause (iii) is similar to (ii) except that it is the objects that are searched for that are in the same nominal classification.

Clauses (iv) and (v) are facts stating that the nouns 'word' and 'pattern' belong to the nominal classification 'file_bit'.

Now consider a request for a component that 'finds particular words in a specified file'. Ideally this would be converted to a Prolog goal of the form:

search(Comp,file,word).

Using its built-in search mechanism and pattern-matching facilities, Prolog tries to prove this true in its database of known information. To do this, the goal must either match (Note 4 above) against a fact or match against the head (left-hand side of the ':–' symbol) of a rule in which case the body (right-hand side) becomes the new goal(s) which has to be proven.

A match is sought in a top-down manner through the database: the relative order of facts and rules is therefore important to the meaning of a Prolog program. Searching for a match for the above goal fails with clause (i) since 'word' fails to match 'pattern'. Assuming there are no other component facts which match the goal, the search reaches clause (ii). The goal matches the head of the clause with the variables 'Require_Where' and 'What' being instantiated to the constants 'file' and 'word' respectively in the process. The criteria for a match have been relaxed by replacing the requirement that the component searches files by the requirement that the component searches objects that are in the same nominal classification as file.

We now have a conjunction of goals, to satisfy, namely:

    search(Comp,Comp_Where,word),
    noun(file,Nominal),
    noun(Comp_Where,Nominal).

The first goal fails since there is no component that searches anything for words, i.e. there are no facts with 'word' as their third argument. This path of the search has been exhausted and therefore Prolog employs its built-in backtracking mechanism, undoing all instantiations of variables until an alternative path in the search for a 'proof' is found.

This is found by matching the original goal with clause (iii) instantiating 'Where' to 'file' and 'Require_What' to 'word'. In this case the search has been relaxed by replacing the object that is searched for by its nominal classification. This time the new goals are:

    search(Comp,file,Comp_What),
    noun(word,Nominal),
    noun(Comp_What,Nominal).

Prolog now proceeds from the start of the database, searching for a proof for each of these goals in succession. search(Comp,file,Comp_What) matches clause (i) with 'Comp' becoming instantiated to 'grep' and 'Comp_What' to 'pattern'. The goal is therefore proven and removed from the goal list. Since the instantiations are perpetuated through the conjunction of goals the third goal becomes noun(pattern,Nominal). The second goal, noun(word,Nominal), is next to be proven, matching against clause (iv) with the result that 'Nominal' is instantiated to 'file_bit'. This leaves the third goal, now noun(pattern,file_bit) which matches clause (v). The body of clause (iii) has been proven true therefore the head is deduced to be true. Since 'Comp' was instantiated to 'grep' in the process, the original goal succeeds as:

    search(grep,file,word).

In this way the system finds the component 'grep' which may satisfy the user's requirement.

A simple example of how knowledge may be built into the Prolog database in the form of a rule might be:

search(Comp,Where,What):– edit(Comp,Where).

This rule states that if a component that searches objects of type 'Where' is required, then a component that edits objects of type 'Where' may be of use. This reflects the general ability of editors to search for specified patterns. This rule would be positioned in the Prolog database so that it was used after all components that perform a search action had been sought.

9.   PROBLEMS IN DEVELOPING PROTOTYPE SYSTEM

Any classification scheme, be it based on keywords or action/object relationships, is somewhat arbitrary and dependent on the classifiers' experience and understanding. This can be partially overcome by discussion and experimentation with a range of interested parties in an attempt to reach consensus. Our approach to classification, whereby items are classified in as many classes as possible, overcomes this to some degree. Contextual ambiguity is also handled by classifying items in all the classes in which the could occur.

A fundamental problem in the development of any component catalogue is the testing of the system. Testing should be done by non-developers. Since it is only feasible to provide a limited catalogue of components, the tester has to be guided to what type of component exist. This guidance has to be some sort of description of the software components available, this inadvertently providing the tester with a form of request for the components. Related to this problem is the general lack of reusable software components with which to build a components catalogue. Ideally the system would be used by an organisation such as a software house developing its own software so that it could be reused in future, storing it in the catalogue for later reference. Development of a general library of software components to test the system is infeasible, so we are dependent on showing that the system performs adequately with the Unix components and that the methods used are general enough to be applied in other areas of software use.

A potential weakness of the developed system is that software components are not described in enough detail. It would be a simple task to extend the component representation so that components could be distinguished by environment features as well as their function. Similarly, the software function frame could be extended to include modifier slots in order that actions and objects are described in more detail. This is not necessary in our limited library of components, but in the interests of generality they should be added. An example of how modifier slots might be added to the software function frame is:

```
comp(Name,verb(Verb,Verb_Mod,Action),
    noun(Noun,Noun_Mod,Nominal),...).
```

Thus verbs and nouns would be represented by clauses which grouped together the item, its modifier and its classification. A completed frame with modifiers for the component 'cc' which 'compiles C programs' would look like:

```
component(cc,verb(compile,_,compile),
    noun(program,c,nom_prog),Dest_Lang).
```

The verb has no modifier (it is ignored using'_') but the object that is compiled, program, is described by the modifier 'c'.

10.   CONCLUSIONS

We have presented an overview of a prototype implementation of our ideas. The aim has been to develop a representation for software component descriptions and software component requests which captures their *meaning*. We described an approach used in natural language understanding to represent the semantics of situations known as conceptual dependency. Following this method we recognised the main concepts of the software component domain, namely the function performed and the objects manipulated by the function. The relationship between the function and objects is represented by what we have termed software function frames. This representation if particularly suitable for information retrieval in the software component domain for three reasons. Firstly, compared to other areas of information retrieval, the software component domain has only a limited dictionary of terminology. Secondly, this domain has clearly recognizable concepts that characterize software components. Thirdly, these concepts have clearly defined relationships, that is, functions operate on objects producing objects. Whether this approach would be suitable for other areas of information retrieval is dependent on the satisfaction of these three criteria.

We argue that, since a system based around these ideas attempts to capture the meaning of descriptions and requests, it has a better capability for matching the two than that provided by independent keywords. In fact, in the worst case, the system behaves as if it were keyword-based. We have shown how it is possible to build knowledge about software components into the system. Although the interface is simplisitic, it meets our initial requirement in that it is straighforward to use. The system is also flexible and extensible. It is a simple matter to add new conceptual actions or conceptual nominals — there is no predefined classification scheme into which new classes have to be accommodated.

Although we have argued that by representing software component concepts the developed system should result in better recall and precision than that provided by a keyword system, we recognise the importance of a systematic evaluation to confirm this. As stated above, evaluation is not straightforward. As well as the problem of not being able to provide users with a comprehensive catalogue and therefore having to describe the available components in some way, there is the added problem of what capabilities a 'keyword system' should have in order to compare the two. Currently we are developing a keyword system with a range of capabilities and see evaluation taking into account user reaction to system usability as well as recall and precision.

Experimentation and evaluation have produced a number of ideas for development in future versions. Firstly, we would like to extend capabilities of the user interface to the system. One way this will be done is to allow users to describe their requirements in the form of simple sentences or phrases, the system questioning the user over any ambiguities of other problems. Secondly, the interface will be extended to make full use of the window-based graphics of the SUN workstation.

We intend extending the descriptive capability of the software function frame by storing modifiers with their related nouns and verbs. We have shown how this might be done above with the example of a 'C' compiler. Another example might be the type of sort a sort component performs, e.g. quicksort, heapsort, etc. Furthermore, we aim to increase the 'knowledge' built into the system by storing sub-functions of typical software components as well as their primary function. Examples might be the editors have search and substitution capabilities, navigation systems have sub-systems for calculating latitude and longitude, and so on.

Another possibility is to add learning capabilities to the system. Learning capabilities would make use of feedback information from the user regarding the success of failure of the cataloque to satisfy his/her requirements. This would involve the introduction of a weighting system where components were attributed a weight and a function, the weight indicating the degree to which the component was described by a function. On a failure to satisfy a user, this weighting would be reduced; on success, it would be incremented. Furthermore, if a user specifies an orginal query which is unsuccessful and then a further query retrieves interesting components, a relationship could be set up between the original query and the components that were eventually retrieved. This relationship would have a low weighting which would be increased if the process was repeated by another user.

ACKNOWLEDGEMENTS

The work described here was funded by the Alvey Directorate, UK. Thanks are due to our collaborators in the ECLIPSE project, namely Software Sciences Ltd, CAP Industry Ltd, Learmonth and Burchett Management Systems Ltd, The University of Lancaster and the University College of Wales at Aberystwyth. Thanks also to Roy Davies and Professor John Campbell for their constructive comments on the first version of this chapter.

REFERENCES

Alderson, A., Falla, M. E. & Bott, F. (1985) An overview of ECLIPSE. In: McDermid, J. (ed) *Intgrated Project Support Environments.*London, Peter Peregrinus.

The Alvey Report (1982) A programme for advanced information technology. The Report of the Alvey Committee. London, HMSO.

Boehm, B. W. (1979) Software engineering. R. & D trends and defense needs. In: Wegner, P. (ed) *Research directions in software technology.* Cambridge (Mass.), MIT Press.

Boehm, B., Penedo, M. H., Stuckle, E. D., Williams, R. D. & Pyster, A. B. (1984) A software development environment for improving productivity. *Computer* **17** (6), 30–42.

Lehman, M. M. (1980) POrograms, life cycles and the laws of software evolution. *Proc IEEE* 68 (9) 1060–1076.

Lehnert, W. G. (1978). *The process of question understanding.* Lawrence Erlbaum Associates, Inc.

Prieto–Diaz, R. (1983) Knowledge representation applied to library cataloging. In: Perrotti, S. (ed), *Anais do XVI Congresso National de Informatica, SUCESU, Sao Paulo, Brazil, October 1983*, pp. 42–47.

Prieto-Diaz, R. (1985) A software classification scheme. Ph.D. thesis, University of California, Irvine, USA.

Ritchie, D. M. & Thomson, K. (1978) The Unix time-sharing system. *Bell Sys. Tech., J.* **57** (6) 1991–2020.

Schank, R. C. (1972) Conceptual dependency: a theory of natural language understanding. *Cognitive Psychology* **3** 552–631.

Waltz, D. L. & Goodman, B. A. (1977) Writing a natural language data base system. In: *5th International Joint Conference on Artificial Intelligence*, pp. 144–150.

2

Library manager: A case study in knowledge engineering

Helder Coelho, Centro de Informatica, Laboratorio Nacional de Engenharia Civil 101, Av. do Brazil, 1799 Lisboa, Portugal

1. INTRODUCTION

Early computers had fairly limited power and were difficult to program. Since that time, hardware technology advances have increased the computational power of the typical computer by several orders of magnitude. Some of this additional computing power has been used to make computers easier to program by developing assemblers, compilers, operating systems, and so on. Meanwhile, effective Artificial Intelligence (AI) techniques have been developed, mainly in the last 20 years. These techniques work in practice; but the resources required, particularly processing time and memory, were until recently prohibitive for many real-world applications (Duda *et al.* 1980). With the falling cost of processing power and memory capacity, this is no longer the case. The R&D programmes on fifth generation computers, under progress from 1982, also opened new ways of knowledge processing.

Moreover, recent advances in many fields suggest a new role for AI, quite different from the traditional view. Two key notions of this new role are the conceptual interface between programs and human users and the idea of knowledge refinement. Programs have been developed that can apply specialist knowledge at least as well as the human expert.

This chapter will examine the actual relevance of knowledge engineering for the future of informatics, by illustrating it with a case study drawn from the work of the Computational Logic Group at LNEC.

2. ADVANCED INFORMATION PROCESSING: KNOWLEDGE ENGINEERING

Answering questions about a specific knowledge domain is the first step taken by a human being learning to become an expert in the art of problem-solving in that domain. The same method is chosen when designing and building systems that enhance such abilities and become helpful problem-solvers and consultants.

A critical problem facing teachers in an educational environment and designers of expert systems is the acquisition, integration, and application of vast amounts of knowledge. Increasing the amount and complexity of knowledge can cause major difficulties, but it may lead to new theoretical developments, as evidenced in the historical progression of knowledge engineering.

Knowledge engineering (a term coined by Donald Michie), or the automatic utilization of knowledge, is a field of study within the area of AI covering the process of building expert systems, i.e. programs that embody and acquire domain-specific knowledge from an expert and apply it to produce useful inferences (Michie 1979). Till now, its main area of application has been medicine (medical diagnosis); however, applications exist in other areas, such as geology (mineral exploration), education (electronic circuits), mass spectroscopy, chemistry (enumeration of atom-bond graphs), mathematical symbol manipulation, model building, engineering (fault-handling and structural analysis), molecular genetics, plant pathology, automated manufacturing, industrial robotics, information sciences (library management) and informatics (computer systems configuration).

The numerous applications of practical importance worked out during the last decade exhibit several important features of knowledge-base programming. As general features, we point out the following: vehicle for communicating expertise, incremental updating of knowledge bases, separation of permanent and temporary information, separation of the domain-specific knowledge from the inference mechanism that does the search and applies that knowledge to the data of individual cases, modularity of control structures and direct response to observed patterns in the environment. As particular features, we point out: non-determinism, declarative representation, modular organization, pattern-invocation, control strategies (data or event driving, intelligent backtracking), and goal hierarchies.

The attractiveness of expert systems stems from two main causes: (1) conceptual clarity (which encourages reading by naive computer users and incremental development, and makes the knowledge base accessible); and (2) its explanantion capabilities (the program can list the steps which led to a conclusion). These aspects disclose the actual relevance of knowledge engineering for the future of informatics. In fact, informatics, and computing technology in general, is mainly concerned with the processing and storage of information, with no emphasis on representing the information in conceptualized form. On the other hand, the human brain is oriented towards conceptual representations. Work in knowledge engineering is concerned with making computing systems act as concept-processors (Michie 1980) approaching the power and intelligence of the human brain.

The relevance of knowledge engineering may be summarized by indicating its impact in the following areas:

(1) development of a wide variety of new features for programming languages, such as abstract data structures (data abstraction is a high-level process which ensures that users and designers focus on data properties

as such and do not get distracted by questions of implementation), control structures, pattern matching (as the amount of knowledge is increased, the importance of effective use of appropriate matching grows, particularly in domains, such as speech, that are characterized by noise, error, ambiguity, and incompleteness), formalisms for encoding and representing uniformly knowledge (e.g. logic, frames, procedures, networks);

(2) principles of system architecture: research on multiple processors, diverse memory structures, global, hierarchical organization could eventually lead to practical systems with novel architectures;

(3) problem-solving attitude, such as rule-based 'advice-taker' representations, which are right for human interaction (human in style, perfectible to super-human completeness, reliability and effectiveness) as compared to those normally used in informatics, i.e. database representations, which are fast but too shallow for fruitful human interaction, and algorithmic representations, which, as they are too deep to be easily understandable, may result in slow, unfruitful, human interaction;

(4) alternative user-modes, such as getting answers to problems (user as client), improving the system's knowledge (user as tutor) and harvesting the knowledge base for human user (user as pupil).

Apart from those impacts, knowledge engineering also presents advantages to the user community, because computer systems that incorporate human judgemental expertise make it widely shareable and relieve the demand for highly trained and experienced personnel (Marshall 1980).

In summary, knowledge-based systems differ from most traditional programs in two ways: (1) they emphasize manipulations of symbolic rather than numeric information (so do many conventional programs used in libraries); (2) they use largely informal or heuristic decision-making rules gained from real-word experience rather than mathematically proved algorithms. At a higher level, these tools of symbolic processing are used to construct understandable lines of reasoning in solving problems and to interact with human users in the decision process.

3.   A CASE STUDY FROM LNEC'S WORK

TUGA (Coelho 1979) is a library manager, i.e. an interactive knowledge-based system which converses in Portuguese to provide a library service for the field of AI. It assists in the acquisition of linguistically and logically consistent knowledge from persons requiring computer processing of information dependent on this knowledge.

TUGA allows AI workers, even naive computer users, to ask questions, classify documents, and make bibliographies based on an AI system of catagories (as in Fig. 1) and on a collection of documents which have already been classified.

In addition, the user can make changes in the document collection, and also modify the classification system by inserting new ground categories. In

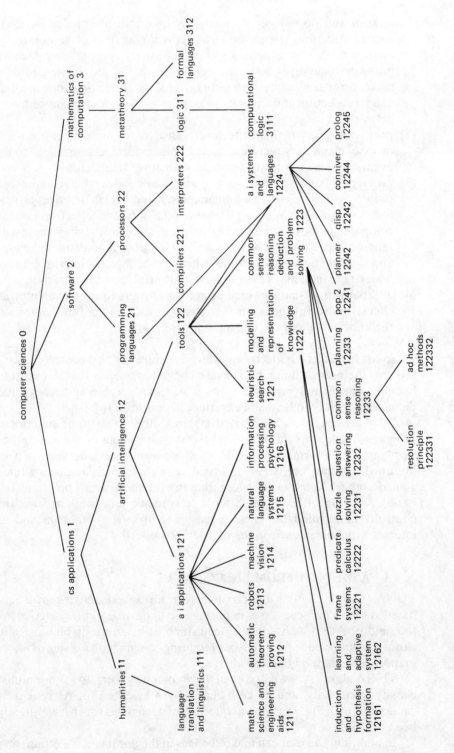

Fig. 1 — The classification scheme.

certain situations, the system takes the initiative by posing questions to the user. It lets the user's answers constrain the system's subsequent response by making proposals about the appropriate classification of a document. It gathers document specifications, it diagnosis incomprehensible sentences, it expands the internal dictionary of Portuguese, and it creates the stock of knowledge shared by the system and its users. All of this is done in straightforward, natural Portuguese.

This is the first example of an AI system (more specifically one supporting natural language dialogue) being designed for use in libraries. The service is supported by a method for classifying documents. It consists of getting a list of categories for maximum of three references, quoted in the bibliography of the document to be classified. Some of these cataegories will probably be valid for this document too. The user discusses the context of that list, and may propose alterations to it.

3.1   Knowledge and tools

TUGA relieves the user of the burden of learning a programming language or query language or the formats of the database. By having two levels of grammar, one for individual Portuguese sentences and the other for dialogues, the system 'knows' various natural ways that a library's user may refer to the particular objects of the library world. Also, it plays two specific roles in the library world: librarian and clerk. Its knowledge includes the specification of each document and the system of classification. Thus it reasons like a librarian by means of heuristics for classifying documents and supplies expert advice to users about those classifications. Furthermore, it can translate a user query into a logical structure which is interpreted in terms of the contents of the database. An appropriate answer (or question) is thereby generated according to the query form and to the retrieved data items.

$$\text{NL Sentence} \xrightarrow{\text{translation}} \begin{array}{c} \text{Logical Structure} \\ + \\ \text{Database} \end{array} \xrightarrow[\text{understanding}]{\text{evaluation}} \text{Answer}$$

The processing of Portuguese queries is done in two successive stages:

(1) Translation: Each user's query is transformed into a list of words and punctuation marks, and a check is made that every word is known. Syntactic plus semantic analysis is performed by a definite clause grammar (DCG) (Pereira & Warren 1978) for Portuguese (Coelho 1979) on the list in order to translate it into a logical structure. The Portuguese DCG, an extension of a context-free grammar, is able to extract from a set of possible readings the appropriate reading: the grammar, being of Portuguese, recognizes if the input sentence belongs to that subset, and it establishes a relation between the written sentence and its meaning. A set of 60 grammatical rules and a dictionary containing approximately 400 words supports that analysis. The dictionary consists of a selection of general Portuguese vocabulary and AI vocabulary of single and compound English terms.

(2) Evaluation and understanding: The logical structure is evaluated over the knowledge base in accordance with a certain logical system. The logical system differs from predicate logic in that quantifiers are more adjusted to the semantics of a natural language, the variables can denote both individuals and sets, and there is a truth-value 'undefined', besides 'true' and 'false' (see Appendix at end of chapter). The logical system for representing Portuguese has been tested over three conversational worlds: personnel identification, civil engineering legislation and in the library service itself. The evaluation consists of decomposing the sentence into single components. Each one is verified by consulting the database, either to find or to relate the individuals belonging to the arguments of each corresponding relation. The logical structure operates as a program the meaning of which is given by the rules interpreted during execution. An answer or a question is the result of comprehension of the input, and it is generated according to the truth-value found and the data retrieved. The knowledge base contains the document collection, the set of current relations and properties giving access to the collection, the classification system and the classification method.

TUGA is an 'active question-answering system', that is, it can run dialogues based on natural language processing, by interchanging the initiative with the user. The communication is based on pre-defined scenarios, context-driven and governed by a grammar of dialogues. This entire perspective distinguishes TUGA from many other 'passive question-answering systems' which support simple consultations, based upon isolated question–answer pairs, motivated by information retrieval (Dahl 1977).

The central feature of TUGA is the use of predicate logic as the sole programming tool for data and knowledge representation, deductive information retrieval and linguistic analysis (Colmerauer 1977). Compared with conventional programming languages, logic programs written in Prolog (Warren 1977; Coelho 1982; Clocksin & Mellish 1981) present a number of notable features, such as: pattern-matching (unification); multi-output, multi-input, multi-purpose, and non-determinate procedures; procedures may return incomplete results; and program and data are identical in form.

Logic programming (Kowalaski 1979) consists of collecting a set of clauses, each expressing a useful property of the relation to be computed and of its auxiliary relations. In logic, objects are represented by terms. A term is either a constant, or an expression of the form $f(t_1, \ldots, t_k)$ where f is a function symbol and $t_1, \ldots, t_k$ are terms. Both simple bibliographic facts and rules of conversation are represented in TUGA, using Prolog, as shown in the following discussion of data and knowledge structures.

Examples of data structures
(1) book specification by the 7-ary relation 'book' and written in Prolog as:

```
book(winston,1,'psychology of computer vision',
    'mcgraw hill',1975, [1214,1216,1222],[3,4]).
```

This unit clause has the following reading: 'Psychology of Computer Vision, book no. 1 of the collection, was written by Winston and published by McGraw Hill in 1975; it is classified under categories 1214, 1216 and 1222, and has documents (books or papers) as its bibliography'.

(2) Classification category specification by 4-ary relation 'category', and written in Prolog as:

    category('artificial intelligence applications',12,
            'natural language systems',1215).

This unit clause has the following reading: 'the category Natural Language Systems has the number 1215, and is an Artificial Intelligence application'.

(3) The 2-ary relation 'published_after' is written in Prolog as the following set of two clauses:

    published_after(T,Y1):–year_of(T,Y), Y>Y1.
    year_of(T,Y):–book(_,_,T,_,Y,_,_);
                paper(_,_,T,_,Y,_,_).

with the following reading: 'T is a document title published after the year Y1 if there is a document with title T published in the year Y which is greater than the year Y1'.

Notions of constant, variable, function, predicate, logical connective and quantifier are used to represent facts as logical formulae in a subset of logic of horn clauses with negation (as failure). The knowledge base according to this view provides a partial description of the library world. Modifications to the knowledge base occur with the assertion/deletion of logical formulae, which are the atomic units for knowledge manipulation.

Examples of knowledge structures
(1) Conversation rules belong to the grammar of dialogues, the supervisor of the system, i.e. the high level control structure of all processes occurring during a dialogue. Let us consider only the first rules in order to make explicit their meaning:

    <converse> → <opening1>, <converse>
    <converse> → <opening2>, <converse1>
    <converse1> → <converse2>, <continue>
    <converse2> → <dialogue>
    <converse2> → <monologue>
    <dialogue> → <user, program>

A general dialogue, 'converse', is defined as an opening followed by a sub-dialogue which may be followed by more sub-dialogues or closed by user initiative. The user may also temporarily suspend the dialogue without affecting it. This justifies the existence of two kinds of opening: one for dialogue start and the other for re-start. A dialogue is simply a sequence of exchanges or monologues and may be followed by other dialogues of different type.

(2) Context-free phrase structure rules belong to the grammar of Portuguese, which representes the syntactic information about sentence form and the general semantic information:

sentence(S) → noun_phrase(NP,S2,O),
          verb([subject–X|L],01), complements(L,01,02).

(3) Linguistic structure describing the meaning of the following Portuguese sentence:

 Nilsson é o autor de 'Artificial Intelligence'.
(Nilsson is the author of 'Artificial Intelligence'.)
fact(
for([X,typ(V)],
    pr(author(X,[artificial intelligence])),
    if(card(X,equal,1)
        pr(set_equal([nilsson],X))))

the reading of which is: for those (sets of individuals) "X", belonging to the domain "typ" (types: authors and publishers), such that "X" is the author of "Artificial Intelligence", if the cardinality of "X" is equal to 1, then "X" is Nilsson'. The linguistic structure contains the logical description of the meaning, and it is an object clause to be handled by meta-level clauses.

Logic programming is a powerful software framework with an existing set of real applications in compiler writing, architecture design, chemical engineering and chess. It exhibits advantages and strengths when compared to other knowledge representation schemes, such as networks, procedures, and frames. Some of these advantages are:

— availability of inference rules in terms of which one can define proof procedures;
— availability of a clean, well-understood and well-accepted formal semantics;
— simplicity of the notation which leads to knowledge-base descriptions that are understandable;

— conceptual economy which allows each fact to be presented once, independently of its different use during the course of its presence in the knowledge base.

3.2 Expertise

The expertise of TUGA is due mainly to heuristic decision-making rules and symbolic reasoning machinery. Those rules support its competence to converse and make deductions like those a librarian might make regarding the classification of a document. The machinery supports the line of reasoning of a librarian, covering the manipulation of highly complex symbolic structures during the evaluation of meaning expressed by logical structures immersed in a certain scenario. Furthermore, it displays the cooperative power of the system in a human-friendly style. Let us present examples that display the degree of expertise of TUGA.

Example 1: Answering constraint

Answering involves the output of data. Sometimes the amount of data is very large, and it may be unexpected by the user. In such a case, it is convenient to output only the first items, and then inform the user that there are more data to be supplied.

The following dialogue samples illustrate this kind of mechanism (u— = user; s— = system):

u—Quais as categories acima de Prolog?	(What are the categories above Prolog?)
s—As cino primeiries sao: computer sciences, computer sciences applications, software, artificial intelligence e programming languages. Existem mais 2! ⇒Quer mais?	(The first five are: . . . . There are two more! Do you want more?)
u—Sim, quero.	(Yes, I do.)
s—As restantes sao: artificial intelligence tools e artificial intelligence systems and languages	(The remainder are: . . . .)

.
.
.
.

u—Qual é a bibliografia para "Artificial Intelligence"?
(What is the bibliography for "Artificial Intelligence"?)

s—Os primeiros cinco documentos sao:
(The first five documents are:)

livro no. 2 — "problem-solving   methods   in   artificial
intelligence",
livro no. 6 — "a   computational   model   of   skill   and
acquisition",
livro no. 7 — "human problem-solving",
livro no. 10 — "computer power and human reason" e
livro no. 23 — "STRIPS: a new approach to the application of
theorem proving to problem-solving".

Existem mais 3 documentos!   (There are three more
                                        documents!)
⇒Quer mais documentos?   (Do you want any more
                                        documents?)
u—Quero mais dois documentos.   (Yes, I want two more
                                        documents.)
s—Os restantes sao: (The remainder are:
artigo no. 25 — "the CONNIVER reference manual" e
artigo no. 27 — "planning in a hierarchy of
abstraction spaces".

⇒E que mais?   Anything else?)

The system knows that the output of data objects is constrained by their
number. The system outputs the first five objects, states the number of
missing ones and interrogates the user about the output.

Example 2: Dialogue shifting
During a dialogue on a precise topic, the user may give up, and start a new
dialogue:

.
.
.

u—Classifique "Explorations   (Classify "Explorations
in cognition"!   in cognition"!)
s—"explorations in cognition"   ("explorations in
é desconhecido!   cognition" is unknown!
⇒Quer ainda classificá-lo?   Do you still want to
                                        classify it?)

u—Por favor, quero.   (Yes, please.)

s—Vamos classificá-lo!   (Let us classify it!

⇒Por favor, de-me o titulo
de uma referencia do
documento em questao.

Please, give me the
title of a reference from
the document in
question.)

u—Desisto.

(I give up.)

s—Ok. Vamos desiar-nos
desta conversa!
⇒E que mais?

(Ok. Let us change
conversation!
And what else?)

.
.
.

The system recognizes whether the document to be classified is known. In the case of a new document, it interrogates the user to confirm his request, and starts its classification by asking pre-defined questions, such as that one on the title of a reference. The decision process of classification is defined by a set of strategies involving rules of experience and judgemental knowledge adopted in a library environment.

Example 3: Gathering missing information about the document
After the user has decided the store a newly classified document, the system is able to go about acquiring the missing relevant document specification. The system knows what to ask, and is able to respond to the user. The system is also able to handle user changes of mind, contradictions and repetitions occurring during the corresponding dialogue. The following dialogue illustrates some aspects of this kind of mechanism:

.
.
.

s—Por favor, deseja arquivar
este documento na Base de Dados?

(Would you like to
store this document
in the Database?)

u—Por favor.

(Yes please.)

s—Por favor, qual o nome do
autor do documento?

(Please state the name of
the author of the document.)

u—Brazdil e 1978.

s—Por favor, qual o tipo do
documento?

(What kind of document
is it?)

u—artigo.

(paper.)

s—O novo documento no. 50
com a restante informacao
adicional foi arquivado!

(The new document no. 50
with the other
information has been stored!

E que mais? Anything else?)

.
.
.

It was unnecessary for the system to ask a question about the date because the user gave that information with the name of the author.

Example 4: Handling the classification method

During the process of classifying a document, the system presents intermediate results to the user in a form that allows the search process to be guided, interrupted, stopped, or re-directed. It is able to simplify the set of categories of its references. It verifies any repeated ones, and it consults the classification system to find redundant categories, i.e. those situated above other categories belonging to that set. The following dialogue shows that and also shows how the system supplies expert advice on how to classify a document:

.
.
.

s—...

.
.
.

De-me 3 categories no maximo! (Give me a maximum of three categories)

u—12, 121 e 312.
O documento ficou classificado (The document has been
nas categorias: classified under the categories:

121—"ai applications" e ....
312—"formal languages"
A categoria 12 foi eliminada, The category 12 was
porque está em cima de 121. eliminated beacuse it is immediately above 121 in the classification.)

.
.
.

u—Classifique "A structure (Classify "A structure
for plans and behaviour"! for plans and behaviour"!)

s—"a structure for plans ("a structure for plans
and behaviour" é desconhecido! and behaviour" is

Quer ainda classificá-lo?

u—Sim, quero.

s—Vamos classificá-lo!
_Por favor de-me o titulo
de una referencia do
documento em questao.

u—"Computational semantics".
s—"computational semantics"
é conhecido, e está
classificado nas categorias!
1215—"natural language
systems" e
312—"formal languages".
Por favor, de-me o titulo
de outra referencia do
documento em questao.

u—"Computer models of
thought and language".

s—"computer models of
thought and language" é
conhecido, e está
classificado nas categorias:
1215—"natural language
systems" e
1222—"modelling and
representation of knowledge".
s—Por favor, de-me o titulo
de outra referencia do
documento em questao.

u—"Computer power and human reason".

s—"computer power and human
reason" é conhecido, e
está classificado na
categoria:
1215—"natural language
systems".
Vamos utilizar o metodo de
classificacao que consiste
em sugerir como categorias

unknown!
Do you still want
to classify it?)

(Yes, I do.)

(Let us classify it!
Please give me the title of
one reference from
the document in question.)

("computational semantics"
is known, and is
classified under the
following categories:
....

Please give me the title of
another reference from the
document in question.)

("computer models of
thought and language" is
known, and is classified
under the categories:
.....

Please give me the title of
another reference from the
document in question.)

("computer power and
human reason" is known, and
is classified under the
category:
.....

Lue us adopt as
classification method the
one that consists

para o documento em
questao, as obtidas das 3
referencias fornecidas
pelo utilizador!
Assim, proponho que o
documento fique classificado
nas categories seguintes:
1215, 312 e 1222.
Por favor, faca a sua
escolha tendo em atencao
and categories sugeridas
e as que julgar mais apropriadas.
De-me 3 categorias no
maximo!

of suggesting as categories
of the document in question,
the one obtained from the
three references given by
the user!
I therefore propose that the
document be classified
under the following
categories: ...
Please choose from the
suggested categories and
the ones that you think most
appropriate.
Give me a maximum
of three!)

u—1222.

s—O documento ficou classificado
na cataegoria:
1222—"modelling representation
of knowledge".
Pr favor, deseja arquivar
este documento na Base
de Dados?

(The document has been
classified under the category:
. . . . .

Please do you want to
store this document in
the Database?)

u—Ok.

.
.
.

Example 5: Diagnosis of incomprehensible sentences
During the dialogue the system may not inderstand the user's sentence. This
may be due to the following causes:

(1) the user has failed to type a word properly;
(2) the user has employed a word unknown to the system;
(3) the user has adopted a syntactical construction unknown to the system
(4) the user has made semantic errors for any reason.

In the two first cases, the system discovers the unknown word(s), asks the
user about it(them), and is able to increase its dictionary with the new word
if it is a proper noun:

.
.
.

u—Ronald é um autor?   (Is Ronald an author?)

s—Nao compreendo esta frase porque a palavra "ronald" é desconhecida! Por favor, preste atencao à frase que escrevue!

⇒Exists algum erro sintatico na escrita da sua frase?

(I don't understand this sentence because the word "ronald" is unknown! Please, observe with care the sentence you have typed! Is there any syntactical mistake?)

u—Nao existe.

(There is none.)

s—Está bem!
⇒A palavra desconhecida "ronald" é um nome proprio?

(All right! Is the unknown word "ronald" a proper noun?)

u—É.

(It is.)

⇒Qual é o genero de "ronald"?

(What is the gender of "ronald"?)

u—Masculino

(Masculine)

⇒A qual dos tipos, autor, titulo, livreiro ou categoria pertence a palavra "ronald"?

(To which type, author, title, publisher or caregory, does the word "ronald" belong?)

u—Autor.

(Author.)

s—A resposta à sua pergunta sobre "ronald" é:
Nao.
.
.

(The answer to your question about "ronald" is: No.)
(i.e. no known document has "ronald" as its author.)

In the third case, the system asks the user to paraphrase his sentence:

.
.
.

u—Está Logic ligada com Prolog?
(Is Logic linked with Prolog?)

s—Nao compreendo esta frase porque a sua construcao sintactica é desconhecida. Corrija a sintaxe ou construa outra parafrase. Repita a pergunta por favor!
(I don't understand this sentence because its syntactic format is unknown. Correct the syntax or re-phrase the sentence. Please, repeat the question!)

u—Logic está ligada com Prolog?
   (Logic is linked with Prolog?)

s—Nao.
   (No.)

u—Logic está ligada à "Computational Logic".
   (Logic is linked with "Computational Logic".)

s—Concordo.
   (I agree.)

.
.
.

Finally, in the fourth case the system rejects some sentences because it detects semantic anomalies by using a tree of semantic types or by word-sense disambiguation:
The sentence,

Penguin publicou na Elsevier.
(Penguin published by Elsevier.)

is rejected because Penguin is a publisher and not an author, and the verb 'publicar eḿ (to be published by) accepts only members of the domain of authors for subject.
The sentence,

As artigos classificadas...
(the classified authors...)

is rejected as it lacks gender agreement: the article 'as' (the) and the adjective 'classificadas' (classified) are in the feminine plural and the common noun 'artigos' (papers) is in the masculine plural form.

Example 6: Linguistic reasoning
A typical case of linguistic reasoning is the following piece of dialogue:

u—Brown é o autor do artigo.
   (Brown is the author of the paper.)

s—A sua frase pressupoe outros factos, logo um contexto. Como nao possuo informacao sobre o que foi dito anteriormente, a sua frase é ambigua. E, portanto, nao consigo responder-lhe!
(Your sentence presupposes other facts, therefore a context. As I have no information about what was said previously, your sentence is undefined. And, therefore, I cannot answer you!)

This dialogue illustrates another feature of the system. TUGA evaluates the logical structure and finds that the truth value is undefined. The user's sentence reveals a definite noun phrase anaphora. The noun phrase 'o artigo' (the paper) is meaningless in a context where no paper has been suggested previously: the sentence is isolated. Also, there are no co-reference sentential restrictions and the noun phrase cannot be interpreted as referring to a certain paper. The presupposition introduced by the definite article is solved but not found.

4. CONCLUSION

The objective of designing an expert system, such as the library manager TUGA, was the development of a feasible method for consulting and creating databases in natural Portuguese. It had been proved already that expert systems may be applicable in commercial databases (very large, relatively simple in structure), since client's demands include facilities for inferential retrieval. TUGA demonstrated that the AI concepts and programming techniques are advanced enough to produce useful tools, at least when applied to a limited speciality. This example of competence improved the credibility of AI and praved the way for other such systems. Moreover, logic programming based upon Prolog appears to be a positive tool for databases designed with 'expert system' extensions in mind.

This is the first time Portuguese has been used in such a practical application. Our work extends the interest of linquistic engineering, i.e. man-machine communication in natural language, by showing that it need not be restricted to English, the language most widely studied and adopted. The subset of Portuguese optimizes intelligibility to both the user and the system.

The approach that has been taken stresses the use of predicate logic to represent knowledge. We chose this programming language on account of its outstanding features, such as closeness to natural language, modularity, one language for program and data, logical variable, computation of relations, economy, understandability, learnability and inbuilt search strategy. These features enable us easily to adapt the program to other knowledge domains, because modifying clauses in Prolog is easier than modifying procedures in other programmming languages.

TUGA program runs on DEC-10 systems, or on any other computer having Prolog interpreters or compilers. The Prolog interpreter occupies only about 12K on the DEC-10, and the program itself needs another 50K of memory. The listing of the program is 54 pages long, and it has 400 horn clauses, 388 unit clauses and 322 grammar rules. On the DEC-10, the CPU time for parsing a question by the compiled program is on average 40 milliseconds.

APPENDIX

In order to set up the logical system for representing Portuguese, we followed closely Colmerauer's system (Colmerauer 1977). Changes were made in the vocabulary of the syntax and in the definition of articles.

Terms

variables:		x	with $x \in X$
	constants:	k	with $k \in K$
	compound terms:	$coord(x)$	with $x \in X$
		$disj(1)$	*with 1 as a list of*

$x \in X$
e_i, s_i, n_i statement formulae:
         relational symbols: r with $r \in R$
$those(x, e)$ quantifier:
logical connectives:
and, not

Individual constants were chosen to treat proper nouns. Compound terms were chosen to treat coordinated proper nouns and the disjunction of proper nouns. Relational symbols were chosen to treat verbs, adjectives and nouns.

Note that the meaning of $those(x,e)$ is 'those xs which satisfy statement e', and that the only combinations considered are those formed by two rules: conjunction and negation.

Definition 1. The occurrence of an individual variable x in a formula f is free if it does not arise inside a sub-formula of the form $those(x,e)$.

Definition 2. A formula which contains no free individual variable occurrence is closed.

Having formalized the language, we formalize the notions of situation and truth, the necessary apparatus for determining the truth-value of any closed formula.

Definition 3. A situation g is an application which, to each relational symbol $r \in R$ of degree n, associates a n-ary relation $p=g(r)$, of which the arguments k_i are individuals or the subsets of the set of proper nouns K, and of which the value $(p(k_1,k_2,...,k_n)$ is either 'true', 'false' or 'undefined', according to the values of the k_i.

Definition 4. Let g be a situation:

the value $\text{val}(e_i)$ of a closed set formula e_i is defined by:

(1) if $s_i = c$ with $c \in K$ then

$$\text{val}(s_i) = (c)$$

(2) if $s_i = x$ has been substituted by the formal representation of a set E then

$$\text{val}(s_i) = E$$

(3) if $s_i = \text{those}(x,e)$ then

$$\text{val}(s_i) = \text{the union of all the subsets } E \text{ of } K:$$

$$\text{val}(e_{x \leftarrow E}) = \text{true}$$

where $e_{x \leftarrow E}$ represents the formula e in which a formal representation of the set E has been substituted for every free occurrence of x.

the value $\text{val}(n_i)$ of a closed integer formula n_i is defined by:

(1) if $n_i = j$ where j is a non-negative integer then

$$\text{val}(n_i) = j$$

(2) if $n_i = \text{card}(s_j)$ then

$$\text{val}(n_i) = \text{number of elements of the set val}(s_j)$$

The semantics of a closed statement, set or integer formula f are simply the variations of its values $\text{val}(f)$ in different situations.

This logical system presents a unique quantifier, $\text{those}(x,e)$, which allows explication of the domain of variable x. This feature does not belong to first-order predicate logic where variable x is not restricted and its implicit domain remains always the same. Also, this feature allows operations of predicate logic and enables us to establish a better definition of articles.

The procedure for operating upon the well-formed formulae of this logical system demands they be set in a convenient form, by appealing to a sole quantifier. Thereby, a new quantifier 'for' is introduced, and defined in terms of quantifier 'those(x,e)':

$$\text{for}(x,e_1,e_2) = e_2$$
$$x \leftarrow \text{those}(x,e_1)$$

i.e. the value of 'for' is equal to the value of e_2 when we substitute all free occurrences of x in e_2 by those(x,e_1).

The quantifier 'for' allows the explication of the domain of a variable. This feature improves the definition of articles, and in so doing contributes to a better translation of natural language sentences. The quantifier 'for' records the difference of meaning of the articles, and expresses them in terms of only some well-defined concepts.

The equalities in Fig. 2 establish the definitions of some of the articles considered in our subset of Portuguese.

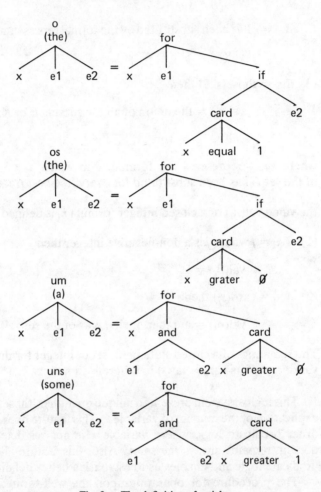

Fig. 2 — The definition of articles.

REFERENCES

Coelho, H. (1979) A program conversing in Portuguese providing a library service. Ph.D. thesis, University of Edinburgh.

Coelho, H. (1982) *How to solve it with Prolog*, 3rd edn. LNEC.

Clocksin, W. & Mellish, C. (1981) *Programming in Prolog*. Springer-Verlag.

Colmerauer, A. (1977) An interesting natural language subset, Université d'Aix-Marseille.

Dahl, V. (1977) Un système deductif d'interrogation de banques de données en Espagnol, Thèse de troisième cycle, Université d'Aix-Marseille.

Duda, R., Nilsson, N. & Raphael, B. (1980) State of technology in Artificial Intelligence, SRI International, Technical note no. 211.

Kowalski, R. (1979) *Logic for problem solving.* Amsterdam, North-Holland.

Marshall, M. (1980) Artificial Intelligence: on the brink. *Electronics* **53** 20.

Michie, D. (1979) *Expert systems in the micro-electronic age.* Edinburgh, Edinburgh University Press.

Michie, D. (1980) P-KP4: expert system to human being in conceptual checkmate of dark ingenuity. *Computing* **8** 29.

Pereira, F. C. N. & Warren, D. H. D. (1978) Definite clause grammars compared with augmented transition networks. University of Edinburgh, DAI Research report no. 58.

Warren, D. H. D. (1977) Implementing Prolog — compiling predicate logic programs. University of Edinburgh, DAI Research report no. 44.

3

Cataloguing as a Domain for an Expert System

Roy Davies, The University Library, Exeter

1. INTRODUCTION

Anyone who is not a librarian may be forgiven for imaging that the cataloguer's task is perfectly straightforward: the compilation of an inventory of books. For this, an ordinary database rather than an expert system may appear more than adequate, particularly in view of the fact that the use of sophisticated mathematical techniques for stock management in libraries is fairly rare. Nevertheless, if any inventory listed thousands or even millions of distinct 'products', it is unlikely that the problems involved in its design and maintenance would be regarded as completely trivial.

In fact, the functions of a catalogue are considerably more extensive than those of a mere inventory. As enunciated by the American librarian C. A. Cutter these functions are:

(1) To enable a person to find a book of which either (a) the author or (b) the title or (c) the subject is known.
(2) To show what books the library has (a) by a given author or (b) on a given subject or (c) in a given kind of literature.
(3) To assist in the choice of a book on the basis of (a) its edition or (b) its character (literary or topical).

Actually, most libraries do not endeavour to satisfy all Cutter's aims in full solely by means of the catalogue. Notes on a book's literary character or contents are often omitted, thus saving the cataloguer's time and improving productivity. Access via title is usually restricted in conventional card catalogues to certain categories, e.g. books with editors and periodicals, in order to limit the size of the file.

Traditionally, whether cards, microfilm or microfiche are used, records are arranged in alphabetical order under headings such as author's name and other access points, and therefore there may be several copies of a record, one under each appropriate heading. In an online catalogue, however, it is more natural to store a single copy of each record in an unsorted file and rely on extensive index files for access. This arrangement is strangely similar to that advocated in the middle of the 19th century by Crestadoro (1856) and applied by him in public libraries in Manchester. Nevertheless, whatever form a catalogue takes, its utility is determined by the quality of the data of which it is comprised.

In the construction of catalogues numerous problems are encountered which, when considered in isolation, may seem readily capable of ad hoc solution, but the inevitable inconsistencies concomitant with such an approach would seriously limit the product's usefulness. Some relatively simple but common problems are described below.

How should names be filed? At first sight the answer appears obvious. However, names of many classical and medieval authors require different treatment from those of modern writers, as the almost universal use of surnames was a relatively late development in European history. In China and in Hungary it is the first name, not the last, which identifies a person's family. The choice of filing element in names containing prefixes such as 'von Neumann' or 'de Gaulle' varies according to nationality, and in some countries would depend on whether the prefix were a preposition, an article or a contraction of an article and a preposition. Compound surnames are also a problem, particularly those without hyphens, e.g. 'Lloyd George'.

Forenames and initials are another potential source of confusion. The Danish writer generally called 'Hans Andersen' in Britain is known by his full name 'Hans Christian Andersen' in the United States but is referred to as 'H. C. Andersen' in his native land. The larger the catalogue and the more common the surname, the more likely it is that inconsistency in the use of initials would lead to entries for works by different authors being interfiled. Some other factors complicating the cataloguer's task of collocating all the works of each author are the use of pseudonyms, change of name (e.g. of women on marriage), and use of ecclesiastical titles or titles of nobility, e.g. the physicist William Thomson is also known as Lord Kelvin (or Baron Kelvin of Largs, to be exact). Collocation of names of organisations with all their departments, committees, working parties, etc. is also difficult, particularly when complex hierarchies of subordinate bodies are inolved, as is often the case with government publications.

Even the use of titles is not always straightforward. Christopher Evans' book 'The Mightly Micro' was subsequently published in the United States under the title 'The Micro Millenium'. It is desirable that a cataloguer in a library with only the American edition ensure that any reader with a reference to the original title will not imagine that it is a different book. Similarly, a reader wishing to know which versions of the Bible a library possessed would not be very pleased if it proved necessary to look up 'New English Bible', 'Good News Bible' and every other single version in a different part of the catalogue. Apart from being time-consuming, it is likely that lesser-known versions would be overlooked.

The solution adopted where copies of the same work or different versions of it have different titles is to use a standard or 'uniform' title. Thus, in the case of the Bible, one copy of each record would be filed under the uniform title 'Bible' and another under the proper title of the particular version.

Problems considerably more complex than those outlined here are sometimes encountered, but the foregoing discussion should suffice to indicate the need for a consistent, methodical approach. Nevertheless, in the middle of the nineteenth century the controversy over cataloguing at the British Museum was so great that it became the prime concern of a Royal Commission established to investigate the Museum's constitution and administration. Critics maintained that the cataloguing of the Museum's holdings could be accomplished much more rapidly if it were not for the complexity of the code of 91 rules, published in 1841, which was drawn up under the direction of Panizzi, Keeper of Printed Books and later Principal Librarian.

It was argued that cataloguing should be more a matter of common sense than of following rules. However Panizzi received the staunch support of the mathematician Augustus De Morgan, after whom two of the basic equivalence rules of logic and set theory are named. Being himself an eminent bibliographer with a special interest in books on arithmetic from the invention of printing onwards (De Morgan 1847), he fully appreciated the difficulties facing Panizzi and in his evidence to the Commission stated, 'I am perfectly satisfied of this, that one of the most difficult things that one can set himself to do, is to describe a book correctly' (De Morgan 1850).

Panizzi was fully vindicated by the Royal Commission and his code had a profound influence on subsequent developments. The most widely used code in use today, the Anglo-American Cataloguing Rules, 2nd edn (AACR2), has more than 20 times as many rules as Panizzi's and may therefore appear to be a somewhat bureaucratic implement. However, a reasonably comprehensive system of rules should help to make cataloguing more of an automatic proces than it otherwise would be, thereby removing much of the difficulty that so impressed De Morgan.

Claims of this nature may be made for sets of rules regulating administrative activities in many spheres. As the great German sociologist Max Weber (1948) put it, 'the fully developed bureaucratic mechanism compares with other organizations exactly as does the machine with the non-mechanical modes of production'. In a similar vein, one systems theorist has argued that bureaucracies, not expert systems, are the most ubiquitous and successful examples of mechanical cognition today (Lee 1983). Therefore it is possible that lessons learnt in attempts to develop expert systems for cataloguing may have relevance in areas beyond the bounds of libriarianship.

2.   AACR 2

The analogy with a mechanical process suggests that the creation of an expert cataloguing system would be a relatively straightforward task. After all, the rules have already been codified. However, in assessing the suitability of AACR2 as a knowledge base it should be remembered that the rules were devised for human application and the librarians who drew them up never envisaged the possibility of cataloguing being performed by a machine.

AACR2 is in two parts. The first consists of rules specifying the content of catalogue records and the second deals with access points or keys to the records. Not all the detail in catalogue entries is equally important, and as libraries vary in their requirements three different levels of description are allowed, though only the first two levels are specified precisely. The second or fuller of these levels, including the symbols which serve as field and sub-field markers, is shown below.

> Title proper [general material designation]=parallel title: other title information/first statement of responsibility; each subsequent statement of responsibility. — Edition statement/first statement of responsibility relating to the edition. — Material (or type of publication) specific details. — First place of publication, etc.: first publisher, etc., date of publication, etc. — Extent of item: other physical details; dimensions. — (Title proper of series/statement of responsibility relating to series, ISSN of series; numbering within the series. Title of subseries, ISSN of subseries, numbering within subseries). — Note(s). — Standard number.

The third level of description may be regarded as the second plus any other details specified by any applicable rule. Not all the elements of the second and third levels are releant to every item. For example, not all books are part of a series. One field does not apply to any books at all. This is the 'material specific details' area, which is used only for cartographic materials and serials (journals). The scale of a map or the volume numbers of a journal would be recorded here. The statement of responsibility would include the name(s) of the author(s) or editor(s) of a book, the composer(s) or performer(s) of a musical work, the cartographer who designed a map, etc.

The terminology used for the different fields is of a rather general nature as AACR2 is meant to be applicable to books, periodicals, microfilms, manuscripts, sound or video recordings, motion pictures and recordings of computer programs and data files as well as anything else that may be catalogued by a library. Actually, the code is less satisfactory for some of these materials than for others and consideration is being given to re-writing the chapter on software.

All records conform to a basic pattern or template. This template could be treated like the frames used in some applications of artificial intelligence. In addition to the most general bibliographic frame based on the second level of description, there would be frames of a still more specific kind, e.g. for monographs which were government publications. Therefoe, by using prompts or screen forms based on the appropriate frame, it would be possible to guide the cataloguer in entering data.

A natural further development would be the provision of extensive help facilities. If a cataloguer had a problem with any part of a record, a table indicating the topics covered by rules applicable to that field could be displayed. On selection of the appropriate option the relevant rule would be displayed, possibly with an example to clarify its meaning. Some sub-fields could be filled by default. The ISBN prefix identifies the publisher and, indirectly, the probable place of publication. Admittedly this is a trivial sort of inference, but it would help to ensure consistency and save time. A system with all these facilities would certainly be very user friendly but could hardly be described as an expert system. However, there is far more to cataloguing than simply selecting and transcribing data.

The most difficult part of a cataloguer's job is to ensure that copies of records of each item are to be found in the places where any sensible reader is likely to look for them. The means to this end are specified in part 2 of AACR2. In general, the rules belonging to this section are conditional instructions, and many are expressly stated in the form 'IF x is true THEN perform y', like the production rules which are used in many expert systems. A typical example is rule 21.4Cl which states:

> If responsibility for a work is erroneously or fictitiously attributed to a person, enter under the actual personal author or under title if the actual personal author is not known. Make an added entry under the heading for the person to whom the authorship is attributed, unless he or she is not a real person.

This rule, like all the others of AACR2, is stated in categorical non-probabilistic terms. It is true that in the literature on expert systems there has been a considerable emphasis on probability as, in many domains, knowledge is uncertain. Nevertheless both DENDRAL (which is used for identifying certain types of organic compounds from their spectra) and XCON (which configures VAX computers) use catagorical rather than probabilistic rules. Therefore the categorical nature of cataloguing rules is no reason for not using expert system techniques. Many of the rules contain a number of premises and actions as in the above example. The final proviso of rule 21.4Cl is intended to eliminate such 'authors' as Winnie the Pooh or Donald Duck. This highlights the need for common sense, a quality not easily imparted to computers. Consequently, it is necessary to decide on a rational division of labour between the human cataloguer and the computer.

Certain rules depend on readily ascertainable conditions such as the number of authors a book has. The tests for these conditions could be made automatically if the names were counted as they were input, though occasionally the cataloguer's time would be wasted since the rules state that if a book has four or more authors, the name of the first only would be recorded unless any one, two or three of them were primarily responsible for the work. However, detection of erroneous or fictitious authorship would be quite a different matter. The cataloguer would have to tell the system if the condition applied. A similar situation exists in other domains. A few expert systems do read data directly from instruments, but most currently existing gather information by interrogating the operator.

Anyone with any experience of cataloguing will realize that long chains of reasoning are rarely involved. Normally, only a few rules are consciously applied, although a large number are potentially relevant to fields which are present in most records, such as the title and the statement of responsibility. Consequently, it could be an excessively time-consuming process if the system attempted to establish which rules apply by asking about possible conditions, one question at a time.

There are two ways around this difficulty. One would be to assign probabilities to the likelihood of various conditions occurring, so that the system would enquire about the more common possibilities first. The probabilities would be used purely to control the order in which the rules were examined and would not effect the conclusions. It would even be possible to endow the system with the ability to learn by making it keep track of the rules which it applies and adjust the probabilities accordingly. Thus, if a university were to establish a new department of music, as the library acquired relevant material the probabilities attached to the rules for music would rise gradually.

A problem with that approach is that either it would be necessary to examine in detail a large, representative collection of records in order to calculate probabilities for each rule, or alternatively one could guess the values and then rely on the system's learning ability in the hope that, once a sufficient number of items had been catalogued, realistic adjustments to all the figures would have been made.

A simpler method of preventing an excessive amount of time being spent on consideration of inapplicable conditions is to present several alternatives simultaneously in the form of a menu rather than sequentially. Within a limited, pre-determined context, a menu system does allow the user to volunteer information, as non-applicable alternatives are simply ignored. This is the method that was chosen by Brian James in an investigation into the feasibility of an expert cataloguing system which he carried out for an M. Phil. degree at the University of Exeter (James 1983, Davies & James 1984).

3.   THE EXETER FEASIBILITY STUDY

The approach James followed requires the that alternative bibliographic conditions be grouped together in a logical way to form menus which would be linked by appropriate pathways. In fact a detailed route through the maze of part 2 of AACR2 had been worked out previously by staff of the School of Librarianship and the Educational Technology Unit of Leeds Polytechnic who developed two algorithms for selecting headings and determining their precise form (Shaw *et al.* 1980). These algorithms were intended for use in teaching cataloguing, but their availability was a factor in the choice of a menu system.

Existence of an algorithmic solution is often regarded as an indication that expert system techniques are inappropriate, but the AACR2 algorithms have a great number of terminating points in contrast to those used in typical problems of a mathematical kind. Their complexity is illustrated by the fact that the flowcharts representing the two cataloguing processes together occupy over 100 pages.

Successive decisions along a false branch of a flowchart may be represented by different options in a menu, while those in a true pathway would correspond to choices in linked menus. The equivalence of the menus, flowcharts and production rules is demonstrated by Figs. 1 and 2 below.

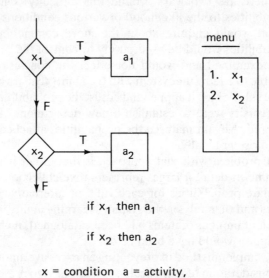

if x_1 then a_1

if x_2 then a_2

x = condition   a = activity,

i.e. display another menu or screen form

Fig. 1 — Alternative selections: flowcharts, production rules and menus.

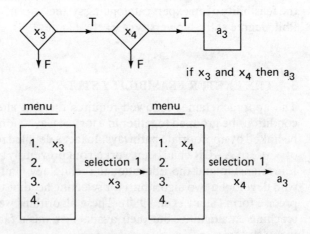

if x_3 and x_4 then a_3

Fig. 2 — Successive selections: flowcharts, production rules and menus.

A typical pathway through the system is shown in the following diagrams. Initially the cataloguer would be presented with the menu in Fig. 3 and would have to indicate the nature of the item being catalogued. If this were a book then the appropriate selection would lead to the menu in Fig. 4. The 'Why?' selection would have resulted in a message stating that the questions were necessary for the determination of the correct access points.

```
Add new record mode
Document specification
1=Books, pamphlets, printed sheets
2=Serials
3=Maps
4=Manuscripts
5=Music
6=Microforms
7=Other
8=End
Enter selection:            (default=1)
Enter control number (e.g. ISBN):
```

Fig. 3 — Initial cataloguing menu.

```
Add new record mode
Material: books, pamphlets and printed sheets
Main entry distinction
1=Unknown, uncertain or unstated authorship
      including works of probable authorship
2=Erroneous or fictitious authorship
3=Work is a collection
4=Mixed authorship
5=Shared authorship
6=Authorship attributed to personal author/
      corpoate body
7=Why?
Enter selection:
```

Fig. 4 — Initial menu for books, pamphlets and printed sheets.

Option 1 in Fig. 3 would lead to the more detailed questions about authorship shown in Fig. 5.

Once this stage in the cataloguing process is reached it is possible for the system to explain what is going on by referring to specific rules. Thus the 'Why?' option would lead to the display shown in Fig. 6. This facility would be helpful to novice cataloguers and students of librarianship.

Finally, supposing that the book had a single known author with an ordinary name, selection 6 in Fig. 4 would lead to another menu and then a screen form for data entry as shown in Figs. 7 and 8.

Add new record mode
Material: books, pamphlets and printed sheets
Main entry distinction
1=Authorship in the form of initials or numerals
2=Authorship indicated by typographical marks, e.g. !, @, M***, etc.
3=Authorship characterized by a word or phrase, e.g. 'by a physician'
4=Probable author indicated by reference sources
5=Authorship attributed in reference sources to one or more authors
6=None of the above
7=Why?
Enter selection:

Fig. 5 — Unknown, uncertain or unstated authorship.

Rule 51.5C states for selection:
1.   Main entry=initials/numerals
     Added entry=title
2.   Main entry=title
3.   Main entry=word or phrase
     Added entry=title

Rule 21.5B states for selection:
4.   Main entry=probable author
     Added entry=title

Rule 21.5A states for selection:
5.   Main entry=title
     Added entry=each attributed author
6.   Main entry=title of work of unknown authorship

Press C/R to return to previous menu

Fig. 6 — Explanation of rules for unknown, uncertain or unstated authorship.

Actually, since certain fields in catalogue records may exhibit considerable variations in length, it may not be possible to fit all the data in one
screen display. Therefore, instead of using a screen formatted like an entire
record, it might be better if the system were designed to prompt the
cataloguer to input one named field at a time. Whether VDU forms or a
series of prompts were used, the guidance provided would be specific for the
type of item concerned, i.e. book, journal, sound recording, etc., and would
be based on part 1 of AACR2.
It is possible to extend this process by developing highly specific
templates for types of documents which frequently present problems.
Publications intended to accompany Open University courses are a case in
point. The courses are broken down into blocks which consist of units.

Add new record note
Material: books, pamphlets and printed sheets
Main entry distinction
1 Corporate body
2 Head of State or high government or ecclesiastical
official
3 Personal author with surname and forenames
4 Personal author with other type of name
5 Why?

Fig. 7 — Type of name.

Add new record mode
Material: books, pamphlets, printed sheets
Responsibility: personal author (with surname)
Enter Surname: . . . .
        Forename(s): . . . .
Enter Title: . . . .
        Subtitle: . . . .
        Edition (if not first): . . . .
Word(s) denoting responsibility if present (e.g. 'by')
Enter Place: . . . .
        Publisher: . . . .
        Date: . . . .
Enter No. of pages: . . . .
Enter Series: . . . .
Enter Circulation system Copy Number: . . . .
Enter Class No: . . . .
Press C/R to skip inapplicable fields

Fig. 8 — Screen form for data entry.

Publications may or may not bear a block title and may consist of one or more units. Any group of units may be given a collective title. The various possibilities are shown in the decision tables in Fig. 9 below.

For the guidance of cataloguers in Exeter University Library, seven model records corresponding to the feasible combinations identified by the decision table rules are used. Templates corresponding to these models could be devised. Not all the conditions involved are mutually exclusive and therefore if presented in menu form it would be necessary to remind the cataloguer to select all those which apply, not just one of them.

Although decision tables are normally thought of in the context of conventional data processing they have been used in expert systems dealing with rheumatism (Weiss & Kulikowski 1983) and eye diseases (Barr & Feigenbaum 1982). Furthermore, van Melle (1981) has observed that the

Table 1

block title?	Y	Y	Y	N	N	N
collection title?	Y	N	N	Y	N	N
single unit?	N	Y	N	N	Y	N
Type						
1a or 1b			X			
2		X				
3				X		
4						X
5					X	
6	X					
Go to table 2				X		

Table 2

block complete?	Y	N
type 1a		X
type 1b	X	

Fig. 9 — Decision tables fof Open University course units.

rules of EMYCIN, which is probably the best-known tool for building expert systems bear some resemblance to extended entry decision tables. He also claimed that much of the rule set of SACON, which is used for guidance in the solution of structural analysis problems, could be more concisely and lucidly expressed using decision tables (van Melle 1981).

In order to test the ideas outlined above, it was hoped to implement an experimental cataloguing system on an ICL perq, but various problems were encountered. Initially James wrote a screen editor in Prolog, but execution of the program proved far too slow and therefore a different approach had to be tried. The solution adopted was to use another language for all the input/output operations while retaining Prolog for the actual processing of the data. In order that these input/output routines could function as an interface to the York Prolog interpreter, they were written in the same language as the interpreter itself, namely Pascal.

This interface known as TLOG (Template interface to PROLOG) allowed the designation of variable fields for the input of numeric and alphanumeric data and error fields too. TLOG also incorporated a protection facility to prevent the user from corrupting variable fields and an automatic tabbing facility for making the cursor skip forward or backward into unprotected variable fields. There was also a window area at the end of each template which was not available to the user when the template was being built or amended but was reserved instead for the display of system messages from Prolog.

Blinking fields could have been used to attract the operator's attention. Another desirable feature would have been notification of the depression of certain special keys so that mistakes such as keying CTRL/A for aborting a transaction instead of CTRL/E for ending it would not go unnoticed. However, owing to lack of time neither blinking fields nor special key depression notification were included.

The interface worked well. However, before the proposed experimental expert cataloguing system could be implemented, it would have been necessary to tackle problems of garbage collection to ensure that sufficient memory was available for the system itself and for files containing records featuring a reasonably representative collection of bibliographic conditions. As this was not possible in the time available the system was not implemented.

Nevertheless James performed a useful function in exploring the opportunities available for the use of knowledge-based techniques in this domain and his work serves as a suitable starting point for consideration of the factors which would influence the succes or failure of any expert cataloguing system intended for routine, practical use.

4.   EFFICIENCY AND USER-FRIENDLINESS

Experience in other areas shows that it is one thing to create an expert system which works; but creating one which will gain widespread acceptance by its intended users is another matter altogether. By the mid-1980s expert systems for a wide range of different tasks had been designed and implemented but many were simply prototypes. No system is likely to go into routine use unless the relevant knowledge has been extracted efficiently, and that is a difficult task except in quite simple domains.

What factors would determine the acceptability of an expert cataloguing system? This question needs to be considered from the viewpoint of the individual user and also in terms of the library's goals. The response at the level of the individual will depend on the latter's role in relation to the machine, while from the organizational viewpoint cost-effectiveness will also be a decisive factor.

The individual cataloguer requires knowledge of the following types:

(1) the bibliographic characteristics of different media, as without the ability to recognize these features it would be impossible even to select the relevant rules;
(2) the cataloguing code used, e.g. AACR2;
(3) local policies, e.g. regarding the treatment of specific types of material, or the level of description (i.e. the amount of detail to be included);
(4) filing rules which cover matters such as the choice of word-by-word or letter-by-letter order, etc.,
(5) the principles of bibliographic classification;
(6) the structure of the particular classification scheme used;
(7) a certain amount of subject knowledge, as, unless the cataloguer is able

to recognize the topics with which a book is concerned, correct classification is impossible.

Where computers are used in cataloguing, two additional requirements are:

(8) knowledge of the system's facilities and commands for using time;
(9) knowledge of the particular record format used, e.g. MARC (a very complex record structure developed as a standard so that bibliographic records could be interchanged and adapted by different libraries).

The burden of filing is eliminated in those automated systems where the catalogue is online or is output on microfilm or microfiche. A few systems are also capable of assigning MARC codes to different fields and sub-fields. We have seen that the rules of AACR2 could be embodied in a knowledge base and that by means of properly constituted templates it would be possible to cater for local policies. Furthermore, the proposed menu system with its help facilities would be largely self-explanatory. That still leaves the problems of recognizing relevant bibliographic features and all those involving classification.

The first of these limitations could be rather irritating to the operator. A mere glance at the title page enables a cataloguer to identify the names of the author(s) and publisher(s), the title and other salient features of a book. An experienced cataloguer dealing with a straightforward item can tell straightaway how the record should be constructed, in which case the need to go through those menus which determine the access points required would seem a waste of time. A way of overcoming this difficulty would be to allow more scope for volunteering information.

Although the flowcharts are very lengthy, diagrams showing the overall structure of the two algorithms from which the menus are derived occupy a page each in the book by Shaw *et al.* (1980) and could be displayed on a VDU. It is possible to envisage a system in which the structure of the access point selection process would be displayed and the cataloguer invited to indicate where he or she wished to begin. Similarly, before starting on the menus for determining the precise forms of the headings, the second structure diagram would be shown.

The cataloguer would still be faced with the task of classification. Choosing a subject from a menu may seem to have no significant advantages over looking it up in a printed index. However, as titles are often a good indication of the subject, it is possible that a program could make use of the information they contain. Key words from the title could be matched against terms in the classification schedules and the results displayed for selection by the cataloguer who could override them completely if necessary. In order to cope with synonyms, a thesaurus could be included in the system. By using terms from the contents list as well as the title, the chances of success would be improved greatly.

The analogous but much more ambitious proposition of extracting knowledge from journal articles was considered by Buchanan and Shortliffe

(1984) in the course of experiments with MYCIN and its various descendants. The proposal was to use the parser of an experimental natural language interface to MYCIN, called BAOBAB, to read simplified transcriptions of journal articles. However, they concluded that the task of transcribing the articles would involve as much intellectual effort as formulating the rules directly, and therefore the idea was not pursued. Nevertheless, Cambell (1985) has suggested that the extraction of knowledge might prove a feasible proposition after preliminary processing of the type used in automatic production of summaries of texts (Tait 1985).

Actually, a little of the sophistication of the knowledge extraction approach would be desirable in a program for classification. It is not enough to pick out key words. Syntax is also of importance in titles such as 'the role of the United States in the reconstruction of Italy'. A program for parsing titles and making sense of them ought to have sufficient intelligence to distinguish between a title and the name of the author. Therefore it may be possible to tackle the problems of identifying bibliographic features and classification by similar means.

Naturally the need to make bibliographic distinctions is, in simple cases, less burdensome than the need to input the data via a keyboard. The amount of typing necessary would be increased considerably if contents lists had to be processed for the purpose of classification. Therefore it is likely that these facilities would be worth incorporating only if optical character recognition replaced or supplemented the keyboard.

Books come in a wide variety of type fonts and therefore any optical character reader would have to be fairly versatile. Exactly the same pattern-recognition problems had to be overcome in order to produce a device for converting print into sound or Braille for the benefit of the blind. A prototype of an omnifont character reader with speech output was demonstrated by Raymond Kurzweil in 1975, and by the early 1980s thousands of reading machines were in use in American libraries, schools, government departments and agencies for the blind (Rice 1984). As a by-product of Kurzweil's original research, a data entry machine was developed which has attracted considerable interest among librarians because of its potential for converting card catalogues into machine-readable form.

Omnifont optical character readers have also been developed by various other companies. The OPTIRAM system is claimed to have a number of intelligent features. It can recognize complete words as well as characters and is even capable of reading handwriting. Although the latter takes considerably longer than printed matter, it is capable of learning the characteristics peculiar to a particular hand. Another intelligent feature of the OPTIRAM system is its format-recognition software. The layout of catalogue cards is generally consistent within libraries, even if it varies slightly from one library to another. Consequently, fields can be identified by their position. Typographical information, particularly use of capitals, helps to identify names of authors. Certain characters may also be used to identify data elements: coming after a numeral, 'ed' could stand for 'edition', but after letters would mean 'editor'. Thus by use of clues derived from layout, typography and the prescence of particular characters, the OPTIRAM system is capable of identifying and tagging fields and sub-fields in catalogue cards (Harrison 1985).

At first sight, the task of reading title pages and identifying data elements would be more difficult, as they slow greater variability in layout than catalogue cards and make fairly liberal use of capitals instead of restricting them to names. On the other hand, publishers sometimes use different type fonts for emphasis, whereas on typed, as opposed to printed, catalogue cards, the same typeface is normally used for all fields. Furthermore, while title pages in general display considerable variation, those belonging to books from the same publisher are likely to conform to a particular house style which would help an intelligent system to distinguish between different fields. As an additional check it would be possible to devise rules to assist in the identification of names.

The ending 'son' is a common feature in surnames of English, Norwegian and Swedish origin, while the prefix 'Mac' or 'Mc' is characteristic of Scottish and Irish surnames. Similar rules could be devised for many names used in other countries. There may not be any simple rule whereby the character string 'Eliot' considered in isolation could be identified as a surname, but if preceded by 'T.S.' it would be recognizable as such, since capital letters followed by full stops would probably be initials. Furthermore, data could be checked against tables of surnames, forenames, names of organizations, etc. The authority files which some libraries maintain in order to ensure that cataloguers are consistent could be used for such purposes. The same problem of editing names occurs in the preparation of author indexes to abstracts journals. After spending over 75,000 hours of human effort on this task for the period 1972–1976, the Chemical Abstracts Service decided to develop an automated system for matching names on the basis of a small set of heuristics (Soukup & Hammond 1982). This enabled the next set of quinquennial indexes to be produced much more rapidly.

Once bibliographic elements have been identified, a significant part of the cataloguing task has been accomplished. Software for manipulating appropriately tagged fields to produce records with the formats and access points specified by AACR2 or other codes is an essential part of conventional computer cataloguing systems. However, even if complete accuracy in identification and tagging of bibliographic features could be attained, an expert system would still make mistakes unless it had human assistance or access to certain kinds of general knowledge.

It is true that some meta-rules could be devised to tell the system how to apply cataloguing rules. The treatment of names containing prefixes is a case in point. German names such as 'von Goethe' could be distinguished from French ones like 'de la Fontaine'. However, filing practices depend on the nationality or language of the author and not the origins of the name. Afrikaans names may be indistiguishable from Dutch, but they obey different rules. John von Neumann was a Hungarian with a German name who became an American citizen and, consequently, entries for his works are filed in accordance with English practice. Without this general knowledge, an expert system would probably file the name as 'Neumann, John von' in accordance with the rules for German authors, unless the catalogue or authority file were checked first for previous entries, which is how human cataloguers work much of the time.

In fact, some rules would be impossible to apply automatically without access to an already existing catalogue. For example, in a library possessing works of Lewis Carroll the catalogue should contain a reference from the author's real name, Charles Lutwidge Dodgson, to the pseudonym by which he is better known. Therefore, if any of Dodgson's mathematical works were acquired, it could be inferred from the catalogue that one of the rules for pseudonyms, that covering the predominant name (rule 22.2C2), would apply. Thus the catalogue itself, or the authority file which determined the form of the headings, would constitute a gradually growing extension of the system's knowledge base (Burger 1984).

It seems likely then that a system could be devised capable of carrying out all the congnitive tasks performed by a cataloguer. The occasional mistake would be made owing to insufficient general knowledge, but human cataloguers also make mistakes. A system of the kind described would undoubtedly be more of an autonomous machine than a tool. The residual human role would be limited to ensuring that the title and contents pages were read by the machine and, assuming the system proved reliable, the issue of user-acceptability would be of no more importance than it would be for a photocopier.

Nevertheless, it is doubtful if anyone would consider it worthwhile to create a fully automatic expert cataloguing system using ACCR2 or any of the other major codes in the near future. A certain proportion of the rules could be applied, without the participation of the operator, by a system equipped with an optical reader, but any attempts to increase this proportion until the entire code were encompassed would almost certainly be subject to the law of diminishing returns. This problem is exemplified by rule 24.11A which states: 'If the name of a radio or television station consists solely or principally of its call letters or if its name does not convey the idea of a radio or television station, add the words "Radio station" or "Television station" and the name of the place in which the station is located'.

In the absence of any previous entry in the catalogue it is difficult to see how a program could apply this rule, except when the title or contents list provided clues in the form of words such as 'programme schedules.' Of course a cataloguer can check printed directories and other publications for information about organizations. Conceivably an expert system could also check this information if it were already online, but it would hardly be economic to create such files purely for the purpose of automatically executing rules dealing with problems of rare occurrence.

In view of the expense and difficulty that creation of an autonomous system would entail, it would be more logical to decide on a proper balance of human and electronic cognition and design a system accordingly. This could be done by incorporating OCR hardware and intelligent software in a menu selection system of the kind James worked on at Exeter. Transcription of data would be largely eliminated and the amount of information the cataloguer had to supply would be reduced, thus saving time.

The need to improve efficiency and avoid wasting the user's time is an important issue affecting the acceptability of expert systems in other domains. MYCIN has been criticized on the grounds that users are often required to provide information stored on other computers in the same building. The knowledge that this is the case could antagonize doctors, few of whom like having to type answers to a long series of questions. Buchanan and Shortliffe have argued that, 'with current technology. . .the consultation model increases the cost of getting advice beyond acceptable limits. Clinicians would rather phone a specialist and discuss a case verbally.' (Buchanan & Shortliffe 1984).

Anybody with any common sense, whether a doctor or a cataloguer, would be reluctant to use an expert system for a task which could be accomplished more quickly by other means. Despite this, according to Kidd and Cooper (1985), designers of knowledge-based systems have placed insufficient emphasis on efficiency in real-time interactive consultations. Four ways of ensuring efficient performance have been considered in this chapter:

(1) design of improved interfaces allowing greater scope for volunteered information;
(2) use of OCR equipment for data capture;
(3) use of meta-rules to reduce the amount of information it is necessary to elicit from the cataloguer;
(4) access to existing files, e.g. the catalogue itself (or, in the case of medical systems, medical records).

Apart from the use of OCR equipment, the above-mentioned points would be of fairly general applicability. However, in some respects efficiency would be of even greater concern in mundane areas such as cataloguing than in more intrinsically important domains. Where expertise is a rare and valuable commodity, as in geophysics and certain areas of medicine, knowledge bases which increase the availability of expertise will be of obvious benefit even when used in rather inefficient systems. This is not true of cataloguing expertise which is relatively cheap and not particularly scarce. Consequently, the expense of developing a full scale expert system for routine practical use would be worthwhile only if a considerable improvement over existing methods in terms of speed could be achieved.

5.   THE ECONOMICS OF CATALOGUING AND ARTIFICIAL INTELLIGENCE

According to Randall Davis (1984) expert systems techniques are suitable for use in domains with the following characteristics:

(1) there are recognized experts;

(2) the experts are provably better than amateurs;
(3) the task takes an expert a few minutes to a few hours:
(4) the task is primarily cognitive;
(5) the skill is routinely taught to neophytes;
(6) the task domain has high payoff;
(7) the task requires no common sense.

Cataloguing qualifies on all of the first five counts even though the time taken over the average item would be a lot closer to the lower than the upper time limit. Some doubt may be expressed over whether the sixth and seventh criteria are satisfied. In some cases it may be difficult to draw a line between common sense and general knowledge. The latter is certainly needed at least when the form of a complicated heading which is not already present in the catalogue has to be decided. Even so, unless the system were autonomous whatever common sense is required could be supplied by the operator.

Even though the expertise is not a particularly expensive commodity, catalogue costs constitute a significant proportion of the budgets of many libraries owing to the numbers of books involved and the manpower resources needed to cope with them. The results of a survey of over 800 British libraries published in 1979 showed that the average cost of cataloguing was £3.10 per title (Overton and Seal 1979). For university libraries the figure was £3.45. When multiplied by the number of books purchased in a year the cost is obviously appreciable. Malinconico (1984) estimated that expenditure on bibliographic control in American academic research libraries had reached a level of $140 million per annum. The investment sunk into catalogues of libraries of all kinds is considerable, but much of this investment will have to be written off, as many libraries are attempting to catalogue not just new accessions but also existing stock in order to take advantage of developments in technology.

The need to contain ever-increasing costs caused by the labour-intensive nature of their operations while simultaneously improving services led to a widespread adoption of computers by libraries in the 1970s for the control of circulation (loans) and for cataloguing. Initially the effect on cataloguing was confined to the method of production and, in some cases, the physical form of the output. European libraries have tended to prefer microfilm or mocrofiche in order to eliminate the need for manual filing even though readers are inconvenienced by having to use two systems, for old and new stock, unless or until the entire holdings are re-catalogued.

To avoid such inconvenience many American libraries using computers stuck to output on cards which had to be interfiled manually with the existing catalogue. By the early 1980s, however, a significant number of American libraries, followed by a trickle of European ones, had introduced online catalogues. Consequently, recatloguing is now a live issue on both sides of the Atlantic.

Some of the hopes of the early advocates of automation have been realized, particularly with regard to improved services. As far as costs are concerned, however, the situation is unclear. Such savings as are achieved do not live up to the exaggerated expectations encouraged by the continuing dramatic reductions in the cost of processing power and memory. An explanation for this phenomenon has been advanced which, if true, has implications not just for library automation but also for the commercial prospects for artificial intelligence in any application.

In the course of an investigation of the economics of the performing arts, William Baumol, one of America's foremost economists, developed in collaboration with W. G. Bowen the theory that certain activities are inherently vulnerable to a debilitating 'cost disease' (Baumol & Bowen 1966). This condition, now often referred to as 'Baumol's disease', afflicts certain labour-intensive areas such as local government, education, medicine, live artistic performances, legal services, fire protection and certain library services. Such increases in productivity as can be achieved in these areas tend to occur only sporadically. In contrast, the manufacturing section of the economy has experienced a steady stream of innovation and the resulting productivity increases have been accompanied by rising wages.

Although wages in the sector with limited scope for technological innovation may lag behind, they are bound to catch up periodically. The law of supply and demand will not permit the persistence of growing divergences since labour would move into the better-paid occupations and the ensuing shortages would force up wages in the jobs in which they had previously lagged. Therefore, even in the absence of productivity gains, wages in the services sector will grow and costs will increase steadily in real terms.

At first sight it may appear that, given the growth in the economy as a whole, these increases do not matter. However, the costs in this sector will continue to rise relative to those in the rest of the economy year after year, except when there is resort to temporary expedients, like reducing the quality of services. Owing to this inexorable process, it is likely that eventually there will be changes in the perceived value of those services which are not normally thought of as absolutely essential. Eventually they may come to be regarded as luxuries which can be ill-afforded.

This phenomenon is described by Baumol as belonging, along with the law of supply and demand, to a group of economic forces 'so powerful that they constantly break through all barriers erected for their suppression' (Baumol 1967). Any attempts to offset the cost increases are in the long run merely palliatives which have no significant effect on underlying trends.

Originally Baumol & Marcus (1973) thought that automation would help libraries to escape from the ravages of the cost disease. The formation of networks allowing libraries to copy each other's catalogue records has been a success but is subject to the law of diminishing returns. What extra benefit is gained by existing members if another library joins the 2,000 or so already belonging to OCLC? Improvements in productivity may also be achieved by limited the amount of detail in records but this method cannot be applied repeatedly without abolishing the catalogue altogether.

Consequently, existing solutions may well turn out to be palliatives in the long run. So far, however, automation has been applied mainly to routine processes, e.g. copying and amending records. Greater scope for economies exists in the more highly paid professional tasks, but automation in this sphere would require more than the use of conventional data processing techniques. Artificial intelligence then, may appear to be a remedy for Baumol's disease; but it has been claimed recently that computing itself may become susceptible to the same ailment.

Hardware costs have been declining at a spectacular rate over a long period but as they do so their importance in relation to the costs of software also declines. Owing to this trend future savings will apply to an ever-shrinking proportion of the total costs. Therefore Baumol and Blackman (1983) arrive at the conclusion that 'paradoxically, the extraordinary rate of technological progress in the field of electronics and the probability that this rate of progress will continue, implies that the remarkable decline in computation costs is likely to "self-destruct", conceivably leaving this activity vulnerable to the cost disease'.

Whether this scenario will prove to be accurate remains to be seen. Baumol and Blackman acknowledge that if computers are themselves able to take over the task of software creation to such an extent that software costs are held to something like their original share of the total then the downward trend in the unit cost of computation would continue. From this point of view efforts to develop a new generation of computers would appear to be more of a prerequisite for ensuring the continuation of the economic progress of all nations than merely a means whereby certain countries or firms may gain a competitive edge.

Paradoxically, although artificial intelligence could be a possible cure for Baumol's disease in many activities now dependent on human intelligence, the development of full scale working expert systems covering reasonably large domains is a prime example of a very expensive knowledge-intensive activity which libraries already suffering from the cost disease may be unable to afford.

6. FUTURE PROSPECTS

The same objection would not apply to a gradual osmosis of new techniques into the area of library automation. Cogent arguments for a deliberate blurring of the distinction between expert and ordinary systems have been put forward by Basden (1983) who has suggested that systems designers should adopt a more electic approach and select techniques from conventional computing and artificial intelligence purely on the basis of suitability rather than provenance. If this were done, systems with a fairly conventional design would incorporate knowledge-based routines for appropriate tasks. An example of a library application would be use of one of the more sophisticated types of optical character reader for input of data to a conventional system.

There is plenty of scope for gradually increasing the intelligence of existing catologuing systems. Very much more could be done in the way of automatic validation of bibliographic data. It was estimated in the late 1960s that about half of all errors could be detected in this way (Dolby *et al.* 1969). Nevertheless, many cataloguing systems in use in the 1980s are capable of detecting errors in two fields only, the ISBN and the copy number for the circulation system, both of which incorporate check digits.

In some respects, many automated systems make it more likely that mistakes will be made, since the need to assign and input MARC codes correctly introduces a potential source of error that is not present in non-automated systems. However, rules for assigning MARC codes can be implemented in programs and this method is already used in the DOBIS/ LIBIS (McAllister & McAllister 1983) and URICA (Goodram 1984) systems.

The changeover from ACCR1 to AACR2 in the early 1980s meant that libraries had to altar a considerable number of the existing fields in their catalogues. In many libraries with machine-readable catalogues, amendments to each affected record had to be input separately. At least one attempt to write software to perform the conversion automatically was abandoned because of the complexity of the task. Of the success a noteworthy example was the British Library's conversion program which utilized some intricate sets of 'if–then' type rules (Brindley 1981).

The automatic assignment of MARC codes and the conversion of catalogues to conform with new rules illustrate that small but useful amounts of knowledge can be incorporated in conventional programs. Use of decision tables to represent categorical or definite knowledge is a long-established data processing technique which, as mentioned earlier, has also been applied in certain expert systems. Incremental improvements along the above lines would add at least a rudimentary amount of intelligence to existing systems.

Eventually it is probable that computers which are much more suitable for knowledge-based applications will be available at affordable prices, as it is unlikely that the various fifth generation projects being pursued in different countries will all end in total failure. By then the process of developing large expert systems should be more of an economic proposition than at present, assuming that costs follow a typical learning curve over time.

A policy of incremental improvements to existing systems could possibly help to reduce the disruptive effects of the transition to a new generation of technology when the latter becomes available. It is often argued however, that it is a mistake to perpetuate previous practices in a superficially sleeker, more efficient guise. Hjerppe (1984) has suggested that prototype expert cataloguing systems with knowledge bases comprised of small subsets of existing codes could be used as tools for the study of cataloguing. Any conflicts or lacunae would soon become apparent and improved rules could be devised. Although creation of an expert system for the provision of assistance to catalogue users would be a desirable development, it would be sensible to rationalize our present codes rather than rely on intelligence in the searching system to compensate for design defects in the catalogue.

Hjerppe and Olander (1985) in the ESSCAPE project (Expert Systems for Simple Choice of Access Points for Entries) developed two expert systems based on EMYCIN and Expert–Ease for studying the execution of certain formulations of selected cataloguing rules. As a result of their investigations they concluded that AACR2 was flawed by the weaknesses listed below.

(1) Much too much is taken for granted.
(2) The basic entities are not properly defined.
(3) Some concepts overlap and as a result the rules are poorly constructed.
(4) Alternatives are not exclusive and precedence rules are not formulated.
(5) Distinctions and exceptions seem to have been made on an ad hoc basis.
(6) The hierarchical structuring of the code has been poorly executed.
(7) The relationships between general and specific rules have not been properly thought out.
(8) The number of distinctions made in the catalogue are fewer than those made in the cataloguing process. A many-to-fewer mapping results.

Conversion of AACR1 to AACR2 proved an expensive exercise for many libraries and the revision of the code was undertaken without any systematic study of the costs and benefits involved. Any successor to AACR2 ought to be planned in the light of the capabilities and limitations of computers. If an optimum balance between human and artificial intelligence could be struck, the adoption of a new code might prove to be cost-effective. In order to exploit to the full the capabilities of future computer systems, the successors to AACR2, RAK (which is used in German-speaking countries) and other codes could be designed as knowledge bases for use in intelligent systems. Encouragement, by the bodies responsible for the codes' of further research of the kind initiated by James in Exeter (Davies & James 1984) and that being vigorously pursued by Hjerppe and Olander (1985) in Linköping would be a prerequisite for the achievement of this goal.

REFERENCES

Barr, A. & Feigenbaum, E. A. (eds) (1982) *Handbook of artificial intelligenc*, Vol. 2. Los Altos, William Kaufmann, pp. 212–216.
Basden, A. (1983) On the application of expert systems, *International Journal of Man–Machine Studies* **19** (5) 461–477.
Baumol, W. J. (1967) Macroeconomics of unbalanced growth: the anatomy of urban crisis. *American Economic Review* **57** (3) 415–426.
Baumol, W. J. & Blackman, S. A. B. (1983) Electronics, the cost disease and the operation of libraries. *Journal of the American Society for Information Science* **34** (3) 181–191.
Baumol, W. J. & Bowen, W. G. (1966) *Performing arts — the economic dilemma*. New York, Twentieth Century Fund.
Baumol, W. J. & Marcus, M. (1973) *Economics of academic libraries*. Washington D. C., American Council on Education.

Brindley, L. (1981) The British Library's approach to AACR2. *Journal of Library Automation* **14** (3) 150–160.

Buchanan, B. G. & Shortliffe, E. H. (eds) (1984) *Rule-based expert systems.* Reading (Mass.), Addison-Wesley.

Burger, R. H. (1984) Artificial Intelligence and authority control. *Library Resources and Technical Services* **28** (4) 337–345.

Campbell, J. A. (1985) Personal communication.

Crestadoro, A. (1856) *The art of making catalogues of libraries.* London, Literary, Scientific and Reference Office.

Cutter, C. A. (1876) Rules for a printed dictionary catalog. In: US Bureau of Education, *Public libraries in the United States,* Part 2. Washington D.C., Government Printing Office.

Davies, R. & James, B. (1984) Towards an expert system for cataloguing: some experiments based on AACR2. *Program* **18** (4) 283–297.

Davis, R. (1984) Amplifying expertise with expert systems. In: Winton, P. H. & Predergast, K. A. (eds), *The AI business: the commercial uses of artificial intelligence.* Cambridge (Mass.), MIT Press.

De Morgan, A. (1847) *Arithmetical books from the invention of printing to the present time.* London, Taylor & Walton.

De Morgan, A. (1850) [Evidence to the Royal Commission]. In: Report of the Commission Appointed to enquire into the Constitution and Government of the British Museum. (House of Commons Parliamentary Papers, 1850, vol. 24 question 5815.) London.

Dolby, J. L., Forsyth, V. J. & Resnikoff, H. L. (1969) *Computerized library catalogues: their growth, cost, and utility.* Cambridge (Mass.), MIT Press.

Goodram, R. J. (1984) The AWA URICA system and TULIPS: its application at the University of Tasmania Library. *Program* **18** (1) 46–65.

Harrison, M. (1985) Retrospective conversion of card catalogues into full MARC format using sophisticated computer-controlled imaging techniques. *Program* **19** (3) 213–230.

Hjerppe, R. (1984) What artificial intelligence can, could and can't do for libraries and information services. In: *Proceedings of the 7th International Online Information Meeting, London 1983,* Oxford, Learned Information, pp. 7–25.

Hjerppe, R. & Olander, B. (1985) *Artificial intelligence and cataloging.* Linköping, LIBLAB Linköping University.

James, B. (1983) Expert systems for library cataloguing functions. M. Phil. thesis, University of Exeter.

Kidd, A. L. & Cooper, M. B. (1985) Man–machine issues in the construction and use of expert systems. *International Journal of Man–Machine Studies* **22** (1) 91–102.

Lee, R. M. (1983) Expert vs management support systems: semantic issues. *Cybernetics and Systems* **14** (2/4) 139–157.

Malinconico, S. M. (1984) Catalogs and cataloging, innocent pleasures and enduring controversies. *Library Journal* **109** (1) 1210–1213.

McAllister, C. & McAllister, A. S. (1983) A case for conversational cataloguing. *Electronic Library* **1** (1) 59–67.

Overton, C. M. & Seal, A. (1979) Cataloguing costs in the UK. BLRD report 5477. Bath, Bath University Libray.

Rice, J. (1984) The conversion of library records to machine-readable form. In: *Encyclopaedia of library and information science,* Vol. 37, supplement 2. New York, Marcel Dekker, pp. 48–65.

Shaw, M. *et al.* (1980) *Using AACR2: a step-by-step algorithmic approach.* London, Library Association.

Soukup, K. M. & Hammond, S. E. (1982) Author name processing at Chemical Abstracts Service: name matching using nonunique bibliographic identifiers. *Journal of Chemical Information and Computer Sciences* **22** (3) 172–176.

Tait, J. I. (1985) Generating summaries using a script-based language analyser. In: Steels, L. & Campbell, J. A. (eds), *Progress in artificial intelligence.* Chichester, Ellis Horwood, p. 303–311.

Weber, M. (1948) From Max Weber: essays in sociology. London, Routledge & Kegan Paul.

Weiss, S. M. & Kulikowski, C. A. (1983) *Practical guide to designing expert systems.* London, Chapman & Hall.

van Melle, W. J. (1981) *System aids in constructing consultation programs.* Ann Arbor. UMI Research Press.

Part II

Information retrieval

The amount of information available in bibliographic databases is growing rapidly, but access to these databases is beset with problems, as explained by Ingwersen in his chapter in Part IV. Methods of lessening these difficulties range in sophistication from the use of simple interfaces for routine tasks such as logging on, transmitting stored search stategies and downloading on the one hand, to the development of expert retrieval systems on the other. One example of the latter is RUBRIC (RUle-Based Retrieval of Information by Computer). The designers of RUBRIC found that many of the rules they had formulated defined alternative terms, expressions and spellings of the same concept, and therefore they suggested that the performance of the system could be improved by incorporating a more general thesaurus (McCune *et al.* 1985).

However, there are numerous thesauri already in existence. One of the best known, MeSH (Medical Subject Headings), has long been used for indexing most of the world's medical literature, and therefore Pollitt decided to exploit this advantage to the full, as he describes in his chapter on CANSEARCH, a system for retrieving information about cancer. The wisdom of exploiting rather than ignoring the existence of MeSH is confirmed by Rada (1985) who has also considered ways of using the thesaurus in a knowledge base.

CANSEARCH is meant to enable doctors to search part of the MEDLINE database without any assistance from intermediaries such as librarians. In tests of its performance, the results obtained by intermediaries tended to be slightly better. It is possible that further development work might alter that verdict, but as good intermediaries are not continuously available in all hospitals and surgeries, any easy-to-use system with a reasonably good performance should improve access to information. Our word 'thesaurus' comes from the Greek word for 'storehouse' or 'treasure-house'. This same word, borrowed by the Romans, was used by the anonymous classical author of a work on rhetoric, in defining memory as 'the treasure-house of the ideas supplied by Invention' (Caplan 1944). By 'invention', the rhetoricians meant the art of finding plausible arguments. Pollitt's work suggests that the thesaurus, which has long been a tool of the indexer and librarian, may yet help to turn our electronic memories into treasure-houses for those needing information.

One possible limitation of systems like Pollitt's is the static nature of the thesaurus and associated database. Contrast this with the dynamic organization of human memory:

> The brain is primarily an organ for storing information, but the storing that takes place is done according to selective criteria. The brain evaluates the information that comes to it by way of the senses. It filters it, sorts it, compares it with information already on hand, recombines it, and finally assigns it to its place. Karl Popper sees this selective process as inherently deductive and thinks it analogous to the 'learning process' of evolution, in which mutations resulting from genetic misreadings are subjected to a constant testing of their viability and, with few exceptions, are proved to be 'false' readings. (Eigen and Winkler 1981, p. 21)

Actually, the way in which we store information in our minds depends on how we learnt it. If we learn something off by heart we are unlikely to form the same kind of associations that we do when truly understanding and mastering the topic and are less likely to recall the information if its relevance is not obvious. Storage in a static system is comparable to rote learning, but Lebowitz describes how it is possible for a computer to create a pattern of associations automatically, in a manner somewhat more analogous to the way we do when we effectively understand new material.

Lebowitz's work on RESEARCHER is related to earlier investigations of natural language understanding, e.g. giving computers the capability of reading and 'understanding' newspaper stories on a particular topic. Scripts are one form of knowledge representation often used in such work. They are similar to the frames discussed in the Introduction. A script describes a typical series of events occurring in a routine situation and thus provides a context which facilitates comprehension of points which are not made explicitly. Scripts are separate fragments of knowledge even though some may have certain features in common. As generalization, and hence learning, depends on noticing resemblances, these common features need to be linked. Memory Organisation Packages (MOPs) are a means of representing knowledge that facilitates generalization (Bonnet 1985) and RESEARCHER make extensive use of a very closely related technique.

Of the two approaches described in this section, Pollitt's would appear more likely to result in the development of practical systems in the short term, as it makes greater use of existing facilities, but Lebowitz's may eventually lead to more powerful ones if its promise is fulfilled. However, a powerful system applied in a reasonably broad field maight encounter problems with terms capable of having more than one meaning and may require some sort of thesaurus or dictionary. Therefore, the two approches could turn out to be complementary in the long run. Certainly both deserve to be pursued.

REFERENCES

Bonnet, A. (1985) *Artificial intelligence: promise and performance*. London, Prentice-Hall.

Caplan, H. (translator) (1944) *Ad C. Herennium de ratione dicendi (rhetorica ad herennium)*. London, Heinemann.

Eigen, M. & Winkler, R. (1981) *Laws of the game: how the principles of nature govern chance*. London, Allen Lane.

McCune, B. P. *et al.* (1985) RUBRIC: a system for rule-based information retrieval. *IEEE Transactions on Software Engineering* **11** (9) 939–945.

Rada, R. (1985) Gradualness facilitates knowledge refinement. *IEEE Transactions on Pattern Analysis and Machine Intelligence* **7** (5) 523–530.

4

A rule-based system as an intermediary for searching cancer therapy literature on MEDLINE

A. S. Pollitt, Department of Computer Studies and Mathematics, Huddersfield Polytechnic

1. RETROSPECTIVE DOCUMENT RETRIEVAL IN THE INFORMATION TRANSFER CYCLE

The information transfer cycle employs many mechanisms to record, transport, store and retrieve information in serving the needs of a user community. A well-established part of this cycle, applicable to most sizeable user communities, is represented in Fig. 1, adapted and extended from Lancaster (1979, p. 2), where information is contained in documents published in journals and is distributed directly or indirectly to the user community.

A user's need to search for relevant documents may arise directly from a current or anticipated problem or be a planned activity as part of a programme of work, such as at the start of a research project. The retrospective document search and retrieval activity, shown as 'Search' in Fig. 1, may be carried out by the actual user or by an information search intermediary in the information centre on behalf of the user. The search activity of the user may comprise the manual scanning of personally held journals and photocopies or of journals held in the local information centre, together with scanning the lists of references in the indexing journals.

The research reported here investigated the possibility of computer searching carried out directly by the user as represented by the dotted line on Fig. 1. The contention is that computerized searching services will not have their full impact upon user communities until direct user searching is widespread. At the present time many users are unable to make full use of available computer searchable databases, as these require knowledge of both the mechanisms of performing a search and of the way a controlled vocabulary may be used to express a document search request. This research sought to design a front-end system to interpose between the user and an existing searching system, which would enable the user to undertake good quality searches without the knowledge or training demanded of the professional search intermediary.

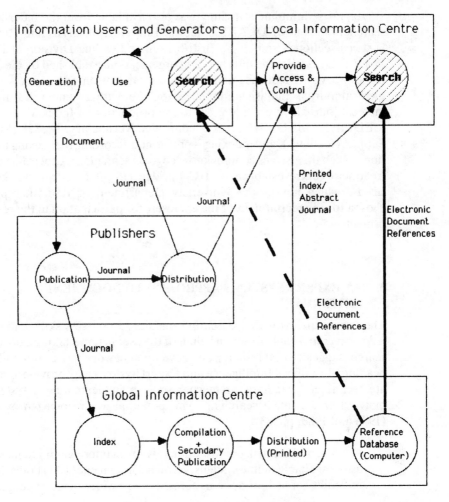

Fig. 1 — Part of the information transfer cycle.

2. DOCUMENT RETRIEVAL FOR CLINICAL CANCER THERAPY

The specific subject area chosen for research into the provision of an intermediary system is that of clinical cancer therapy. The research was carried out in collaboration with the Oncology Information Service based in the Medical Library at the University of Leeds.

The main function of the Oncology Information Service (OIS) is to generate regular monthly awareness bulletins containing references to recently published material relevant to workers in cancer therapy and research. In addition the Oncology Information Officer provides the skills and knowledge needed in using the abstracting and indexing journals and performing searches of the equivaent computer-held collections. The principal database consulted is MEDLINE generated by the National Library of Medicine, the computerized equivalent of Index Medicus.

Expertise in online searching was also available from the indexers and searchers in the MEDLARS (Medical Literature Analysis and Retrieval System) section based at the British Library Lending Division at Boston Spa. MEDLARS is the international organization established by the National Library of Medicine, and the section at Boston Spa indexes all the medical journals published in the UK together with a number of European medical journals to provide input to the production of Index Medicus and MEDLINE. MEDLINE uses a controlled vocabulary, MeSH (Medical Subject Headings), and indexing is performed according to indexing instructions which themselves contain knowledge on searching. A specialist cancer treatment centre established at Cookridge Hospital, on the outskirts of Leeds, which houses the University Department of Radiotherapy was chosen for the recruitment of the end users for participation in the research project.

3. AN EXPERT SYSTEMS APPROACH TO DOCUMENT RETRIEVAL

The requirement for the search intermediary to possess skills and knowledge, so as to be able to act on behalf of the user in undertaking a document search, suggested that research and development work carried out under the heading of Artificial Intelligence and Expert Systems may provide appropriate techniques, methods or mechanisms for implementing a system for maive user document searching. This potential was recognized by Smith (1976 and 1980, p. 383).

At present the end user must often rely on an intermediary to make use of available online systems. Artificial intelligence (AI) holds the possibility of making systems accessible to a wider range of people.

The majority of expert systems developed to date have been self-contained. The representations of knowledge embedded in them are consulted and applied either in the course of an interactive session, as in MYCIN for disease diagnosis and therapy recommendation or in PROSPECTOR for assessing geological sites with regard to mineral deposits, or without a user system dialogue, as in R1, the system which configures DEC VAX Computer Systems. One system, RITA (Rand Intelligent Terminal Agent/Rule-directed Interactive Transaction Agent) (Anderson & Gillogly 1976), developed by the Rand Corporation, was different in that it provided a language for defining intelligent interfaces to external data systems, and so contained knowledge and the ability to carry out tasks on a second system.

RITA represented the first attempt to use a program which embodied expertise to search a computer-held reference collection, the New York Times Information Bank.

In general RITA

performs routine and periodic services for the user or passes messages back and forth between the user and the system he is accessing, modifying them to make them more intelligible to either the user or the system he is accessing, the net effect is that of a friendly comprehensible system for the user. (Waterman 1978b)

Whilst RITA was able to handle the communications to make for a friendlier system for the user, no attempt was made to embody any knowledge of the subject matter of a document search. Other systems have been built however which advise or mediate on the use of a system. These include SACON (Bennett & Engelmore 1979), which advises on the use of a suite of programs for use in structural analysis.

The knowledge to be embedded in an expert intermediary system could be classified under four headings (Pollitt 1981, p. 27).

System Knowledge — the command language and facilities available in the search system(s) from logging-on and the submission of search statements to the printing of references or abstracts.

Searching Knowledge — relating to the strategy and tactics involved in searching.

Subject Knowledge — particular knowledge which can express typical searches . . . given a thesaurus of terms as a linking framework between the user and the information being sought. . .

User Knowledge — knowledge about each individual user including previous searches, preferred journals and personal reference collection.

An important consideration in the provision of an intermediary system is the nature of the interaction where infrequent computer terminal users may resist the idea of having to type in the details of an information search request. It is also important to recognize that the user is likely to have a poor model of the computerized document retrieval system, the way in which the database is established and maintained and the limited functions and facilities that it can provide for searching. These functions and facilities must be projected by the system for the user to be aware of their existence.

These considerations suggest the use of menus wherever possible with some easy method of selecting items from the menu.

The system should be robust in being able to cope with user errors without the need for any external support. An operational system would also need to be readily available and reliable.

In a key paper by Thompson (1971) it is stated that:

the process of matching or mapping the user's unstructured problem space into the retrieval system's highly structured index space is a complex sophisticated process that man does reasonably well provided he has the necessary information but computers find very difficult to automatically.

This description exemplifies the kind of problem tackled by research in artificial intelligence (AI) which, according to Duda & Shortliffe (1983, p. 261) has two goals:

> One is the development of computational models of intelligent behaviour, including both its cognition and perceptual aspects. A more engineering oriented goal is the development of computer programs that can solve problems normally thought to require human intelligence.

However Duda and Shortliffe (1983, p. 266) warn researchers 'not to duplicate intelligent human behaviour in all its aspects' but to 'constrain the problems addressed in realistic ways to allow useful solutions to real world problems'.

A general review of possible applications for expert systems in the library or information field has been provided by Clarke and Cronin (1983).

The application or adoption of expert systems approaches or techniques to document retrieval has centred on the role of the human intermediary as an agent who is able to help the user formulate a query and interrogate a database on behalf of the user. RITA, one of the original intermediary agents for document retrieval, mentioned earlier, was developed as a rule-based programming language (Waterman 1978a). RITA (Rule-directed Interactive Transaction Agent) could be used to:

> act as an interface between the user and computer facilities he wants to employ . . . The agent typically displays many of the characteristics of a human assistant. For example, it may have the ability to carry on a dialog with either the user or external computer systems . . . it may have specific knowledge about particular users.

RITA was patterned closely after MYCIN (Shortliffe 1976), which many people regard as the classic expert system.

Waterman (1978a p. 205) makes a distinction between active and passive agents:

> An active agent stands between the user and the external system hiding the characteristics of that system. The agent may carry on a dialog with the user in one language while communicating with the external system in another, never permitting the user to talk directly to the external system . . . In contrast a passive agent passes the user's input directly to the external system and the reply of the system directly back to the user.

The CONIT system (Marcus & Reintjes 1981) can be considered to be an active agent although the agent has a simplified task by presenting what is conceptually a single system interface and language to the user when accessing a number of heterogeneous retrieval systems. However, the fundamental requirements for the user to become aware of a command language and the way in which commands may be used in putting a query to a retrieval system remain. Essentially the CONIT intermediary does not provide a dialogue capability suitable to the end user which it could then convert to a dialogue required by the retrieval system and database being searched. Instead it retains the nature of the dialogue of the retrieval system being accessed.

The first intermediary system to be given the title 'epxert system' was developed by Yip at MIT (Yip 1981) as an extension of the work on CONIT. Entitled Expert-1, the approach taken in the design was 'to model a human expert's search procedures in terms of search strategy formulation and explanation'. The expertise built into Expert-1 included the following abilities:

> to assist the user to formulate his search problem . . . to formulate search strategy based on the concepts and search terms supplied by the user . . . to assist the user to select the appropriate databases to search in . . . to handle different protocols and command languages . . . to assist the user reformulate search strategy based on partial search results

Expert-1 provides no real subject expertise and relies on the user to identify concepts and provide keywords with no attempt by the system to examine or analyse this input. This makes the system a little more advanced than the RIOT system (Hall *et al.* 1972) with respect to the demands placed upon the user in formulating the search. The difference between CONIT and EXPERT-1 has been described by Marcus (1981, p. 270): 'while CONIT — and most of the other intermediary systems — emphasize a command/argument language approach to the unser interface, EXPERT employs only menus and fill-in-the-blank mode of computer–human interaction'.

The functions of a passive agent are characterized by the IIDA system of Meadow *et al.* (1982), which again does not seek to simplify the dialogue, but does monitor the interaction between searcher and retrieval system in an attempt to detect problems in the search process and then offers advice regarding a possible solution.

It is suggested that there is considerable scope for an expert systems approach to the provision of considerable semantic help in the form of an agent along the lines proposed by Thompson.

3.1   Abstracting the search space
MOLGEN, an expert system developed by Stefik (1981) as part of the Heuristic Programming Project at Stanford Univeristy, was designed to assist biologists in planning the design of experiments in molecular genetics.

The analogies with a document retrieval system are not immediately obvious. However, the central hierarchical structure of what are known as planning spaces provides an appropriate framework for the provision of a document retrieval capability. The general concept being one of abstraction which has been described by Stefik *et al.* (1983a, p. 70).

> One of the important skills in problem solving is the ability to focus on the most important considerations of a problem . . . Consider the problem of driving from the San Diego Hilton Hotel to the New

York Hilton . . . Trip planning could be formalised as a search process that starts at the San Diego Hilton and fans out through the streets of San Diego, enumerating non-cyclic paths until the fastest route to the New York Hilton is found . . . Using these ideas and the fastest computer available a driver would never manage to find a route to New York . . . In planning the trip without a computer, a driver would not be busy with street maps . . . but might start instead with a reduced scale map and consider only the main highways that cross the country . . . By searching an abstracted representation of a space, the combinatorics can be reduced. The search of the abstract space is quicker because it is smaller; single steps in the abstract space correspond to big steps in the ground search space . . . This amounts to hierarchical problem solving through various levels of abstraction.

Abstracting the search space was the central technique to be applied in the intermediary system whereby the controlled vocabulary of a database is an abstraction of the contents of all of the documents in the database. The laborious examination of all the routes in the problem described above may be seen to be analogous to examining every single document in a collection. However, unlike the driving problem which can at least apply such heuristics as 'head in a north-easterly direction', the document searching problem has numerous dimensions and no tangible directions to speak of in solving the problem.

3.2   The domain of the access system

The well-bounded domain required as the basis of the expert system has been defined as the retrieval of documents concerned with clinical cancer therapy stored on the MEDLINE database. By comparison with the expert systems which contain the knowledge sought by the user within themselves, such as MYCIN, the boundary of knowledge regarding the access system is much less distinct. It is perhaps useful to distinguish the domain as perceived by the user from that perceived by the access system designer. It is suggested that the user does not clearly distinguish the accessing aspects of the system from the document references being retrieved, and as such the domain of the system is the domain of the documents in that system. The designer, on the other hand, is concerned with access mechanisms and the vocabulary of the documents to be retrieved, never entering into the detail of the knowledge contained in any particular document.

In an expert system such as MYCIN or R1, the domain of the system can be physically examined by looking at the rules. In an intermediary or access system, the knowledge sought by the user is outside the system in a database where the sheer volume of material prohibits direct examination and forces the design of selective access mechanisms. The knowledge contined in an access system used by the system designer is not directly applicable in the treatment of a cancer patient. However, this presents certain advantages over the traditional expert system.

The specific treatment for a particular patient may be a matter for debate. This debate can be reflected in the documents without the need to embody or resolve the debate within the access system. Addition of knowledge in the form of a document does not require an immediate change in the access system. The rate of change of the access system will be slower than that of the expert system and as such makes the access system easier to maintain. The problem of certifying elements of knowledge either as facts or rules in the expert system is obviated by identifying documents within an already accepted publication system. Explanation of the knowledge in the user perceived domain is not required, although clarification of vocabulary may be essential in the course of query specification.

The user perceived domain of the access system will be much broader than for the expert system because of the more general nature of its knowledge. This can be illustrated by comparing the number of documents on clinical cancer therapy with the number of documents relating to the subject domain of MYCIN, the antibiotic treatment of bacterial infections of the blood. This is not to say that there is any equivalence between the documents and the knowledge in MYCIN, which in any case ceased development in 1978.

Number of document references on MEDLINE

Subject domain	1980	1981	1982	1983	1984	Total
MYCIN	176	185	195	221	210	987
Clinical cancer therapy	10,029	10,316	11,061	11,625	12,621	55,652

The knowledge for an access system comprises much larger grains than for the expert system, as it cannot usefully represent the same level of detail to be found in the actual documents to which it provides access, as pointed out by Sparck-Jones (1983):

> there is no useful sense in which we can provide the retrieval mechanism with all the knowledge embodied in the document collection. If we may refer to the machine in human terms, it is not at present medically possible to provide the system with the information or knowledge contained in, or represented by, the documents, for direct use in responding to the user . . . Thus we are dealing with an access system. However well indexers or authors may describe documents, we are working, with these descriptions or other document surrogates, with substitutes for the documents which are our real interest, and the real location of the information we seek.

The well-bounded domain in a document access system may be typified in a pragmatic way by suggesting that it refers to a sizable collection of documents accessed by a sizeable user community where specific query characteristics may be analysed to enable subject dependent search techniques to be practically incorporated into the system.

Failure to use the controlled vocabulary in searching the MEDLINE database can be compared to failing to use the 'main highways' in the route-planning problem described by Stefik *et al.* (1983a p. 70). Although the use of free text may be more efficient than looking at every document, recall and precision failures can be expected to be severe. Recall failures would not be evident to the user given that a significant number of relevant documents would still be retrieved.

Intermediary systems which provide a general searching facility requiring the user to supply search terms, will achieve a lower level of retrieval performance than is possible unless the user is aware of the controlled vocabulary and its application.

3.2.1 Facets of cancer therapy queries

A facet or component analysis of cancer therapy queries can be performed both intuitively and by examination of actual queries. A description of the subject area represents a range of potential queries from which general query templates, similar to the scripts mentioned in the CSIN system (Bergman 1981), can be proposed. Previous queries on the topic of cancer therapy, as listed in the report of the evaluation of CANCERLINE (Pollitt 1977), also provide guidance in the generation of query templates.

For example, an end user may be interested in the use of a particular drug for treating cancer at a particular site. This two-facet query would actually involve two MeSH terms and two subheadings.

i.e. disease-site/DT AND drug/TU

e.g. LIVER NEOPLASMS/DT AND METHOTREXATE/TU

(DT = drug therapy   TU = therapeutic use)

Each of the terms belongs to a different hierarchy in MeSH which at the highest level could be represented by:

cancer at a particular site and chemotherapy

or more generally:

cancer at a particular site and therapy

The appropriate subheadings can be applied by default in the case of therapeutic use of a drug. However, the application of the drug therapy subheading to the disease term is a consequence of the selection of chemotherapy. The appropriate term has been synthesized from knowledge of the indexing rules.

This first query template with the two facets of disease-site and drug can be viewed with different levels of facets. If any use of a drug in the treatment of cancer is the query, then the facet value of all cancers is needed in place of cancer at a particular site. This, for efficient searching, uses a searching feature known as 'pre-explosion'. In this case, the system performs a search for all documents indexed by any term in the C4 hierarchy of MeSH whenever documents are added to the database, the resulting set of indentities being stored against the code for the exploded neoplasms term, thereby saving searching time. The new query formulation is:

NEOPLASMS(PX) AND METHOTREXATE/TU

(PX = 'Pre-explosion')

Similarly, the query may be for any chemotherapy of liver cancer:

LIVER NEOPLASMS/DT AND EXP ANTINEOPLASTIC AGENTS/TU

This statement uses the 'explode' (EXP) facility to dynamically access the identities of all the documents indexed by terms in the atineoplastic agents hierarchy and restricts retrieval to those with the subheading 'therapeutic use'. In the above example, further simplification may reduce the query to LIVER NEOPLASMS/DT.

The general template can be extended to take this most abstracted form, the top level of the menu hierarchy:

all cancers   OR   cancer at a particular site
cancer of a particular histologic type

therapy   OR   multimodal therapy

patient details
miscellaneous concepts

3.2.2   The hierarchy of menus

The use of a hierarchy of menus for search statement generation has been described elsewhere (Pollitt 1982, 1983).

The first menu displayed to the user represents the top level of the abstracted search space where the selections of each option would normally lead to another menu at the next level in the hierarchy, the only exception at the top level being the term 'all cancers', which is effectively an end-term where no further detailed specification is necessary to complete this facet of the search.

The end-term may appear at any level of the hierarchy and is usually a choice between all terms or a particular term or set of terms, such as within the drugs hierarchy when the option is available to select from:

particular antineoplastic drug/s or drug classes
all antineoplastic drugs

The choice of 'all antineoplastic drugs' effectively selects all of the terms in the tree beneath that point in the hierarchy using appropriate short-hand mechanisms, such as pre-explosion or explosion of a particular term, without the user knowing.

The option of 'cancer at a particular site', presented at the top level menu, requires further specification to determine whether the query concerns either primary or secondary cancer or both. Rather than create two separate trees with site terms and allow selection from both to satisfy the third option, a qualifier is preselected on the site menus to indicate whether the site being selected is as a primary or secondary site. Conceptually this represents two separate hierarchies.

The full hierarchy is presented in Fig. 2.

3.2.3   Example query

To demonstrate the principle of end-user term selection for query specification, the frames and selections are presented for the query used to instruct the doctors prior to their experimental sessions. The query was for '5–FU in the treatmet of breast cancer'.

The system was designed to use a touch terminal where the user could directly select a term by touching the screen of the terminal, either with a finger or a pen or pencil. The touch terminal was able to identify indicated locations on the screen to a single character.

Fig. 3.1 presents the first frame (frame2) prior to any user item selection. The user touches the item 'cancer at a particular site'*, and the selection is indicated by reversing the video and redisplaying the chosen item as shown in Fig. 3.2.

Further selections are made to complete the top level specification of the search topic. In this example, 'therapy' is selected, Fig. 3.3, after which the command 'CONTINUE' is selected.

Frame15 is displayed in response to the selection of 'cancer at a particular site'*, Fig. 3.4, so that further specification regarding the nature of the site(s) can be established. After selecting 'specific primary site(s)'* on frame15, the top site frame (frame15a) is displayed, Fig. 3.5. Note that the term 'primary' at the top of the frame has been preselected following from the selection made on frame15. 'breast' is selected to complete the specification of site. This demonstrates how a search specification may not require the user to reach the end frames down a particular branch of the hierarchy shown in Fig. 2. End terms can be present for selection on frames prior to the end of a branch.

The next frame to be displayed is the top therapy frame, frame3, Fig. 3.6, and 'chemotherapy' is selected.

Fig. 3.7 presents the top-level chemotherapy frame, frame4, where 'particular antineoplastic drug/s or drug classes'* and 'therapeutic use' are selected.

Drugs have been classified into five classes, which are presented on frame5, Fig. 3.8. 'antineoplastic antimetabolites'* is chosen. Examples of the drugs to be found in each class are included in the menu to aid the user in selecting which class a particular drug belongs in. 'fluorouracil' is selected from frame9, Fig. 3.9, completing the specification of drug treatment and the topic of the search.

The resulting search statement formulation is then displayed, Fig. 3.10.

The sequence of frames visited is shown on Fig. 4, where the frames displayed are highlighted and the sequence of frames is given as circled numbers.

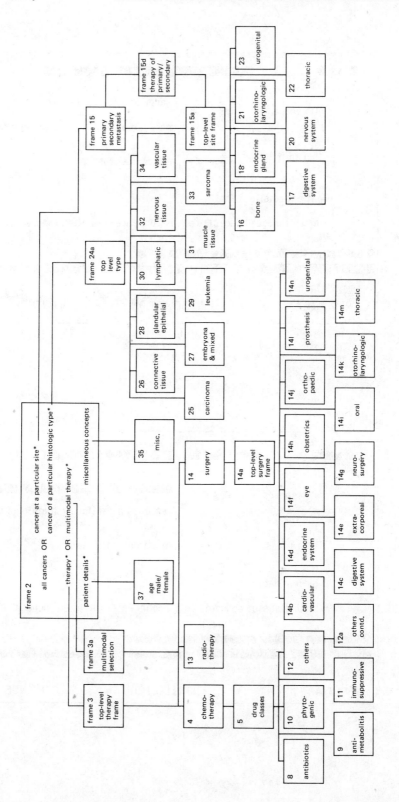

Fig. 2 — The menu hierarchy.

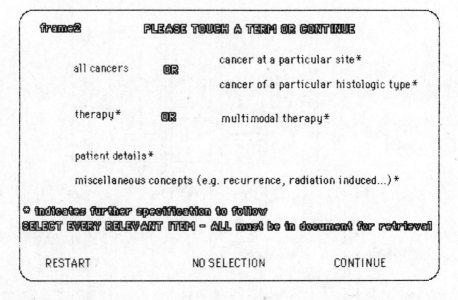

frame2   PLEASE TOUCH A TERM OR CONTINUE

all cancers   OR   cancer at a particular site*

cancer of a particular histologic type*

therapy*   OR   multimodal therapy*

patient details*

miscellaneous concepts (e.g. recurrence, radiation induced...)*

* indicates further specification to follow
SELECT EVERY RELEVANT ITEM – ALL must be in document for retrieval

RESTART   NO SELECTION   CONTINUE

Fig. 3.1.

frame2   PLEASE TOUCH A TERM OR CONTINUE

all cancers   OR   **cancer at a particular site***

cancer of a particular histologic type*

therapy*   OR   multimodal therapy*

patient details*

miscellaneous concepts (e.g. recurrence, radiation induced...)*

* indicates further specification to follow
SELECT EVERY RELEVANT ITEM – ALL must be in document for retrieval

RESTART   NO SELECTION   CONTINUE

Fig. 3.2.

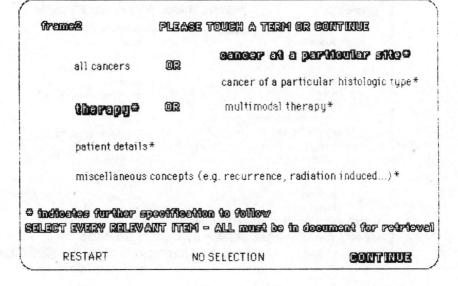

Fig. 3.3.

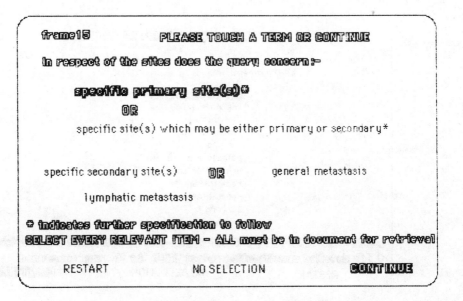

Fig. 3.4.

```
frame15a              PLEASE TOUCH A TERM OR CONTINUE
                as primary    /    as secondary
        abdominal                      head and neck
          peritoneal                   mouth*
          retroperitoneal              nervous system*
        anal gland                     orbital
        bone*                          otorhinolaryngologic*
        breast                         pelvic
        digestive system*             skin
        endocrine gland*                 sebaceous gland
        eye                              sweat gland
          conjunctival               soft tissue
          eyelid                     splenic
          uveal                      thoracic*
        choroid                      urogenital
        facial
  * indicates further specification to follow
  SELECT ALL RELEVANT SITES - ANY one is sufficient for retrieval
     RESTART            NO SELECTION              CONTINUE
```

Fig. 3.5.

```
frame3              PLEASE TOUCH A TERM OR CONTINUE


        all treatment methods

                chemotherapy*
                cryotherapy
                diet therapy
                fever therapy
                nursing
                palliative treatment
                prevention and control
                radiotherapy *
                rehabilitation
                surgery *
                terminal care

  SELECT ALL RELEVANT TREATMENTS -ANY is sufficient for retrieval
  * For detailed specification select ONLY the therapy concerned
     RESTART            NO SELECTION              CONTINUE
```

Fig. 3.6.

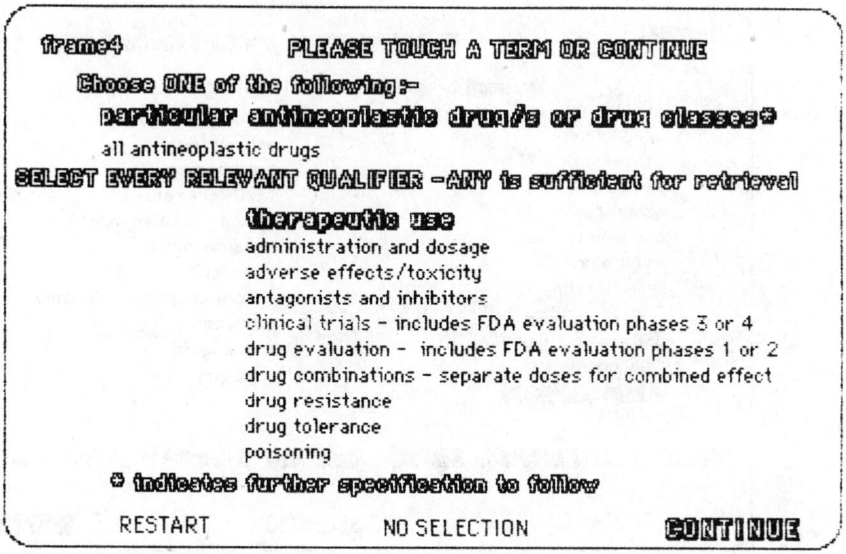

frame4   PLEASE TOUCH A TERM OR CONTINUE

Choose ONE of the following:-
        particular antineoplastic drug/s or drug classes*
    all antineoplastic drugs
SELECT EVERY RELEVANT QUALIFIER -ANY is sufficient for retrieval

                    therapeutic use
                    administration and dosage
                    adverse effects/toxicity
                    antagonists and inhibitors
                    clinical trials - includes FDA evaluation phases 3 or 4
                    drug evaluation - includes FDA evaluation phases 1 or 2
                    drug combinations - separate doses for combined effect
                    drug resistance
                    drug tolerance
                    poisoning
        * indicates further specification to follow

        RESTART   NO SELECTION   CONTINUE

Fig. 3.7.

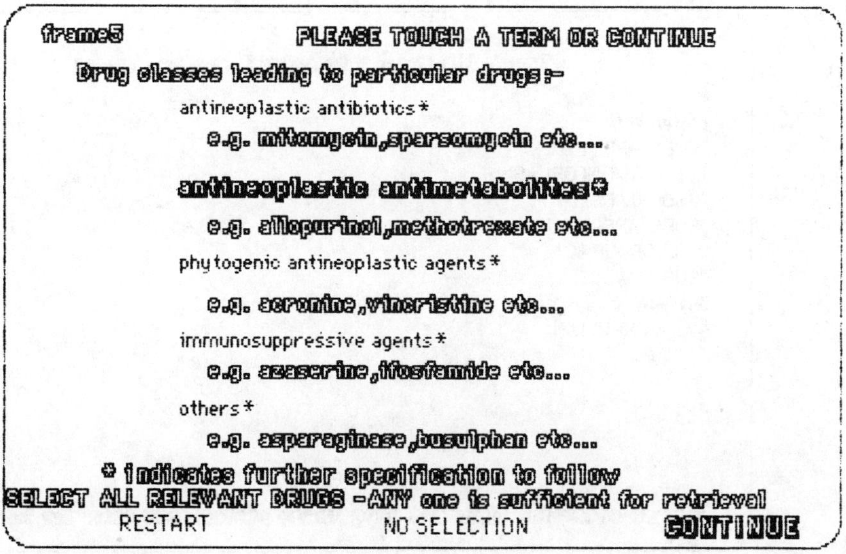

frame5   PLEASE TOUCH A TERM OR CONTINUE

Drug classes leading to particular drugs:-
        antineoplastic antibiotics*
            e.g. mitomycin,sparsomycin etc...

        antineoplastic antimetabolites*
            e.g. allopurinol,methotrexate etc...

        phytogenic antineoplastic agents*
            e.g. acronine,vincristine etc...

        immunosuppressive agents*
            e.g. azaserine,ifosfamide etc...

        others*
            e.g. asparaginase,busulphan etc...
        * indicates further specification to follow
SELECT ALL RELEVANT DRUGS -ANY one is sufficient for retrieval
        RESTART   NO SELECTION   CONTINUE

Fig. 3.8.

frame3   PLEASE TOUCH A TERM OR CONTINUE

                    all antineoplastic antimetabolites
        allopurinol   folic acid antagonists
        azaguqnine   aminopterin
        azaserine   methasquin
        azathioprene   methotrexate
        azauridine   tetrahydrohomofolic acid
        bromebric acid   mercaptopurine
        cytarabine   butocin
          cyclotidine   puromycin aminonucleoside
        3-deazauridine   thioguanine
        diazooxonorleucine   toyocamycin
        fluorodeoxyuridine   tubercidin
        fluorouracil
          ftorafur

    SELECT ALL RELEVANT DRUGS - ANY one is sufficient for retrieval

        RESTART   NO SELECTION   CONTINUE

Fig. 3.9.

                    Touch the screen to submit another query or stop

    statement
    "SUBS APPLY DT
    1 : BREAST NEOPLASMS
    "SUBS CANCEL
    "SUBS APPLY TU
    2 :FLUOROURACIL
    "SUBS CANCEL
    3 :1 AND 2
    4 :3 AND HUMAN

    Please enter the time and copy these statements onto the form

Fig. 3.10.

3.3   CANSEARCH: program design and implementation

The program to provide the intermediary system was given the title CANSEARCH, a name which has since been used to refer to the whole system.

3.3.1   *Language-independent program design, rules and the use of blackboards*

The CANSEARCH program design is based on sets of rules which carry out matching functions on user selections and internal messages (sometimes referred to as tokens), and perform actions appropriate to the conditions signified by the match. These rules represent knowledge of search statement formulation for the retrieval of cancer therapy related references from the MEDLINE database.

The internal messages and eventually the actual MEDLINE search terms are written to working storage areas, called blackboards, where each board is concerned either with some facet of the query or with an element of control.

The original rules were written in a language-independent fashion, each rule being applicable in a particular context. The following rules demonstrate the basis of the program design.

To initialize the blackboards prior to processing a new query, the message 'start' is written on the control board. The highest level of rule context in the dialogue portion of the program is that which determines which frame to display. The first rule in this context cleans all the boards and displays the top level menu, frame2:

```
IF 'start' on control board
THEN  erase 'start' from control board
         clean all boards
         display frame2
         context frame2
```

The change of context at the end of the rule passes control to the set of rules which process the selections made by the user from frame2. There are two types of rule in this lower context. The first is concerned with consistency in user selections and will force the user to correct inconsistent selections. For example, if a user selects both 'all cancers' and 'cancer at a particular site', this forces reselection through exercising the following rule:

```
IF 'all cancers' is selected
AND 'cancer at a particular site' is selected
THEN  display 'select all cancers or particular cancers' reselect
```

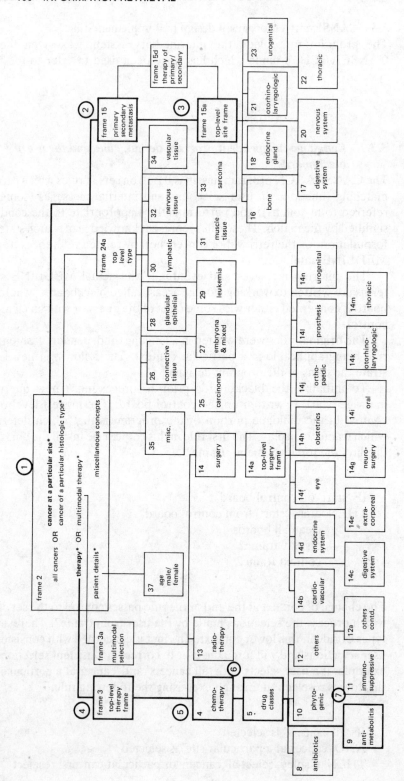

Fig. 4 — Trace of the example query.

The second type of rule in this context is only reached if none of the consistency-checking rules can be applied. The general form of the rule is to match user selections and update the contents of appropriate blackboards. For example, if the user selects 'cancer at a particular site', the following rule wil be exercised:

> IF 'cancer at a particular site' is selected
> THEN deselect 'cancer at a particular site' write 'site to specify' on site
>   board

When all of the selection processing rules have been exercised, or failed to match, the context is changed by a general rule at the end of the set of rules. This rule always succeeds as it does not have to match any data:

> IF TRUE
> THEN context frame selection

A second rule from the frame selection context would then be seeking to match with the message left by the lower level rule:

> IF 'site to specify' on site board
> THEN erase 'site to specify' from site board
> display frame15
> context frame15

Another rule from the user selection context will write the MeSH search term on the blackboard:

> IF 'ear' is selected
> THEN deselect 'ear'
>   write 'EAR NEOPLASMS' on primary site board

WEhen a large number of such rules are required they can be written in a general form by introducing variables:

> IF Site is selected
> THEN deselect Site
>   write Site & 'NEOPLASMS' on primary site board

Site, the variable, will take the value of any user selection not processed. Rules handling exceptions to the general rule need to be placed before it.

The third context for rules is that which applies when the selection process has been exhausted and no further frames can be displayed. These rules deal with the generation of search statements. One example of a rule from this context shows matching, again using variables, to determine whether a command to establish a subheading needs to be generated:

IF Subheading on therapy subheading board
    AND EITHER Site is on primary site board
    OR   Type is on type board
THEN generate 'SUBS APPLY' & Subheading

The rules are all data-driven and forward-chaining. The overall architecture is presented in Fig. 5.

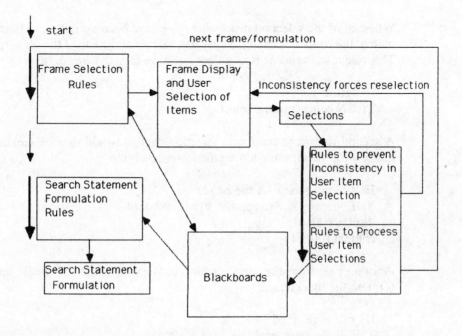

Fig. 5 — Rule-based architecture of CANSEARCH.

3.3.2 Implementation in Prolog
Prolog (Clocksin & Mellish 1981) provides a programming language suitable for carrying out the necessary matching functions described in the above rules.

Implementation was achieved on a Prime 750 time-shared minicomputer in Portable Prolog (Spivey 1982), a Prolog interpreter written in Pascal at York university, which was written to comply with the Edinburgh syntax.

3.3.2.1 The use of blackboards in Prolog
The following is a list of the main blackboards as they are named in the Prolog program:

```
control_board
site_board
primary_site_board
secondary_site_board
type_board
therapy_board
therapy_sub_board
drug_therapy_board
radiotherapy_term_board
surgery_therapy_board
drug_sub_board
surgery_sub_board
patient_board
misc_board
```

In the program development version of CANSEARCH, a feature was built in to allow the contents of any blackboard to be examined through the use of a 'BOARDS' command at the foot of each frame. This command could be touch selected at any time during the search specification dialogue. When selected, a menu of all the blackboard names would be displayed.

Writing, reading and erasing the contents of a blackboard in Prolog is straightforward. Writing the message 'site_to_specify' on the site board uses the built-in prediocate 'assert':

```
assert(site_board(site_to_specify))
```

Checking whether a particular message is on a board, such as the 'site_to_specify' message, is done by stating the blackboard name and the message as a predicate:

```
site_board(site_to specify)
```

This predicate will evaluate to true if 'site_to_specify' is a message on the site_board.

Cleaning a message from a board uses the built-in predicate 'retract':

```
retract(site_board(site_to_specify))
```

This will clean the message 'site_to_specify' from the site_board.

Variable names can be used to match with a message or term on a board. The variable name in this version of Prolog must begin with a capital letter. For example:

```
primary_site_board(Site)
```
_will match Site with a term on the primary_site_board. The value matched by a variable will be associated with that variable within a rule, so that a

particular item may be acted upon within a rule and then removed without
having to refer to its actual value, using 'retract':

    retract(primary_site_board(Site))
_This will remove the term in Site from the primary_site_board.
    Given the easy-to-read predicates and simple rule syntax, the program
rules were developed directly in Prolog, instead of in a programming
language-independent form as described earlier.

3.3.2.2   Frame selection rules

The frame selection rules (master_select) examine the blackboards to
determine which frame should be displayed. Before a new query is to be
processed, the initial condition is established by placing the message 'start'
on the control_board. The first rule detects the presence of this message and
cleans all the blackboards presenting the user with frame1, which allows the
user to stop the session or submit a query. If there is a query to process, then
the message 'frame2' is placed on the control_board and 'start' is removed.
This second rule provides the pattern for the majority of master_select rules.

```
master_select:-control_board (frame2),
                retract(control_board (frame2)),
                fdisplay(f2),
                user_select1,
                f2cr,
                !,fail.
```

Given the matching of the item on the board, in this example 'frame2' on the
control_board, retract the message from the board, display the appropriate
frame, fdisplay(f2) displays frame2, request user selections and then process
these selections with the frame rules. f2cr is the controlling rule to cycle
through the f2 rules in the above example.

```
f2cr:-repeat,
      f2r.
```

The same pattern of rule can be seen where there is also system selection
of a displayed item. In this example the primary site(s) of the cancer are
about to be specified:

```
master_select:-site_board(primary),
                retract(site_board(primary)),
                fdisplay(f15a),
                select('as primary'),
                user_select1,
                f15acr,
                !,fail.
```

As mentioned earlier, general reference can be made to the contents of boards using variable names, names starting with a capital letter, such as 'Type' for the type of cancer which requires a more detailed frame to be displayed and further specification to take place. This can be expressed in general instead of explicitly for each expanding type:

```
master_select:-type_board(Type),
              expand(Type),
              next_frame(Type, Frame),
              fdisplay(Frame),
              user_select1,
              rulesapply(Frame, Framerules),
              call(Framerules),
              retract(type_board(Type)),
              retract(expand(Type)),
              retract(next_frame(Type, Frame)),
              !,fail.
```

'Type' picks up an entry on the type_board and 'expand' determines whether this term requires further specification. This fact was established if, in the key fact, there was a frame number stored against the item, as described in the next section. The frame number for display is picked up in 'Frame', and the standarized naming of the rules which process user item selection allows this name to be generated for this frame and the rules exercised using the built-in predicate 'call'. The use of variables in this way dramatically reduces the number of master_select rules that would otherwise be required to manage the display of frames.

When no master_select rule matches with the data on the blackboards the final master_select rule is encounterd:

```
master_select:-true
```

This allows control to proceed and exercise the rules which carry out search statement formulation.

3.3.2.3   Rules to process user item selections

At the completion of specification from a given frame the 'CONTINUE' command is selected. Rules which examine what selections have been made update the contents of the blackboards, e.g.:

```
f2r:-rselected('cancer at a particular site*'),
     assert(site_board(site_to_specify)),
     !,fail.
```

where 'rselected' has been defined as:

```
rselected(Termlist):-selected(Termlist),
                retract(selected(Termlist)).
```

If an item has been selected by a user, then in the rules processing selections it is identified and removed by 'rselected' and a blackboard is updated using 'assert'. In the above example, the board is updated to ensure another frame display to further specify the site of the cancer. A message will be detected by one of the 'master_select' rules which determine the frames to be displayed. Once the above rule has fired, the retract in 'rselected' ensures that the firing is not repeated.

Final search terms are also written to the blackboards, e.g.:

```
f26r:-rselected('osteogenic sarcoma'),
      add_type_board('SARCOMA, OSTEOGENIC'),
      !,fail.
```

This example demonstrates the conversion from the alphabetic ordering chosen from display for the user of CANSEARCH, to the legal inverted form from the Medical Subject Headings Thesaurus (MeSH).

When inversion is not taking place, then a catch-all rule is introduced, e.g.:

```
f26er:-add_type_direct(Termlist),
       !,fail.
```

where 'add_type_direct' has been defined as:

```
add_type_direct(Termlist):-
               rselected(Termlist),
               upercase(Termlist, Upper_Termlist),
               name(Medline_Term, Upper_Termlist),
               assert(type_board(Medline_Term)).
```

More significant translation takes place where the presented item defines the underlying MeSH term more precisely than the term itself, a common example being the use of the qualifier 'general' proceding a term, e.g. 'general bone neoplasms' which translates into the MeSH term 'BONE NEOPLASMS'. This is to discourage the use of the 'BONE NEOPLASMS' term when there are more specific terms.

3.3.2.4   Search statement formulation rules

The search statement formulation rules are in two parts: the first deals with the combination of terms within blackboards, whilst the second creates the search statements which combine the contents of different blackboards.

There are two principle types of blackboard contents. One contains the controlled vocabulary terms of MeSH, such as to be found on the primary_site_board at the end of the specification; the other contains the subheadings applied to qualify MeSH terms, such as on the therapy_sub_board. If more than one MeSH term is on a particular blackboard, the terms will either be ORed or ANDed together, depending on the contents of other boards.

ORing terms together is achieved by the repeated firing of a rule transforming the multiple term contents of a blackboard, e.g.:

'INTESTINAL NEOPLASMS' and 'CECAL NEOPLASMS'

on the primary_site_board into:

'INTESTINAL NEOPLASMS OR CECAL NEOPLASMS'

using the following:

```
    or_primary_site_terms:-repeat,
or_primary_site_terms2.

    or_primary_site_terms2:-
                primary_site_board(TERM1),
                primary_site_board(TERM2),
                not(Term1=Term2),
                or_together(Term1, Term2, Term3),
                assert(primary_site_board(Term3)),
                retract(primary_site_board(Term1)),
                retract(primary_site_board(Term2)),
                !,fail.
    or_primary_site_terms2:-true.
```

At the end of the ORing and ANDing operations, the rules which generate the actual search results are exercised. The general form, whereby a rule fires if it matches the contents of the blackboards, remains as with the previous rules, except that these rules do not typically change the contents of the blackboards. The blackboards need to remain intact as they are consulted by different rules. This requires some more direct control of rule-firing, to prevent repeated firing of the same rule from always being able to match its conditions with the current state of the blackboards.

The control is provided by testing for the presence of a rule flag on entry to a rule. If the flag is present then the rule cannot be exercised; if not, then the flag is set and the rule entered, e.g.:

```
    /* Rule b Asserts Site or Site-Type then ANDS */
    s_s_g:-enter(b),
            primary_site_board(Site),
            assert_inc(Site),
```

```
                    type_board(Type),
                    assert_inc(Type),
                    and_last_two,
                    !,exit(b_2).


            assert_inc(Statement):-
                    assert(statement(Statement)),
                    inc_statement_number.
```

The predicate 'assert_inc' saves a numbered search statement as a fact on the 'statement' blackboard and increments the search statement number. In the above example, it will save a statement containing the primary site terms. If type terms are also present, then a further statement is saved, and then a boolean statement combining the previous two statements is generated and saved using the 'and_last_two' predicate.

Typically, the rules to be found in seach statement formulation are more complicated than those found elsewhere in the CANSEARCH program. Some rules are concerned with the establishment of subheadings during the course of the search, using the 'SUBS APPLY' command, e.g.:

```
            /* Rule a, subheadings for site, site&type, type */
            s_s_g:-enter(a),
                    therapy_sub_board(Subheading),
                    (primary_site_board(Site);
                      type_board(Type)),
                    set_therapy_sub(Statement),
                    assert(statement(Statement)),
                    !,exit(a).


            set_therapy_sub(Statement):
            thrapy_sub_board(Statement_subs),
            name(Statement_subs,Subslist),
            append(""SUBS APPLY"", Subslist,Statement_list),
            name(Statement,Statement_list).
```

Commands which implement subheadings do not use a statement number. This way of implementing subheadings using commands is a feature of the software used to search MEDLINE at the National Library of Medicine. This situation is made simpler when the subheadings can be treated more like normal terms within the search statements, as in the software provided for searching MEDLINE on the Data-Star host.

Each rule which fires should leave the lastest statement as combining all previous search statements up to that point. The result of the search so far should be the result of the last search statement.

4.   AN EXPERIMENT TO TEST CANSEARCH

4.1   Objectives of the experiment

The main objective of the experiment was to determine whether the CANSEARCH approach to document retrieval by naive end users was feasible. To satisfy this objective the following questions needed to be answered:

(1) Could doctors, with no training or assistance, use CANSEARCH to specify the subject of a query concerning cancer therapy?
(2) Would CANSEARCH be able to generate legal MEDLINE search statements which corresponded to the subject of the query?
(3) Would relevant documents be retrieved from the MEDLINE database using the search statements generated by CANSEARCH?
(4) Would CANSEARCH be as effective as a human information search intermediary?

In testing CANSEARCH to answer these questions it was also possible to satisfy other objectives, notably to identify the reasons for failure, in particular with reference to vocabulary coverage which could be used in any further development to improve the performance of CANSEARCH.

4.2   Test queries

Forty queries were provided by the following information services/libraries:

John Squire Medical Library,
Clinical Research Centre,
Medical Research Council,
Harrow.

The Library,
Institute of Cancer Research,
Royal Cancer Hospital,
London.

The Medical Library,
Christie Hospital & Holt Radium Institute,
Machester.

Oncology Information Service,
School of Medicine,
University of Leeds,
Leeds.

The Medical Library,

Wessex Regional Library Service,
Southampton General Hospital,
Southampton.

All these queries had at some time been presented to one of the above information service/libraries and had resulted in an online search.

The queries were grouped into three classes. Class 1 queries, listed in Table 1, co-ordinated concepts of cancer and therapy which were contained in the CANSEARCH program; Class 2 queries co-ordinated concepts of cancer and therapy where at least one concept was not contained in CANSEARCH; and Class 3 queries included other concepts in addition to those on cancer and therapy. Class 2 and Class 3 queries are listed in Table 2.

The division into classes recognized the limited scope of CANSEARCH and the limited development that was possible in the time and with the resources available. Only Class 1 queries were used in tests associated with answering question 3 because of the predictability of retrieval failure for Class 2 and Class 3 queries.

These queries were genuine user queries, and could be considered to be representative of the population of potential queries that might be encountered in different libraries or information centres, or more appropriately in different hospitals, where terminals providing access to cancer therapy documents could be located.

4.3   The doctors
Eleven Doctors were recruited from Cookridge Hospital, a cancer treatment centre on the outskirts of Leeds. A copy of the CANSEARCH program was mounted on a Prime 9750 computer, belonging to Leeds University's Computing Service, and a special communications line was made available to enable the Touch Terminal to be sited in an office in the Tunbridge Building at Cookridge Hospital, the main building of the Department of Radiotherapy. Siting the terminal at the Hospital was seen as essential in encouraging or attracting doctors to participate in the experiment with the very minimum of inconvenience and disruption to their very busy schedules.

The doctors included Consultants, Senior Registrars and Registrars, with a range of ages and experience. it was anticipated that individual specialisms, experience and interests would impact on the doctors' attitude towards each test query and that their previous information-seeking activity, especially of online searching using an intermediary and manual searching of Index Medicus, would influence their use of the CANSEARCH interface. Problems could also be anticipated because the Doctors were having to interpret someone else's search requirement. However, no analysis was made of doctors as it was felt that these end users reflected a significant number of the intended end user population. The differences between doctors was levelled to some extent by using repeated measures, the same

Query Number	Query
1	Cis-platinum in ovarian cancers
4	Clinical trials for colonic neoplasms
10	Hyperthermia used in cancer therapy
11	Use of cis-platinum for head and neck neoplasms
12	Therapy of cancer of paranasal sinuses
13	Chemotherapy of ovarian neoplasms
14	Complications of mitomycin therapy of stomach cancer
19	Treatment of breast cancer using megavoltage radiotherapy
20	Treatment of lung metastasis
23	Vincristine therapy of bladder neoplasms
25	Surgery of pulmonary lyumphoma
27	Treatment of parotid neoplasms
28	Treatment of mesothelioma
29	Chemotherapy of neuroblastoma or carcinoid tumours
32	Drug therapy of prostatic cancer
33	Pre and post operative radiotherapy of esophageal cancer
35	Bilateral adrenalectomy for secondary carcinoma from the breast
36	Ovarian granulosa cell cancer treatment
37	Therapy of cervix neoplasms
40	Surgery, radiotherapy or chemotherapy of testicular cancers

Table 1 — Class 1 Test Queries.

Query Number	Query
	Class 2
2	Autologous bone marrow transplantation in malignant disease
3	Interferon in multiple myeloma or plasmacytoma
5	Tumour regression after cryotherapy or fulguration
7	Use of cyclophosphamide or DTIC by infusion or continuous administration in the treatment of malignant disease
9	lacrimal gland tumours and radiotherapy
15	Effects of ricin and abrin on melanoma
16	Methods of treating melanoma of the groin nodes
17	malignant melanoma treatment with endolymphatic therapy
18	Comparison between conservative and radical surgery combined with radiotherapy in the treatment of breast cancer
21	Endocrine treatment in breast cancer
22	Management of fungating tumours
24	Total body irradiation or bone marrow transplantation and acute leukemia
30	Drug therapy of sacral chordoma
31	Management of borderline ovarian tumours
34	Therapy of Stage I and Stage II seminoma of the testes
	Class 3
6	Economics and effectiveness of cancer chemotherapy
8	Obstructive uropathy or ureteric obstruction as radiation complication of radical radiotherapy in carcinoma of the cervix
26	Psychological ill-effects of cerebral irradiation in young children
38	Radiation myelitis, radiation myelopathy in radiotherapy
39	Ethambutol hydrochloride inhibited by radiation therapy

Table 2 — Class 2 and 3 Test Queries.

query being processed by different doctors with overall and average measures being made.

Each doctor was allocated eight queries randomly selected from the test set, with four from Class 1, three from Class 2 and one from Class 3. The queries were placed in a random sequence to take account of sequence effects by averaging these out across the different doctors.

The experimenter was present during the experiment to initialize the system, cope with system or program errors and record the resulting search formulations. Each doctor was presented with a single page introduction, Fig. 6, which included an example search which the doctor was intended to work through, using CANSEARCH, before being presented with the test queries. The time taken on this introduction was noted along with whether or not the example search was carried out. The time taken to generate each formulation was recorded.

Cansearch
Instructions to Users

Words and phrases displayed on the screen can be selected by touching the screen with a finger (or pencil). the selection is indicated by lighting the word or phrase.
Now touch "TOUCH THIS TO SUBMIT A QUERY"
and touch "CONTINUE" (the display changes to a new frame).
Touch "cancer at a particular site"
touch it again to deselect it so that this phrase is no longer lit. The selections will not be processed until "CONTINUE" is selected.

Using an example query:
    "5FU in the treatment of Breast Cancer"

frame2:	Touch "cancer at a particular site*"
	Touch "therapy*"
	Touch "CONTINUE"
frame15:	Touch "specific primary site(s)*"
	Touch "CONTINUE"
frame15a:	Touch "breast"
	Touch "CONTINUE"
frame 3:	Touch "chemotherapy*"
	Touch "CONTINUE"
frame4:	Touch "particular antineoplastic drug/s or drug
classes*"	
	Touch "therapeutic use"
	Touch "CONTINUE"
frame5:	Touch "antineoplastic antimetabolities*"
	Touch "CONTINUE"
framme9:	Touch "fluorouracil"
	Touch "CONTINUE"

The program then formulates and displays the search statements that would be sent to the MEDLINE Database. Touch the screen to return to the starting frame.

NOTES:
1. In submitting a search ALL the words and phrases that are relevant on a frame should be selected before touching "CONTINUE".
2. The program uses a sub-set of the Medical Subject Headings and may not be able to process some of the test queries — could you do your best with the available vocabulary.

Fig. 6

4.4 The information search intermediaries
Seven different intermediaries, at four of the Libraries and Information Centres listed above, generated search formulations for test queries excluding those queries originally provided for the experiment by their library/ information service.

A straightforward comparison between the performance of CAN-SEARCH when used by a doctor with the intermediary, using all available resources to aid the search formulation, would not have taken into account the limited scope of CANSEARCH, so test queries were randomly selected for either normal search formulation by the intermediary or for search formulation when the intermediary was limited to using an extract of the Medical Subject Headings (MeSH), associated subheadings and check-tags. This MeSH extract had formed the basis for the CANSEARCH program. The presentation of the terms in the extract was as in the tree section of the printed version of MeSH.

4.5 Generation of search formulations
The time taken by each Doctor in following through the example search in the instructions (Fig. 6), with details of the time taken to generate and record search formulations for both doctors and intermediaries, is presented in Tables 3 and 4. The instructions for the example search were not always followed accurately, and in spite of intending that the use of CANSEARCH should be by using only the written sheet of instructions, a constraint which was explained to the doctors, there were inevitably additional questions, and further verbal explanation was given.

One doctor (4) had used the system several months earlier as part of a pilot trial and did not require any introduction.

4.6 Search formulation quality assessment and ranking
Search formulations were assessed to provide both absolute and relative measures of quality, using absolute quality to assess them on their own merits, and using both absolute quality and ranking, with respect to other formulations for the same query, to provide relative measures.

4.6.1 The assessors
Two experienced indexers from the MEDLARS Section at the British Library Lending Division in Boston Spa assessed the absolute and relative quality of each search formulation. These assessors were effectively providing a 'Gold Standard' for query formulation, given that their training and experience in indexing and online searching exceeded that to be expected from the normal information search intermediary.

In assessing the quality of search formulations the experiment is similar to that undertaken by Harter (Robertson 1981, p. 22), who was comparing automatically derived indexing with human indexing, defining human indexing as good and using that as his 'gold standard'. In this experiment, the concept of the expert search intermediary is used. Although an expert from the MEDLARS section had been involved in the development of the CANSEARCH program, neither of the assessors was aware of the details of the CANSEARCH program.

Class 1 Queries – Time taken to formulate search statements in minutes

Inst. – instructions &
& Ex. – example search

Time taken with:
- a – formulation abandoned
- c – program crash (out of space)
- e – error in formulation
- r – formulation repeated
- x – formulation excluded
- n – no time given
- – random selection

Inst. & Ex.	Doctor & CANSEARCH (C1)											Intermediaries & MeSH Extract (C2)				Intermediaries & All Available Resources (C3)				
Query	1	2	3	4	5	6	7	8	9	10	11	1	5	7	8	2	3	4	6	9
Inst. & Ex.	7	3	6	0	8	4	4	4	4	4	5	4	1	2	2		2	8	20 nx	3
1							4				5r 3									
4	4													2			2		5x n	
10	1r	2						1	6			3					9x 1		11	
11				1c 4		2					1	2			2		1		n	
12			5	3				2	3						6		1	5		3
13		3		4					7					e		3	7	7		
14												2	1	1			2			
19		3			3a 5	5	2a 3			3	6				5				nx nx n	
20										3			1	1	1				n	
23			4	6				1	4			2	1				2			2
25									6r 5	4r 3	3	1			3					2
27	8a 8							6r 7				4	4	5			2	20		2
28		5										4		e	n		1	5	3	2
29	10	3		6								1			3		2	5	3	
32			2c 2				3													

Table 3

Class 2 & 3 Queries – Time taken to formulate search statements in minutes

a – formulation abandoned c – program crash (out of space) e – error in formulation n – no time given r – formulation repeated x – formulation excluded – random selection

Query	Doctor & CANSEARCH (C1)											Intermediaries & MeSH Extract (C2)				Intermediaries & All Available Resources (C3)				
	1	2	3	4	5	6	7	8	9	10	11	1	5	7	8	2	3	4	6	9
2	6e		2								2		4	n	8	7		15	6	3
3							2r 2					3	4				10	15	30x n	
5					5e				5e								6	15		
7				3r 5				3c 3						7			6			
9				3						4				n		1	6			
15		4e	3e				3					7							11 nx	4
16				4r 5			3			1a 3e		21		5 nx						
17							1					12							19	
18		4r 2c 4					1													
21								5e			3e		6	n	4	10			36	
22	5a	3a 1				2a 5			9			4				5		5	12	
24						4c					2							25		
30																4				
31										2r 4		4	3		4					8
34	6 4c		4r 7r 6c 8																	
6			4r 3	2e 6e		4	4	2r 2r 2			4	4	5	4	8	5	15	15	37 nx	5
8										1e								20		
26									5									5		
38	2a				2a 2							5	5						18 nx	
39	1a											3	3	n						5

Table 4

The assessors were independently supplied with sets of formulations for each test query, each formulation being word-processed onto a separate sheet (Fig. 7). The formulations were in random order within each query

Query 36   Ovarian granulosa cell cancer treatment   Rank 4 =

1:OVARIAN-NEOPLASMS WITH (SU OR DT OR RT)
2:GRANULOSA-CELL-TUMOR WITH (SU OR DT OR RT)
3:1 AND 2
4: . . L/3 HUMAN=Y

Formulation 1   Quality = (Very Good) : Good : Average : Poor : Very Poor

Fig. 7 — Example of quality assessment of a search formulation.

and the set of test queries were presented in a random order. Each formulation was headed by the query number and query description with no indication of the condition giving rise to the formulation.

All formulations were written using the same search statement syntax, that used for searching the MEDLINE database on the Data-Star host. Although CANSEARCH generated formulations in NLM acceptable syntax, most intermediaries had used Data-Star syntax in their formulations. In addition, the searching element of the experiment was to be carried out on the Data-Star host.

The scale of absolute quality was listed at the foot of each formulation and the appropriate grade was circled by the assessor. The formulations were then placed in rank order and the rank was written in the top right hand corner of the formulation sheet. Equal rankings were possible.

The absolute quality assessments for both assessors are presented in Tables 5 and 6.

4.6.1.1   Conclusions on scoring relative quality assessments
Doctors using CANSEARCH (C1) do, on some occasions produce better quality search formulations than both Intermediaries using MeSH extract (C2) and using all available resources (C3), although the latter two produce better quality search statements more frequently.

Averaging the Rank Score, Quality Score and the Difference in Average Quality score for both assessors:

Class 1 Queries – Absolute Quality Assessments

Key: VG – Very Good   G – Good   Av – Average   P – Poor   VP – Very Poor

Doctor & CANSEARCH (C1)

Query	1	2	3	4	5	6	7	8	9	10	11
4	P	Av					P	Av			
10	VG	VG					VG	VG			
11				Av	Av	Av	Av				
12				G	G	Av	Av				
13			Av	G				Av	G		
14			Av	G							
19		P	Av						P	Av	
20		VG	VG	P	VP				Av	Av	
23		VG	VG	G	G						
25								VG	VG		
27							P	P	P	P	
28									P	P	
29				G	G				G	G	
32			G	VG	G			VG	VP	P	VG
33	Av	Av	Av	Av						Av	
35	VG	VG	Av	Av							
36	VG	VG									
37					G		VG	VG			
40			VG	VG			VG	VG			

Intermediaries & MeSH Extract (G2)

Query	1	2	3	4	5	6	7	8
4	VG	VG	G	G	G		G	G
10	VG	VG	VG	G	VG	G	G	
11	Av	Av	Av					
12	VG		VG					
13							G	G
14			P				P	P
19			VG				6	Av
20								VG
23					6			VG
25	VG	VG						
27	VG				VG			
28	VG				VG			
29	6				G			
32	VG				VG			
33		P	P		P		P	
35		VG	VG	G	P		P	6
36		VG	VG	G	G	6	G	Av
37			VG	VG		VG		
40			VG	VG	VG	VG		Av

Intermediaries & All Available Resources (C3)

Query	2	3	4	6	9
10					Av G
19					VG VG
27			6	6	
28	P				
32			6		P Av
33			6		P Av
37					VG VG
40				VG VG	VG VG

Table 5

Class 2 & 3 Queries – Absolute Quality Assessments

Key: VG – Very Good   G – Good   Av – Average   P – Poor   VP – Very Poor

Query	Doctor & CANSEARCH (C1)											Intermediaries & MeSH Extract (C2)								Intermediaries & All Available Resources (C3)				
	1	2	3	4	5	6	7	8	9	10	11	1	5	7	8	2	3	4	6	9				
C 2		VP YP									VP YP	P P	P P	P P										
13	P P				VP P		P P	Av Av	VP YP			Av Av P P			YP P	VG VG	VG VG	Av Av Av	P P	VG VG				
a 5				Av Av						Av Av			P P	G G		G G	G VG	Av Av						
s 7			Av Av	P Av				P Av					P Av	P Av		P Av Av Av	G VG Av Av	Av						
2 9	VP YP VP YP																							
15		VP YP VP YP					YP YP		YP YP			YP VP												
16				P P			Av Av	P P				P P	Av Av	Av Av	P P	Av Av	G G	G G	G G	Av Av				
17							P VP	VP		P VP		P VP												
18	G G							P P			P P	G G	G G	P P		VG VG	G VG	YP VP	VG VG	VG VG				
21	YP YP P P								YP YP		YP P	YP VP	YP VP						Av G				
22	VP YP P P					Av Av	Av Av		YP YP	VG					Av Av	Av Av Av	Av Av	YP VP	Av 6				
24						YP VP			YP YP		YP P	P P	YP VP					YP VP	YP VP					
30						Av Av	Av Av				YP P	Av Av	Av			Av Av								
31										G VG										VG G				
34	P P	VP YP				YP YP	YP YP P P	P P	P P		P P	P P	YP YP	P P	P P	G G	P P	P P	P P	VG 6				
C 6		P P							P P		P P	YP VP	YP VP			G G		P P P P	P P					
18		P P	VP YP VP			Av P			P P		Av Av	Av Av			Av Av Av Av	Av Av	Av Av	Av Av	Av Av	Av				
a 26											P P	YP P				Av	YP P	YP P	P P					
s 38					YP VP					YP VP			YP VP											
3 39	YP YP	YP YP VP YP										YP P YP VP	YP P YP VP	YP VP		Av Av	YP YP VP YP	P P Av P	P P	Av				

Table 6

C1 versus C2

Query class	Number of queries	C1 better	C2 better	No difference
1	20	4	14	2
2	15	3	6	6
A11	40	8	22	10

C1 versus C3

Query class	Number of queries	C1 better	C3 better	No difference
1	20	5	13	2
2	15	2	12	1
A11	40	8.5	28.5	3

C2 versus C3

Query class	Number of queries	C2 better	C3 better	No difference
1	20	7	7	6
2	15	2	12	1
A11	40	10	21	9

4.6.2 Judgement of relevance of search results

All the formulations for Class 1 queries were used to search the MEDLINE database on the Data-Star host.

Doctors were invited to act as judges, comparing the system output of Author, Title of Document, Title of Journal and Abstract, when available, with the original query. The following were the guidelines for making relevance judgements:

Each document reference should be identified as belonging to only *one* of the following categories by circling the category listed at the top of each reference.

Category
Relevant — A relevant document is one which, from the available information, bears directly and substantially on the user's query irrespective of the language of the document.
Possibly relevant — may bear directly on the user's query.

Irrelvant — bears not at all on the user's query.

Cannot judge — where insufficient information is avaiable to assign the reference to one of the above categories.

When more than 100 different documents were retrieved from the formulations, a sample was taken, so as to keep the task of judgement reasonable and not demand too much time from the doctors agreeing to judge references. The sample was taken by limiting the union of the total retrieved set using the entry date field until the size of the sample set was in the region of 100. Relevance judgements for the sample for each formulation were extrapolated to the original total. This was necessary in 11 out of the 18 queries, e.g.:

Formulation 1
Original Total Number of Documents=187
Sample Total=67
$R'=29$
$P'=17$
$I'=21$
Extrapolated Relevance
$R''=(29/67)*187=81$
$P''=47$
$I''=59$

The number of references and relevance judgements for all formulations for Class 1 queries have been presented in Table 7. Extrapolated results are marked with an asterisk '*'.

4.6.2.1   Relevance measures

Relevance judgements can be used to derive measures which provide a comparison of the retrieval performance of one formulation with another. The comparison is achieved using the three measures relative recall, precision and relative effectiveness.

These measures have been calculated for two levels of relevance, Broad and Narrow. For Broad relevance, both relevant and possibly relevant references were considered relevant; whilst for Narrow relevance possibly relevant references were classed as irrelevant.

For formulation A versus formulation B in one condition comparison the measures for A are:

Relative Recall=
$$\frac{\text{Num. of Rel. Docs. Retrieved by A}}{\text{Total of Diff. Rel. Docs. Retrieved by A and B}}$$

Class 1 Queries – Number of references and relevance judgements

Legend:
- Total number of references retrieved → n_1
- Number of relevant references / Number of relevant + possibly relevant references → n_2 / n_3, n_4
- Number of irrelevant references → n_4
- * = Extrapolated relevance judgements
- n.a. = Relevance judgements not available

Each cell is given as: total retrieved (n_1) / relevant : relevant+possibly relevant (n_2/n_3) / irrelevant (n_4).

Query	Doctor & CANSEARCH (C1) 1	2	3	4	5	6	7	8	9	10	11	Interm. & MeSH Extract (C2) 1	5	7	8	Interm. & All Available Resources (C3) 2	3	4	6	9
4	1242* 836/177 405						7 3/0 4				91* 65/18 26	182* 128/122 54	106* 59/51 47	106* 59/51 47	97* 70/19 27		97* 70/19 27	163* 76/23 27	270* 194/63 76	69* 46/38 23
10	263 n.a. n.a.	9588 n.a. n.a.		96 n.a.				263 n.a.				319					319		319	
11									0 n.a.			58 n.a.					58		61 n.a.	
12						242* 169/116 73	1844* 654/296 1190					250* 171/110 79				371* 292/189 79	250* 171/110 79		250* 171/110 79	
13				353* 275/179 78							353* 275/179 78			732* 522/268 210			736* 525/270 211			
14			27 22/12 5					27 22/12 5						1 1/1 0		22 22/12 5	1 1/1 0			87 66/44 21
19		3 2/0 1		15 5/4 10					17 15/9 2					90 69/44 21					198* 170 181	
20									456* 327/266 129						489* 388/328 101		489* 388/328 101			58* 52/28 6
23		2 2/1 0						2 2/1 0		2 2/0					2 2/1 0	2 2/1		2 2/1 0		
25						1 10/7					0 0/0	22 19/11 3								
27							1654* 795/0 858			1051* 505/0 546			212* 204/187 8		26 19/13 7				212* 204/187 8	117 102/83 15
28					56* 25/10 31								125* 87/29 38			125* 87/29 38				
29				76* 62/32					76* 62/42 4			83* 68/33 15	171* 119/54 52							
32			200* 173/162 27						0 0/0	24 7/2 17	200* 173/162 27		635* 590/457 45							
33	1 1/0 0									1 1/0						4 4/2 0		8 8/5 0		
35			1 1/0 0										0 0/0	4 4/2			0 0/0			
36	25 18/12 7							43 33/20 10							10 7/4 3	43 34/20 9	50 39/21 11	48 36/21 12	43 34/20 9	
37					1376* 1154/522 222								1613* 1373/974 240	1614* 1374/974 240						
40		88* 70/35 18	801* 733/528 68				801* 733/528 68								2 2/0 0		807* 734/528 73	807* 734/528 73	807* 734/528 73	1653* 1414/985 239

Table 7

Precision=

$$\frac{\text{Num. of Rel. Docs. Retrieved by A}}{\text{Total Number of Docs. Retrieved by A}}$$

Relative Effectiveness=
$1/(1/\text{Relative Recall}+1/\text{Precision}-1)$

The effectiveness measure is a modified version of the measure suggested by Heine (van Rijsbergen 1979, p. 175). The modification makes the maximum effectiveness=1.0 signifying the best performance in line with the best values of Relative Recall and Precision.

4.6.2.2   Conclusions on relevance measures

Overall, CANSEARCH used by Doctors (C1) had a lower relative recall, precision and relative effectiveness than Intermediaries using MeSH Extract (C2) and Intermediaries using all available resources (C3).

Taking the mean of the average Broad and Narrow relevance measures produces the following summary:

Comparison	Relative recall (per cent)	Precision (per cent)	Relative effectiveness (per cent)
C1	58	56	39
versus			
C2	73	64	48
C1—C2	−15	−8	−9
C1	60	56	40
versus			
C3	71	62	50
C1—C3	−11	−6	−10
C2	81	64	55
versus			
C3	76	62	53
C2—C3	5	2	2
Overall average			
C1	59	56	40
C2	77	64	52
C3	74	62	52

However, Doctors using CANSEARCH (C1) did, on a number of occasions, show a better retrieval performance than both Intermediaries using MeSH Extract (C2) and Intermediaries using all available resources (C3), although the latter two do show a better retrieval performance more frequently.

Averaging the performance measures for both Broad and Narrow relevance measures:

Total Number of Queries=18

C1 versus C2

Measure	C1 better	C2 better	No difference
Recall Score	4	10.5	3.5
Precision Score	5.5	6.5	6
Effectiveness Score	4.5	9.5	4

C1 versus C3

Measure	C1 better	C3 better	No difference
Recall Score	5	8.5	4.5
Precision Score	4.5	7.5	6
Effectiveness Score	5	8.5	4.5

C2 versus C3

Measure	C2 better	C3 better	No difference
Recall Score	7.5	5	5.5
Precision Score	5	7.5	5.5
Effectiveness Score	6	6.5	5.5

5. CONCLUSION

The potential of the CANSEARCH approach to naive user document retrieval has been demonstrated in a very testing experiment. The actual analysis of experimental results and statistical testing was more extensive than indicated here and is fully presented elsewhere (Pollitt 1986a). This work is to be continued to provide a fully working system. The suitability of the approach is to be tested in subject domains other than clinical cancer therapy, including computing and engineering.

The ideas exploited in the research programme have also been applied to videotex systems to suggest an improved videotex searching capability using boolean searching from menu selection (Pollitt 1985, 1986), and similarly in the provision of query language facilities for database management systems.

REFERENCES

Anderson, R. H. & Gillogly, J. J. (1976) Rand Intelligent Terminal Agent (RITA): Design Philosophy. Rand Report no. R–1809–ARPA.

Benett, J. S. & Engelmore, R. S. (1979) SACON: a knowledge-based consultant for structural analysis. In: *Proceedings of 6th International Joint Conference on Artificial Intelligence, Tokyo, Japan,* pp. 47–49.

Bergman, R. (1981) Beyond SDI: On-line retrieval scripts in the Chemical Substances Information Network. *Proceedings of the ASIS 44th Annual Meeting* **18** pp. 276–278.

Clarke, A. & Cronin, B. (1983) Expert systems and library information work. *Journal of Librarianship* **15** 4 277–292.

Clocksin, W. & Mellish, C. (1981) *Programming in Prolog.* Springer-Verlag.

Duda, R. O. & Shortliffe, E. H. (1983) Expert systems research. *Science* **220** 4594 261–268.

Hall, J. L., Negus, A. E. & Dancy, D. J. (1972) On-line information retrieval: a method of query formulation using a video terminal. *Program* **6** 175–186.

Lancaster, F. W. (1979) *Information retrieval systems: characteristics, testing and evaluation,* 2nd edn. New York, Wiley.

Marcus, R. S. & Reintjes, J. F. (1981)0 A translating computer interface for end-user operation of heterogeneous retrieval systems. 1: Design. *Journal of the American Society for Information Science* **32** 4 287–303.

Marcus, R. S. (1981) An automated expert assistant for information retrieval. *The Information Community: An Alliance for Progress. Proceedings of the 44th ASIS Annual Meeting* **18** 270–273.

Meadow, C. T., Hewett, T. T. & Avesa, E. S. (1982) A computer intermediary for interactive database searching. 1: Design. *Journal of the American Society for Information Science* **33** 5 3235–332.

Pollitt, A. S. (1977) CANCERLINE Evaluation Project: Final Report BLRDD Report Series no. 5377.

Pollitt, A. S. (1982) A search statement generator for cancer therapy related information retrieval. *Proceedings of the 6th International Online Information Meeting,* pp. 405–413.

Pollitt, A. S. (1983) End user touch searching for cancer therapy literature: a rule-based approach. *Sixth Annual International ACM SIGIR Conference on Research and Development in Information Retrieval. SIGIR Forum* **17** 4 136–145.

Pollitt, A. S. (1985) End user Boolean searching of Viewdata using numeric keypads. *Proceedings of the Ninth International Online Information Meeting, London, December 1985,* pp. 373–380.

Pollitt, A. S. (1986a) An expert system approach to document retrieval. Ph.D. thesis (in preparation).

Pollitt, A. S. (1986b) Extending Viewdata to perform Boolean searching of large scale literature databases. *43rd FID Congress, Montreal, September 1986.*

Robertson, S. E. (1981) The methodology of information retrieval experiment. In: Sparck-Jones, K. (ed), *Information retrieval experiment.* London, Butterworths. pp. 9–31.

Shortliffe, E. H. (1976) *Computer based medical consultations: MYCIN.* New York, Elsevier.

Smith, L. C. (1976) Aritificial intelligence in information retrieval systems. *Information processing and management* **12** 189–222.

Smith, L. C. (1980) Implications of artificial intelligence for end-user use of online systems. *Online Review* **4** 4 383–391.

Sparck-Jones, K. (1983) Intelligent retrieval. *Proceedings of the Aslib Informatics 7 — Intelligent retrieval.*

Spivey, J. M. (1982) *University of York Portable Prolog System. Release 1 User Guide.* York, University of York Computer Centre.

Stefik, M. J. (1981) Planning with constraints (MOLGEN: Part 1). *Artificial Intelligence* **16** 111–139.

Stefik, M., Aikins, J., Balzer, R., Benoit, J., Birnbaum, L., Hayes-Roth, F. & Sacerdoti, E. (1983) Basic concepts for building expert systems. In: Hayes-Roth, F., Waterman, D. A. & Lenat, D. B. (eds), *Building expert systems,* Reading, Mass., Addison-Wesley. pp. 59–86.

Thompson, D. A. (1971) Interface design for an interactive information retrieval sytem: a literature survey and a research system description. *Journal of the American Society for Information Science* **November** 361–373.

van Rijsbergen, C. J. (1979) *Information Retrieval,* 2nd edn. London, Butterworths.

Vickery, A. (1984) An intelligent interface for online interaction. *Journal of Information Science* **9** 7–18.

Waterman, D. A. (1978a) Exemplary programming in RITA. In: Waterman, D. A. & Hayes-Roth, F. (eds), *Pattern directed inference systems.* New York, Academic Press. pp. 261–279.

Waterman, D. A. (1978b) Rule-directed interactive transaction agents: an approach to knowledge acquisition. Rand Report no. R-2171-ARPA.

Yip, M. K. (1981) *An Expert System for Document retrieval. M. Sc. thesis, Massachusetts Institute of Technology.*

5

An experiment in intelligent information systems: RESEARCHER

Michael Lebowitz, Department of Computer Science, Computer Science Building, Columbia University, New York, NY 10027, USA†

1. INTRODUCTION

Traditional work in information retrieval (such as that described in Heaps (1978) and Salton & McGill (1983)) has concentrated on ways of storing and retrieving texts based on their lexical contents with little regard to meaning. While this has led to quite powerful and useful systems, we can hope to still better by applying techniques of artifical intelligence to information retrieval. Specifically, we will describe in this paper how we are using research in the areas of natural language processing and learning to help understand how to develop powerful, intelligent information systems. General discussion of the application of artificial intelligence to information retrieval can be found in Schank *et al.* (1980), DeJong (1983) and Lebowitz (1983a).

In Lebowitz (1983a) and Lebowitz (1983b), we describe the early stages of development of RESEARCHER, a prototype intelligent information system. RESEARCHER is intended to accept information in natural language form, in particular, patent abstracts such as EX1.

EX1 — P137; U.S. patent #4400750; Forestlane Co. Ltd.

A Magnetic read/write head carriage assembly for a floppy disk drive is disclosed for use with double sided floppy disks which permits the head tracking force to be easily and accurately adjusted. The head carriage assembly comprises a coil spring, having a central coil portion and first and second ends, which is mounted in a position between the base and the head support arm of the carriage assembly with the first end coupled to the base and the second end coupled to the support arm. An adjusting

† This research was supported in part by the Defense Advanced Research Projects Agency under contract N00039-84-C-0165. Many people have contributed to RESEARCHER. In particular, the work on generalizing hierarchies has largely been conducted by Kenneth Wasserman and the work on question-answering by Cecile Paris in conjuction with Kathleen McKeown. Comments on an earlier draft of this chapter by J. A. Campbell and Roy Davies were most useful.

screw is mounted on the base adjacent to the first end of the coil spring
for adjusting the position of this end, thereby adjusting the biasing force
applied by the spring to the support arm.

RESEARCHER:

— understands the text (extracts the meaning);
— adds the acquired information to a long-term memory, learning
   through generalization as it does so;
— answers questions about the information in its memory.

Descriptions of complex physical objects such as those in abstracts lead
to special problems in the development of intelligent information systems.
In this paper, we will present an overview of three areas that we are studying
using RESEARCHER that are important in the development of intelligent
information systems:

— learning by generalizing hierarchical descriptions — learning is
important if we wish our systems to be able to return *more* information than
we give them, by comparing the different texts read; physical objects can be
best represented hierarchically;
   — using a long-term memory built up through generalization to assist in
      text interpretation — intelligent information retrieval requires
      robust understanding, and this can only be done with extensive
      application of knowledge, including that which the system acquires;
   — tailoring the system's answers for different users — a truly intelligent
system with a large memory can be most effective by giving answers that are
crafted for each individual user.

We begin by describing the problems of generalizing hierarchically
structured objects, as the creation of a long-term memory is necessary for
our text understanding methods.

2.   GENERALIZING HIERARCHICAL DESCRIPTIONS

Intelligent information systems should be able to return to a user more
information than that contained in any single text. They should be able to
learn from the texts by noticing similarities (among other learning methods).
The patent abstracts that we have been looking at describe the physical
structure of complex objects. Since such objects are naturally represented as
hierarchies of parts, our learning research has addressed the generalization
of hierarchically structured descriptions. To see the input to the generalisa-
tion process, consider EX2, the first part of a typical patent abstract.

EX2 — P37; U.S. patent #4190870; Avina Raymond, Merrell Patrick

A disk drive assembly includes a baseplate housing joined with front and rear covers to enclose a spindle that supports ball bearings and a hub for rotating a stack of magnetic disks ...

Our representation of patent abstracts such as this one includes three classes of information:

— *a parts hierarchy*, that indicates the components of each part;
— *interpart relations*, capturing physical and functional relations between various components;
— *properties* of the objects.

The level of detail needed for each of these classes of information certainly depends on the task at hand. For our purposes, we have concentrated on the parts hierarchy and physical relations (which are represented using a primitive-based canonical scheme (Wasserman & Lebowitz 1983)). We are currently working on classification schemes for functional relations and object properties (such as size and composition), which are crucial in understanding many device descriptions. Fig. 1 shows the representation of EX2 created by RESEARCHER.

```
Text Representation:

            |-------------2                 1 = UNKNOWN-ASSEMBLY# ('ASSEMBLY')
            |-----------AB-3                 2 = DISC-DRIVE#
            |-----------B-5                  3 = ENCLOSURE#
            |-----------D-6                  5 = NUMBER/>1 LOCATION/FRONT,REAR COVER#
-----------C-1|---------CD-7                 6 = DRIVE-SHAFT#
            |-----------E-8                  7 = NUMBER/>1 BALL-BEARING#
            |-----------E-9|-----------10    8 = HUB#
                                             9 = UNKNOWN-ASSEMBLY# ('STACK')
                                            10 = NUMBER/>1 DEV-TYPE/MAGNETIC DISC#

--------------------A-4    4 = BASEPLATE#


A list of relations:

              Subject:             Relation:              Object:

[&REL1/A]  &MEM4 (BASEPLATE#)    {UNKNOWN-PURP-REL} &MEM3 (ENCLOSURE#)
[&REL2/B]  &MEM3 (ENCLOSURE#)    {R-CONNECTED-TO}   &MEM5 (COVER#)
[&REL3/C]  &MEM6 (DRIVE-SHAFT#)  {R-SURROUNDED-BY}  &MEM1 ('ASSEMBLY')
[&REL4/D]  &MEM6 (DRIVE-SHAFT#)  {P-SUPPORTS}       &MEM7 (BALL-BEARING#)
[&REL5/E]  &MEM8 (HUB#)          {P-ROTATES}        &MEM9 ('STACK')
```

Fig. — A typical RESEARCHER representation.

We can see in Fig. 1 all three of the types of information used in representing physical description patents. The backbone of the representation is a parts hierarchy. (The numbers in the hierarchy refer to the objects listed on the right.) Fig. 1 shows an assembly (part 1) composed of a number of parts, including a disc drive, an enclosure, and so forth. One of the components is another assembly (the 'stack') which is composed of a number of discs. There is also a 'loose part', the baseplate, not included in the main assembly. The items in Fig. 1 with #s indicate concepts (e.g. disc-drive#, the concept of a disc drive) as opposed to words (the phrase, 'disk drive').

Fig. 1 also includes several relations between objects. These are shown by letters in the parts hierarchy and enumerated below the hierarchy. For example, the 'B' with the enclosure (part 3, from the word 'housing' in EX2) and the covers (part 5) indicates that they are connected ('joined') to each other.

Finally, the representation of EX2 includes several object descriptions augmented with properties. These are indicated in Fig. 1 in the object descriptions. For example, object 10, the discs, has been modified by making its device-type property 'magnetic'. The object representations of the covers, ball bearings and disc include indications that there is more than one each.

The representation in Fig. 1 is at a level of understanding that many artificial intelligence text processing systems might achieve if applied to this domain. However, full understanding requires that we integrate this representation with existing knowledge in memory. In particular, RESEARCHER has as one of its goals the incremental generalization of descriptions such as that in Fig. 1 by finding similar examples in memory, comparing the new example with them, and abstracting out any similarities. Since there has been considerable work done on generalizing objects described with property values and to some extent relations (Winston (1972), Michalski (1980) and Lebowitz (1983c), among others), we have concentrated on the problems of generalizing hierarchically structured objects.

Generalizing hierarchical representations presents a number of difficult problems. Typical are: the problem of deciding how the components in the objects being compared correspond; dealing with differing levels of description of objects; and structuring memory so that maximal inheritance of the sort used in semantic networks and frame systems (see Barr *et al.* (1982)), which implies minimum space utilization, can be achieved automatically. In this chapter, we will give examples of how the generalization process works, and refer the reader to Wasserman (1984) and Wasserman (1985) for more details.

We can break generalization into two parts: (1) since RESEARCHER is not explicitly being taught concepts, when a new example is presented it must decide what other objects to compare it to, and (2) the process of comparing object descriptions, which includes the abstraction of similarities.

We will look at the comparison process first, as it is involved in the search process. Fig. 2 shows two simplified disc drive patents.† The physical relations and properties involved are not displayed, though they are handled in the generalization process.

---

† Simplified versions are used because the complex nature of real abstracts obscures the generalization process and because text processing problems are thus avoided.

Patent: EX3

(A DISC DRIVE COMPRISING AN ENCLOSURE SURROUNDING THE DISC DRIVE *COMMA*
SAID DISC DRIVE INCLUDES A SPINNING ASSEMBLY A DISC AND A READWRITE HEAD
COMMA SAID SPINNING ASSEMBLY INCLUDES A SPINDLE CONNECTED TO A MOTOR
COMMA SAID ENCLOSURE COMPRISING A COVER ON TOP OF A SUPPORT MEMBER)

Text Representation:

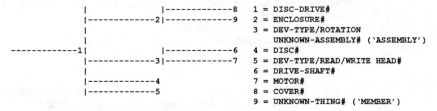

```
            |                    |-------------8     1 = DISC-DRIVE#
            |-------------2|-------------9           2 = ENCLOSURE#
            |                                        3 = DEV-TYPE/ROTATION
            |                                            UNKNOWN-ASSEMBLY# ('ASSEMBLY')
-------------1|                  |-------------6     4 = DISC#
            |-------------3|-------------7           5 = DEV-TYPE/READ/WRITE HEAD#
            |                                        6 = DRIVE-SHAFT#
            |-------------4                          7 = MOTOR#
            |-------------5                          8 = COVER#
                                                     9 = UNKNOWN-THING# ('MEMBER')
```

Patent: EX4

(A DISC DRIVE COMPRISING AN ENCLOSURE SURROUNDING THE DISC DRIVE *COMMA*
SAID DISC DRIVE INCLUDES A SPINNING ASSEMBLY A MAGNETIC ASSEMBLY AND A
READWRITE HEAD *COMMA* SAID SPINNING ASSEMBLY INCLUDES A SPINDLE CONNECTED
TO A MOTOR *COMMA* SAID MAGNETIC ASSEMBLY COMPRISING A DISC *COMMA* SAID
ENCLOSURE COMPRISING A COVER ON TOP OF A SUPPORT MEMBER)

Text Representation:

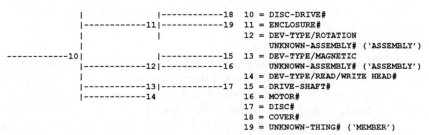

```
            |                    |------------18    10 = DISC-DRIVE#
            |------------11|------------19          11 = ENCLOSURE#
            |                  |                     12 = DEV-TYPE/ROTATION
            |                  |                         UNKNOWN-ASSEMBLY# ('ASSEMBLY')
-------------10|                  |------------15    13 = DEV-TYPE/MAGNETIC
            |------------12|------------16              UNKNOWN-ASSEMBLY# ('ASSEMBLY')
            |                                        14 = DEV-TYPE/READ/WRITE HEAD#
            |------------13|------------17          15 = DRIVE-SHAFT#
            |------------14                          16 = MOTOR#
                                                     17 = DISC#
                                                     18 = COVER#
                                                     19 = UNKNOWN-THING# ('MEMBER')
```

Fig. 2 — Two simple device representations.

As human understanders, we can easily see that patents EX3 and EX4 describe similar objects, particularly after looking at the hierarchical representations. However, to begin to generalize the similarities, RESEARCHER must decide how the parts of the representations correspond — for example, that part 2, the enclosure in EX3, corresponds to part 11, the similar assembly in EX4, and not to parts 12, 13 or 14. Here this is relatively easy, as the assemblies are identical, but we must be able to identify less than perfect matches. RESEARCHER does this with a numerical scoring algorithm, similar to the one in Winston (1980) and related to Evans (1968).

Fig. 3 shows the output of the generalization process of these objects, taken from Wasserman (1985). It is assumed that EX3 is already in memory and EX4 is being compared to it. We can see how RESEARCHER first makes correspondences of the sort mentioned above. One problem arises in dealing with the discs (parts 4 and 17). The disc in EX3 is described as part of

```
(GEN '&MEM10)
Matching &MEM10 against &MEM1 .... 170
Best match is:
(170 ((&MEM1 . &MEM10)
      ((&MEM5 . &MEM14))
      ((NULL# . &MEM13) ((&MEM4 . &MEM17)))
      ((&MEM3 . &MEM12) ((&MEM7 . &MEM16)) ((&MEM6 . &MEM15)))
      ((&MEM2 . &MEM11) ((&MEM9 . &MEM19)) ((&MEM8 . &MEM18)))))
Incorporating into g-tree ...
New generalization created: &MEM22
with variants: (&MEM10 &MEM1)


********************
```

```
                |------------23            22 = DISC-DRIVE#
                |------------24|------------25   23 = HEAD#
                |                              24 = NULL#
                |                |------------27   25 = DISC#
------------22|------------26|------------28   26 = UNKNOWN-ASSEMBLY#
                |                              27 = MOTOR#
                |------------29|------------30   28 = DRIVE-SHAFT#
                                |------------31   29 = ENCLOSURE#
                                              30 = UNKNOWN-THING#
                                              31 = COVER#
```

Fig. 3 — Generalizing the representations in Fig. 2.

the disc drive, while in EX4 the disc is part of a magnetic assembly which is part of the disc drive. To make the representations match, RESEARCHER must insert a 'null' part, which may or may not actually exist in any given object. This is legitimate as we can assume that the descriptions are incomplete or use different levels of aggregation. The null part appears in the generalization of EX3 and EX4 as part 24, shown at the bottom of Fig. 3. The two input representations are stored as variants of the generalized object, recording only how they differ from it (basically, in this case, how the null object is resolved; in real examples there would usually be more differences).

Even with just two hierarchical descriptions to compare, the matching process involves a number of problems in determining how the components of the hierarchies correspond. Typical of such problems is the need to insert levels in a hierarchy to obtain a good match, as described above. (While the insertion of a null level by itself decreases the goodness of a match, it will often greatly increase the value of lower level matches.) The problem is that there are an exponentially large number of places where null levels can be inserted, each requiring a complex, recursive match to test. We have used RESEARCHER to experiment with a variety of different algorithms for deciding where null levels should be inserted for optimal matching, concentrating on ones that only try the most obvious places near the top of the hierarchy.

Since the examples given RESEARCHER are not expressly designed for learning specific concepts (as they would be for a system being taught concepts, e.g. Winston's arch program (Winston 1972)), the program must decide which examples to compare for the purpose of generalization. This is done using a generalization-based memory of the sort in Lebowitz (1983c) and Lebowitz (1983d). A hierarchy of concepts that organizes specific examples is created in memory. A possible memory is shown in Fig. 4, where there are two concepts subordinate to disc-drive#, floppy and hard disc drives. The former has two further sub-concepts. Each concept organizes a

```
disc-drive# --------------------------------> patent A
   |
   > floppy-disc-drive# ----------------------> patents B, C
   |   |
   |   > single-sided-floppy-disc-drive# -----> patents E, F
   |   |
   |   > double-sided-floppy-disc-drive# -----> patents G, H, I
   |
   > hard-disc-drive# -----------------------> patents J, K
```

Fig. 4 — A typical generalization-based memory.

group of instances. Note that: (1) using the techniques outlined in this section, the generalization hierarchy is automatically created by RESEARCHER, not provided to the system in advance (at least this will be the case in a fully developed system; see Lebowitz (1983d), Lebowitz (1984) and Wasserman (1985) for progress to-date); (2) each node in Fig. 4 represents a complete hierarchical description of the kind we have been looking for (in effect, RESEARCHERS's memory is a hierarchy of hierarchies); and (3) information in the generalization notes can be inherited by lower level generalizations and examples, so that information need not be stored repetitively.

In using its generalization-based memory, RESEARCHER takes each new example and searches down the tree for the example or generalized concept most similar to it. This process involves matching generalized concepts with the new example in much the same way as EX3 and EX4 were matched above. RESEARCHER begins by matching the new example with each of the children of the generalization tree's root. It then selects the best match and looks at the node's children. As long as one of the children produces a better match than the parent node, RESEARCHER continues down the tree. Eventually, it either reaches a leaf (an instance already in memory) or a maximally good generalization (i.e. all of the subordinate nodes contain factors that decrease the quality of the match).

RESEARCHERS's search algorithm does not guarantee finding the best match, since it is possible that only an inferior match at an interior node would lead to the optimal match. However, this is viewed as an acceptable compromise in limiting search. An alternative would be to set a threshold match value and search down all branches of the tree that match above this threshold. Again, though, we might still miss the best match. Only experimentation will tell whether one algorithm or the other improves chances of finding a good (if not always best) match.

Sacrificing a guarantee of finding the maximally similar example (in return for computational feasibility) matches the observation that human memory gains robustness by initial heuristic classification of information. (For example, if we first classify a person we meet as an artificial intelligence researcher, we may miss similarities he or she has with our favorite politician.)

Eventually, after a series of matches, RESEARCHER selects the node in memory which it believes the new example best matches, either a previous example or an existing generalization. It then 'factors out' similarities between these represenations, and, if need be, creates a new generalization node. In any case, the new example is stored by recording how it differs from a generalization in memory. This is an optimally space-efficient method of storage, which also captures significant generalizations about the objects in the domain.

The current implementation of RESEARCHER's generalization scheme works quite well on modest-sized example. In addition to disc drive patents, a modified version of the program (CORPORATE-RESEARCHER (Wasserman 1985) has been tested on hierarchical descriptions of corporate organizations. In the future, we plan to address some of the combinatoric problems that arise for large examples, consider whether our approach of abstracting out all possible similarities is too extreme (in particular, determining exactly what the genralized concepts signify) and applying confidence evaluation methods of the sort described in Lebowitz 1982) to refine initial generalizations.

3.   TEXT PROCESSING USING MEMORY

Since intelligent information systems as RESEARCHER have available many examples in memory, it seems natural to make use of this information for text processing (beyond identifying lexical items (Harris, 1978)). If we have intelligent systems with large amounts of information it is vital that text processsing be robust. Patent abstracts, like the rest of natural language, are quite ambiguous (which was somewhat surprising to those of us a bit naive about patents, who expected perfect clarity). We can use the system's updated memory to help resolve many ambiguities.

We feel that the best way to use detailed memory information during text understanding in the context of current systems is to identify specific tasks where a piece of information from memory will be useful. More general methods, such as using memory to determine the interesting aspects of a text to focus processing (Schank 1979, Lebowitz 1981), we leave for the future. We have identified a set of 'questions' that arise during text processing that can most easily be answered (and often can *only* be answered) by accessing long-term memory.

It is important to keep in mind that we are proposing using *memory* for understanding, as opposed to general semantic information about words or concepts (as many other artificial intelligence systems have done). While general information is crucial for our conceptually-based understanding methods, in order to resolve many ambiguities, it will be necessary to look at very detailed information in memory — in our case, how the objects described in patent abstracts are constructed and how their pieces relate to each other. One way of looking at this distinction if that RESEARCHER ends up using similar information to other artificial intelligence systems but much less of it has to be hand-coded initially.

EX5 — A disc head supporting a spindle made of magnetic material.

The first ambiguity in EX5 involves 'disc head'. Although not syntactically ambiguous, an understanding system such as RESEARCHER must determine the conceptual relationship between the nouns. The phrase 'made of magnetic material' is ambiguous in that we do not know whether it attaches to the head or the spindle. Both of these ambiguities can only be resolved by looking at memory. In fact, it would be easy to construct scenarios where different states of memory would cause this example to be understood differently (e.g. whether we knew about magnetic heads or magnetic spindles).

RESEARCHER makes use of relatively simple, but heavily memory-based, techniques for handling ambiguities of the sort in EX5. Its conceptual analysis type text processing algorithm described in Lebowitz (1983b) and Lebowitz (1984), involves identifying object descriptions (usually noun groups) and connecting them with various relational words (usually prepositions — patent abstracts are quite short of verbs) which indicate the various physical, functional and assembly/component relations mentioned in Section 2. Within this processing algorithm, we have identified places where ambiguity can be identified and memory is asked which of several possible physical constructions is more likely or what relation is likely to occur between two objects. Questions in both classes are answered by looking for examples of the possible configurations that already exist in memory.

Fig. 5 lists the various questions that RESEARCHER can currently ask its memory for purposes of disambiguation. They primarily involve prepositional phrase attachment and noun groups with multiple nouns.† Our analysis of these ambiguities shares much with the linguisitc work of Levi (1978) and the application of this work to artificial intelligence in Finin (1982). However, our method of resolving the ambiguities — the use of a dynamic, long-term memory — is rather different. By looking for specific examples in memory (or information generalized from specific examples) we allow RESEARCHER to always use the best information currently

---

† The word types used in Fig. 5 are functional, rather than syntactic. Howver, object words are usually nouns and relation words and part indicators are usually prepositions, although not always in either case.

Form: object-word1 object-word2
Example: An actuator housing ...
Question: What is the relation between object-word1 (actuator) and
object-word2 (housing)?

Form: modifier object-word1 object-word2
Example: A metal drive cover ...
Question: Does the modifier (metal) better apply to object-word1 (drive)
or object-word2 (cover)?

Form: object-word1 object-word2 object-word3
Example: A disc-drive transducer wire ...
Question: Is object-word1 (disc-drive) "related to" (as a part, assembly
or in relation) object-word2 (transducer) or object-word3 (wire)?

Form: object-word1 relation-word1 object-word2 relation-word2
object-word3
Example: A transducer on top of a disc supported by a spindle ...
Question: Does relation-word2 (supported by) connect object-word3
(spindle) with object-word1 (transducer) or object-word2 (disc)?

Form: object-word1 part-indicator1 object-word2 part-indicator2
object-word3
Example: A disc drive including a disc comprising a metal plate (and) ...
Question: Is object-word3 (metal plate) a part of object-word1
(disc drive) or object-word2 (disc)?

Form: object-word1 relation-word object-word2 part-of-indicator
object-word3 (There are several related configurations.)
Example: A disc on a spindle for a disc drive ...
Question: Is object-word1 (disc) or object-word2 (spindle) a part
of object-word3 (disc drive)? (Directly a part, as both are parts
indirectly.)

Fig. 5 — RESEARCHER disambiguation questions.

available. While examples do not always provide resolution of ambiguities
as clearly as pre-defined semantic properties, they have the clear advantage
of minimizing the need for ad hoc, hand-coded information.

   The search for possible examples that answer a given question is a
relatively simple one. Recall that RESEARCHER's memory (Fig. 4) is
basically a hierarchy of object descriptions. In addition to the hierarchy for
the main concept under consideration (e.g. disc drives), there are subsidiary
hierarchies for other objects, such as spindles and discs. RESEARCHER
uses these hierarchies to look for possible assembly/component constructions and physical relations. It begins its search with general object descriptions and searches through more specific descriptions until a relevant
example is found. If several possible constructions (or relations) are found,
the one associated with the most general description is used, as that

represents RESEARCHER's boadest information. RESEARCHER's memory search disambiguation process is described in more detail in Lebowitz (1984).

Our disambiguation methodology bears resemblance to that of Small (1980), Birnbaum and Selfridge (1981) and Hirst (1983), except, crucially, it relies on information from a detailed, dynamic memory for executing disambiguation. Our algorithm does have the side-effect of making under-standing subjective (in the sense of Abelson (1973) and Carbonell (1981)), since new examples will be interpreted to correspond to old ones, but we view this as inevitable if we wish to achieve robust understanding.

To illustrate RESEARCHERS's memory-based disambiguation, we will first consider how the simple noun phrase, 'a motor spindle', is processed. Fig. 6 shows how RESEARCHER processes this phrase with no relevant information in memory.† The program queries memory (indicated

```
Running RESEARCHER at 3:19:26 PM

(A MOTOR SPINDLE)

Processing:

A              : New instance word -- skip
MOTOR          : Memette within NP; save and skip
SPINDLE        : MP word -- memette DRIVE-SHAFT#
  New DRIVE-SHAFT# instance (&MEM0)
  >>> Looking for relation between MOTOR# and &MEM0 (DRIVE-SHAFT#)
  New MOTOR# instance (&MEM1)
  Assuming &MEM1 (MOTOR#) and &MEM0 (DRIVE-SHAFT#) are functionally related
  Establishing UNKNOWN-PURP-REL; SUBJECT: &MEM1 (MOTOR#);
    OBJECT: &MEM0 (DRIVE-SHAFT#) [&REL1]

Text Representation:

---------------------A-0    0 = DRIVE-SHAFT#

---------------------A-1    1 = MOTOR#


A list of relations:

           Subject:              Relation:          Object:

[&REL1/A]  &MEM1 (MOTOR#)        {UNKNOWN-PURP-REL} &MEM0 (DRIVE-SHAFT#)
```

Fig. 6 — 'A motor spindle' with memory empty.

by '>>>' for a plausible relation between a motor and a drive shaft (spindle). Since none is found, it assumes that there is an unknown functional (purpose) relation between the objects, which is its default for concrete objects.

Now we assume that before processing 'a motor spindle',

---

† In Fig. 6 and other examples of RESEARCHER output, the term 'memette' refers to an object concept in memory — literally a small piece of memory. An MP, or Memory Pointer, is a word that points to an object in memory. Normally MPs are concrete nouns.

RESEARCHER had had in memory EX6, shown in Fig. 7 along with its representation. EX6 simply consists of a drive with two parts, a motor on top of a drive shaft.

```
EX6 - A drive with a motor on top of a drive shaft.

Text Representation:

                      |----------------A-1    0 = DRIVE#
------------------0|----------------A-2    1 = MOTOR#
                                           2 = DRIVE-SHAFT#

A list of relations:

              Subject:            Relation:           Object:

[&REL1/A]  &MEM1 (MOTOR#)       {R-ON-TOP-OF}      &MEM2 (DRIVE-SHAFT#)
```

Fig. 7 — Setting up memory.

With EX6 in memory, RESEARCHER process the same noun phrase, 'a motor spindle' as shown in Fig. 8. We can see that when it queries memory

```
Running RESEARCHER at 3:18:11 PM

(A MOTOR SPINDLE)

Processing:

A             : New instance word -- skip
MOTOR         : Memette within NP; save and skip
SPINDLE       : MP word -- memette DRIVE-SHAFT#
  New DRIVE-SHAFT# instance (&MEM3)
  >>> Looking for relation between MOTOR# and &MEM3 (DRIVE-SHAFT#)
  New MOTOR# instance (&MEM4)
  Establishing R-ON-TOP-OF; SUBJECT: &MEM4 (MOTOR#); OBJECT: &MEM3 (DRIVE-SHAFT#) [&REL2]

Text Representation:

----------------------B-3    3 = DRIVE-SHAFT#

----------------------B-4    4 = MOTOR#

A list of relations:

              Subject:            Relation:           Object:

[&REL2/B]  &MEM4 (MOTOR#)       {R-ON-TOP-OF}      &MEM3 (DRIVE-SHAFT#)
```

Fig. 8 — 'Spindle motor' with EX6 in memory.

to try and find known relations between motors and drive shafts, it finds the one from EX6 and assumes it to hold here, as well. Thus, an 'on top of' relation is added to the representation, showing the genuinely dynamic nature of RESEARCHER's text processing.

As a further illustration of RESEARCHER's use of memory in text processing, we will show how to processes part of a real patent abstract, EX7.

EX7 — P58; U.S. Patent #4287445 (abstract)

An electromagnatic linear actuator for positioning a transducer over locations on a rotating magnetic recording disk comprising an actuator housing used as a stationary base for supporting various parts; a coil and cart assembly including a cart, having a rectangular cross section and tubular in construction, adapted at one end to support the transducer.

Although it may not be immediately obvious, the beginning of EX7 is extremely ambiguous. (It may not be obvious because people are so good at resolving ambiguity.) The internal structures of the various noun phrases and the determination of what is a part of what could all be resolved in several ways. Without any information in memory, RESEARCHER would have to rely on general heuristics which might or might not work, but would certainly be quite ad hoc. Instead, we will provide RESEARCHER with a few (admittedly somewhat artificial) examples that it can use. Specifically, we will give it the following decriptions:

A disc drive comprised of an actuator that has a housing; an assembly with a coil.

A cylindrical cart with one modified end and a rectangular crossp-section.

Having given RESEARCHER examples of support mechanisms and double sided floppy disc drives, we let it read EX6. The first part of processing is shown in Fig. 9.

A number of aspects of RESEARCHER's text processing are shown in Fig. 9. We will focus on its use of memory. Each memory access is again indicated by '>>>'. The beginning of the processing of P58 is relatively simple. As we can see in Fig. 9 how RESEARCHER processes the first noun group with a 'skip and save' strategy (Lebowitz 1983e). The words 'electromagnetic' and 'linear' are saved until the head noun, 'actuator' is reached. It then works back through the noun group, applying the modifiers to the actuator. Next to be established are a purposive relation, P-GUIDES, taken from the word 'positioning' (after 'for', which in this case indicates that a purpose word is to follow) and a physical relation, R-ABOVE from the word 'over'. In establishing the R-ABOVE relation, RESEARCHER must decide whether the 'transducer' or the 'actuator' is over the 'locations'. There being no relevant information in memory, and the objects being similar from the point of view of the system's heuristics, the most recent is picked.

RESEARCHER's processing gets more interesting when the noun group 'a rotating magnetic recording disk' is reached. The processing begins similarly to that for the first noun group, saving the modifiers and then

```
Running RESEARCHER at 28-Jul-85 19:37:57
Patent: P58

(AN ELECTROMAGNETIC LINEAR ACTUATOR FOR POSITIONING A TRANSDUCER OVER
LOCATIONS ON A ROTATING MAGNETIC RECORDING DISK COMPRISING AN ACTUATOR
HOUSING USED AS A STATIONARY BASE FOR SUPPORTING VARIOUS PARTS *SEMI* A COIL
AND CART ASSEMBLY INCLUDING A CART *COMMA* HAVING A RECTANGULAR CROSS
SECTION AND TUBULAR IN CONSTRUCTION *COMMA* ADAPTED AT ONE END TO SUPPORT
THE TRANSDUCER *STOP*)

Processing:

AN            : New instance word -- skip
ELECTROMAGNETIC : Memette modifier; save and skip
LINEAR        : Memette modifier; save and skip
ACTUATOR      : MP word -- memette ACTUATOR#
  New ACTUATOR# instance (&MEM8)
  Augmenting &MEM8 (ACTUATOR#) with feature: CONFIGURATION = LINEAR
  Augmenting &MEM8 (ACTUATOR#) with feature: TYPE/PURPOSE = ELECTROMAGNETIC
FOR (FOR1)    : Purpose indicator -- skip
POSITIONING   : Purpose word -- save and skip
A             : New instance word -- skip
TRANSDUCER    : MP word -- memette TRANSDUCER#
  New TRANSDUCER# instance (&MEM9)
  Establishing P-GUIDES relation; SUBJECT: &MEM8 (ACTUATOR#);
    OBJECT: &MEM9 (TRANSDUCER#) [&REL1]
OVER          : Relation word -- save and skip
LOCATIONS     : MP word -- memette LOCATION#
  New LOCATION# instance (&MEM10)
  >>> Refining R-ABOVE OBJECT from &MEM9 (TRANSDUCER#) &MEM8 (ACTUATOR#)
  Establishing R-ABOVE relation; OBJECT: &MEM9 (TRANSDUCER#);
    SUBJECT: &MEM10 (LOCATION#) [&REL2]
ON (ON2)      : Part of indicator
  Assuming &MEM10 (LOCATION#) or &MEM9 (TRANSDUCER#) or &MEM8 (ACTUATOR#)
    is part of the following
A             : New instance word -- skip
ROTATING      : Purpose word within NP; save and skip
MAGNETIC      : Memette modifier; save and skip
RECORDING     : Purpose word within NP; save and skip
DISK          : MP word -- memette DISC#
  New DISC# instance (&MEM11)
  Establishing P-WRITES relation; OBJECT: &MEM11 (DISC#) [&REL3]
  Augmenting &MEM11 (DISC#) with feature: TYPE/PURPOSE = MAGNETIC
  Establishing P-ROTATES relation; OBJECT: &MEM11 (DISC#) [&REL4]
  >>> Selecting comp for &MEM11 (DISC#) from among &MEM10 (LOCATION#)
      &MEM9 (TRANSDUCER#) &MEM8 (ACTUATOR#)
  Assuming &MEM10 (LOCATION#) is part of &MEM11 (DISC#)
```

Fig. 9 — RESEARCHER processing the first part of P58.

applying them to disc#. But here RESEARCHER must decide whether the 'part of' word 'on', indicates that 'locations' or the 'actuator' is part of the disk. (If the second reading is not obvious, imagine the word 'and' before 'on'. This reading is syntactically possible, with or without the word 'and' being present.)

RESEARCHER's first choice of how to resolve this ambiguity is with a memory check. It looks for cases in memory where either the concept location# or actuator# is part of disc#. Finding none, since we have only provided the system with a simple memory for this example, RESEARCHER resorts to its set of heuristics. The relevant rule states that 'virtual' objects, such as location#, which refer to implict parts of objects, are more likely to be parts of solid objects (such as disk#) than are complex objects (such as actuator#).† This sort of processing is related to the use of semantic properties of words for disambiguation, and is integrated nicely with memory search. However, we wish to avoid adding too many ad hoc rules of this sort — the system currently has about six such rules which seem to cover most of the cases where memory is unavailable.

More specific use of memory by RESEARCHER occurs in the processing of the next section of P58, shown in Fig. 10.

```
COMPRISING      : Parts of &MEM11 (DISC#) or &MEM10 (LOCATION#) or &MEM9 (TRANSDUCER#)
                  or &MEM8 (ACTUATOR#) to follow
AN              : New instance word -- skip
ACTUATOR        : Memette within NP; save and skip
HOUSING         : MP word -- memette ENCLOSURE#
  New ENCLOSURE# instance (&MEM12)
  >>> Looking for relation between ACTUATOR# and &MEM12 (ENCLOSURE#)
  Assuming &MEM12 (ENCLOSURE#) is part of &MEM8 (ACTUATOR#)
  >>> Selecting assy for &MEM12 (ENCLOSURE#) from among &MEM11 (DISC#)
      &MEM10 (LOCATION#) &MEM9 (TRANSDUCER#) &MEM8 (ACTUATOR#)
  &MEM12 (ENCLOSURE#) is already known to be a part of &MEM8 (ACTUATOR#)
USED AS         : Phrase
-> USED-AS      : Purpose word -- save and skip
A               : New instance word -- skip
STATIONARY      : Memette modifier; save and skip
BASE            : MP word -- memette BASE#
  New BASE# instance (&MEM13)
  Augmenting &MEM13 (BASE#) with feature: MOBILITY = NONE
  Assuming &MEM13 (BASE#) is part of &MEM8 (ACTUATOR#)
  >>> Refining P-ACTS-AS SUBJECT from &MEM12 (ENCLOSURE#) &MEM8 (ACTUATOR#)
  Establishing P-ACTS-AS relation; SUBJECT: &MEM12 (ENCLOSURE#);
      OBJECT: &MEM13 (BASE#) [&REL5]
FOR (FOR1)      : Purpose indicator -- skip
SUPPORTING      : Purpose word -- save and skip
VARIOUS         : Memette modifier; save and skip
PARTS           : MP word -- memette PART#
  New PART# instance (&MEM14)
  Augmenting &MEM14 (PART#) with feature: NUMBER = SOME
  Assuming &MEM14 (PART#) is part of &MEM8 (ACTUATOR#)
  >>> Refining R-CONNECTED-TO SUBJECT from &MEM13 (BASE#) &MEM12 (ENCLOSURE#)
  Unable to select SUBJECT -- using most recent
  Establishing R-CONNECTED-TO relation; SUBJECT: &MEM13 (BASE#);
      OBJECT: &MEM14 (PART#) [&REL6]
  Establishing P-SUPPORTS relation; SUBJECT: &MEM13 (BASE#); OBJECT: &MEM14 (PART#) [&REL7]
*SEMI*          : Skip (SKIP)
```

Fig. 10 — RESEARCHER processing the second part of P58.

The first noun group processed in Fig 10, 'an actuator housing', includes a noun–noun construction requiring memory access. RESEARCHER must determine the relationship between the two objects described, actuator# and enclosure# ('housing'). There are no syntactic clues or semantic clues as to the relation. So, RESEARCHER goes to memory, finds the assembly-part relation that exists in memory for other instance of these concepts (from an example we gave it), and assumes that this relation holds for the new example. Had there been a more complex construction, say noun–noun––noun, RESEARCHER would have used this same information in memory to determine which objects related to each other.

---

†   Other such virtual objects are side#, top#, etc.

The same assembly/part relation in memory is used to resolve another textual ambiguity. RESEARCHER must determine whether the actuator or the disk 'comprises' the 'actuator housing'. Again, the existing relation in memory resolves this ambiguity, and determines that the housing is part of the actuator. Since this relationship has already been established (while analyzing the noun group) processing simply moves on.

The remainder of Fig. 10 shows more examples of RESEARCHER identifying objects, relating them to each other and accessing memory to resolve ambiguity. Fig. 11 shows further examples of all of these sorts of processing as RESEARCHER completes the first fragment of P58.

One interesting aspect of the processing in Fig. 11 is the handling of the phrase 'coil and cart assembly'. As for the earlier noun–noun constructions, RESEARCHER must determine the relations between the 'assembly', the 'coil' and the 'cart'. Naturally, RESEARCHER accesses memory in each case. In one instance, for the 'coil', it finds the example existing in memory. In the other case, relating 'cart' and 'assembly', RESEARCHER must rely on its heuristic that vague, complex objects, like 'assemblies', usually contain more specific objects as parts. (Actually, to do this example perfectly, we would also have to apply similar techniques to determine the scope of 'and' as a connective.)

Fig. 12 gives the representation that RESEARCHER has derived by using memory to help understand P58. The key point is that a correct representation could not be found from syntactic or semantic rules alone. Some form of object memory is needed. While a larger memory would force us to consider more deeply problems of multiple examples, we feel the approach is a sound one.

We have much left to do in our integration of text processing and memory. However, we feel our general approach is quite promising, as our work in building up memory has a positive synergistic effect on text processing robustness. The identification of specific questions to ask memory seems to be much more effective than looking for more general applications of memory to understanding or developing huge numbers of ad hoc disambiguation rules.

4.   USER EXPERTISE AND QUESTION ANSWERING

Once a substantial knowledge base has been built up by RESEARCHER, it is important that it can be queried intelligently. In Lebowitz (1983b) and Paris (1984) we described an early question-answering module. Recently, our work has concentrated on how RESEARCHER might tailor its answers to the needs of individual users. There are many elements to such tailoring, the goal of the user, for example, but here we will concentrate on just one factor — the user's level of expertise. We have tried to determine the sorts of basic strategies that would be appropriate for expert and naive users of the system.† Eventually, we will also look at how expertise affects other levels

† Actually, user expertise falls into two areas — familiarity with the system and familiarity with the domain. We are concerned here with the latter.

```
A             : New instance word -- skip
COIL          : Memette within NP; save and skip
AND (AND2)    : Skip (SKIP)
CART          : Memette within NP; save and skip
ASSEMBLY      : MP word -- memette UNKNOWN-ASSEMBLY#
  New UNKNOWN-ASSEMBLY# instance (&MEM15)
  >>> Looking for relation between CARRIAGE# and &MEM15 (UNKNOWN-ASSEMBLY# -- `ASSEMBLY')
  New CARRIAGE# instance (&MEM16)
  Assuming &MEM16 (CARRIAGE#) is part of &MEM15 (UNKNOWN-ASSEMBLY# -- `ASSEMBLY')
  >>> Looking for relation between COIL# and one of &MEM16 (CARRIAGE#)
        &MEM15 (UNKNOWN-ASSEMBLY# -- `ASSEMBLY')
New COIL# instance (&MEM17)
Assuming &MEM17 (COIL#) is part of &MEM15 (UNKNOWN-ASSEMBLY# -- `ASSEMBLY')
Assuming &MEM15 (UNKNOWN-ASSEMBLY# -- `ASSEMBLY') is part of &MEM8 (ACTUATOR#)
INCLUDING     : Parts of &MEM15 (UNKNOWN-ASSEMBLY# -- `ASSEMBLY')
                or &MEM8 (ACTUATOR#) to follow
A             : New instance word -- skip
CART          : MP word -- memette CARRIAGE#
  Reference for CARRIAGE#: &MEM16
  >>> Selecting assy for &MEM16 (CARRIAGE#) from among
        &MEM15 (UNKNOWN-ASSEMBLY# -- `ASSEMBLY') &MEM8 (ACTUATOR#)
  &MEM16 (CARRIAGE#) is already known to be a part
    of &MEM15 (UNKNOWN-ASSEMBLY# -- `ASSEMBLY')
*COMMA*       : Skip (SKIP)
HAVING        : Parts of &MEM16 (CARRIAGE#) or &MEM15 (UNKNOWN-ASSEMBLY# -- `ASSEMBLY')
                or &MEM8 (ACTUATOR#) to follow
A             : New instance word -- skip
RECTANGULAR   : Memette modifier; save and skip
CROSS SECTION : Phrase
-> CROSS-SECTION : MP word -- memette CROSS-SECTION#
  New CROSS-SECTION# instance (&MEM18)
  Augmenting &MEM18 (CROSS-SECTION#) with feature: SHAPE = RECTANGULAR
  >>> Selecting assy for &MEM18 (CROSS-SECTION#) from among &MEM16 (CARRIAGE#)
        &MEM15 (UNKNOWN-ASSEMBLY# -- `ASSEMBLY') &MEM8 (ACTUATOR#)
  Assuming &MEM18 (CROSS-SECTION#) is part of &MEM16 (CARRIAGE#)
AND (AND2)    : Skip (SKIP)
TUBULAR       : Memette modifier; save and skip
IN CONSTRUCTION : Phrase
-> IN-CONSTRUCTION : Collecting modifiers
  >>> Looking for memette modified by CONFIGURATION/CYLINDRICAL from
        &MEM18 (CROSS-SECTION#) &MEM16 (CARRIAGE#)
        &MEM15 (UNKNOWN-ASSEMBLY# -- `ASSEMBLY') &MEM8 (ACTUATOR#)
  Augmenting &MEM16 (CARRIAGE#) with feature: CONFIGURATION = CYLINDRICAL
*COMMA*       : Skip (SKIP)
ADAPTED       : Purpose word -- save and skip
AT            : Relation word -- save and skip
ONE           : Memette modifier; save and skip
END           : MP word -- memette END#
  New END# instance (&MEM19)
  Augmenting &MEM19 (END#) with feature: NUMBER = 1
  Assuming &MEM19 (END#) is part of &MEM16 (CARRIAGE#)
  Establishing P-MODIFIES relation; SUBJECT: &MEM19 (END#) [&REL8]
  Establishing R-AT relation; SUBJECT: &MEM19 (END#) [&REL9]
TO SUPPORT    : Phrase
-> SUPPORTS   : Purpose word -- save and skip
THE           : Antecedent word -- skip
TRANSDUCER    : MP word -- memette TRANSDUCER#
  Reference for TRANSDUCER#: &MEM9
  >>> Refining P-SUPPORTS SUBJECT from &MEM19 (END#) &MEM16 (CARRIAGE#)
        &MEM15 (UNKNOWN-ASSEMBLY# -- `ASSEMBLY') &MEM8 (ACTUATOR#)
  Unable to select SUBJECT -- using most recent
  Establishing P-SUPPORTS relation; SUBJECT: &MEM19 (END#);
    OBJECT: &MEM9 (TRANSDUCER#) [&REL10]
*STOP*        : Break word -- skip
```

Fig. 11 — RESEARCHER processing the third part of P58.

of processing (such as lexical choice) as well as other factors that require the tailoring of answers.

In order to get an idea about the kinds of strategies that might be

Text Representation:

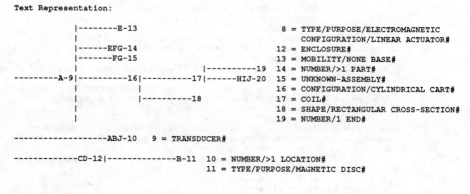

```
          |--------E-13                       8 = TYPE/PURPOSE/ELECTROMAGNETIC
          |                                       CONFIGURATION/LINEAR ACTUATOR#
          |------EFG-14                       12 = ENCLOSURE#
          |------FG-15                        13 = MOBILITY/NONE BASE#
          |                        |----------19  14 = NUMBER/>1 PART#
---------A-9|----------16|----------17|------HIJ-20 15 = UNKNOWN-ASSEMBLY#
          |              |                        16 = CONFIGURATION/CYLINDRICAL CART#
          |              |----------18            17 = COIL#
          |                                       18 = SHAPE/RECTANGULAR CROSS-SECTION#
          |                                       19 = NUMBER/1 END#

------------------ABJ-10    9 = TRANSDUCER#

------------CD-12|-------------B-11   10 = NUMBER/>1 LOCATION#
                                      11 = TYPE/PURPOSE/MAGNETIC DISC#
```

A list of relations:

	Subject:	Relation:	Object:
[&REL1/A]	&MEM8 (ACTUATOR#)	{P-GUIDES}	&MEM9 (TRANSDUCER#)
[&REL2/B]	&MEM10 (LOCATION#)	{R-ABOVE}	&MEM9 (TRANSDUCER#)
[&REL3/C]		{P-WRITES}	&MEM11 (DISC#)
[&REL4/D]		{P-ROTATES}	&MEM11 (DISC#)
[&REL5/E]	&MEM12 (ENCLOSURE#)	{P-ACTS-AS}	&MEM13 (BASE#)
[&REL6/F]	&MEM13 (BASE#)	{R-CONNECTED-TO}	&MEM14 (PART#)
[&REL7/G]	&MEM13 (BASE#)	{P-SUPPORTS}	&MEM14 (PART#)
[&REL8/H]	&MEM19 (END#)	{P-MODIFIES}	
[&REL9/I]	&MEM19 (END#)	{R-AT}	
[&REL10/J]	&MEM19 (END#)	{P-SUPPORTS}	&MEM9 (TRANSDUCER#)

Fig. 12 — The representation of EX7.

appropriate for various users, we have looked at tests that describe objects
and that are aimed at readers with different levels of expertise — several
adult and junior encyclopedias. As described more fully in Paris (1985), the
strategies used in adult and junior encyclopedias are quite different — the
adult encyclopedias, presumably aimed at relative experts, tend to describe
the part structure of objects, while the junior encyclopedias describe the
processes that take place in the device. EX8 and EX9 show this distinction
for descriptions of telephones.

EX8 — The hard-sets introduced in 1947 consist of a receiver and a
transmitter in a single housing available in black or colored plastic. The
transmitter diaphragm is clamped rigidly at its edges to improve the high
frequency repsonse. The diaphragm is coupled to a doubly resonant
system — a cavity and an air chamber — which broadens the response ... (*Collier's Encyclopedia* 1962)

As we can see, EX8, taken from an adult encyclopedia, describes a
telephone by presenting its parts. The description continues in this vein. It is
using a construction quite similar to the constituency schema that McKeown
used in her question-answering work (McKeown 1982), providing an almost
tree-like description of the parts of the object. This is in contrast with a
description aimed at younger readers, EX9.

EX9 — When one speaks into the transmitter of a modern telephone, these sound waves strike against an *aluminium disk or diaphragm* and cause it to vibrate back and forth in just the same way the molecules of air are vibrating ... (*Britannica Junior* 1963)

Here the description is process-oriented. It traces the process of transmitting sound, introducing part descriptions only when necessary. This is clearly a different presentation strategy, and our study of texts indicates that it is much more widely used in texts aimed at less experienced readers. We feel that a process-oriented answer would be appropriate for RESEARCHER to use when dealing with a novice user not likely to know what various parts are used for.

We are currently implementing these two different strategies for describing the same object. Fig. 13 shows how RESEARCHER generates an explanation of a telephone from a hand-coded knowledge base making use of McKeown's consistency schema. This is presumably the kind of explanan-

```
; Description of the TELEPHONE based on the Constituency schema.

; &MEMX are the unique identifiers for the object frames.
; The Constituency Schema was filled by stepping through an ATN.

&MEM1   (TELEPHONE)                                          ; The telephone is
        (*IDENTIFICATION* (VARIANT-OF: DEVICE#))             ; a device.  It consists
        (*CONSTITUENCY* (&MEM2 (TRANSMITTER))                ; of a transmitter,
                        (&MEM16 (HOUSING))                   ; a housing, a line and
                        (&MEM15 (LINE))                      ; a receiver.
                        (&MEM17 (RECEIVER)))

&MEM2   (TRANSMITTER)                                        ; The transmitter is
        (*IDENTIFICATION* (VARIANT-OF: TRANSMITTER#))        ; a kind of transmitter.
        (*CONSTITUENCY* (&MEM6 (DOUBLY-RESONANT-SYSTEM))     ; It has a doubly
                        (&MEM3 (DIAPHRAGM-T)))               ; resonant system and
                                                             ; a diaphragm;
&MEM16  (HOUSING)                                            ; the housing is
        (*IDENTIFICATION* (VARIANT-OF: COVER#))              ; a type of cover;
        (*CONSTITUENCY*)

&MEM5   (LINE)                                               ; the line is a wire;
        (*IDENTIFICATION* (VARIANT-OF: WIRE#))
        (*CONSTITUENCY*)

&MEM17  (RECEIVER)                                           ; The receiver is a
        (*IDENTIFICATION* (VARIANT-OF: RECEIVER#))           ; kind of receiver.
        (*CONSTITUENCY* (&MEM22 (DIAPHRAGM-T))               ; It consists of a
                        (&MEM21 (AIR-GAP))                   ; diaphragm, an air gap
                        (&MEM18 (ELECTROMAGNET)))            ; and an electromagnet.
```

Fig. 13 — A constituency explanation of 'telephone'.

tion we would have RESEARCHER generate for an expert user. In Fig. 13 we can see the various steps of the explanation that RESEARCHER produces, annotated by hand on the right. We are currently interfacing

RESEARCHER with a surface generator that uses a functional grammar Kay (1979) to automatically produce English output.

Fig. 14 shows the first part of another description of a telephone generated by RESEARCHER from the same knowledge base, this time in a process-based manner appropriate for a novice.

```
; The process information gets picked up and printed out for a naive  user.
; &MRX are the unique identifiers to the frames corresponding to the
; meta-relations the program is tracing.

&REL3 (P-SPEAKS-INTO):                    ; When one speaks into the
        subject : (&MEM27) [ONE]          ; transmitter of a telephone,
        object  : (&MEM2) [TRANSMITTER]

    ===>    &MR0 {M-CAUSES}

&REL4 (P-HITS):                           ; the sound waves  hit
        subject : (&MEM28) [SOUNDWAVES]   ; the diaphragm of the transmitter.
        object  : (&MEM3) [DIAPHRAGM-T]

    --------

&REL4 (P-HITS):                           ; This causes
        subject : (&MEM28) [SOUNDWAVES]   ;
        object  : (&MEM3) [DIAPHRAGM-T]

    ===>    &MR1 {M-CAUSES}

&REL5 (P-VIBRATES):                       ; the diaphragm to vibrate
        subject :
        object  : (&MEM3) [DIAPHRAGM-T]

    --------

&REL5 (P-VIBRATES):
        subject :
        object  : (&MEM3) [DIAPHRAGM-T]

    ===>    &MR2 {M-EQUIVALENT-TO}        ; in the same manner as

&REL8 (P-VIBRATES)                        ; the molecules of air
        subject :                         ; are vibrating.
        object  : (&MEM26) [AIR-MOLECULES]
```

Fig. 14 — Process-oriented description of 'telephone'.

Instead of just giving the parts of the telephone, it now describes the operation of the device, primarily by presenting a series of causal links. Our surface generator under development will also produce English text for this example

The manner in which RESEARCHER generates the descriptions of Fig. 13 and Fig. 14 is described in more detail in Paris (1985). In addition to looking at the different generation strategies, we are also studying ways to determine the expertise of a user, since simply asking is not always the appropriate approach, particularly as a user's expertise may vary over different topics of discussion. We are also considering mixed strategies that make use of elements of each of the generation techniques illustrated here.

5. CONCLUSION

We have described here three areas of investigation in the study of intelligent information systems, involving the prototype system RESEARCHER. Our work involves the basic idea of *understanding* the text to be stored in the system's memory. Remarkably little work in artificial intelligence has taken this approach. The system CyFr (Schank *et al.* 1980), which combined FRUMP (DeJong 1979) and CYRUS (Kolodner 1984), worked from a similar perspective as did our earlier work with IPP (Lebowitz 1983c), a system that read news stories about terrorism. Other work applying artificial intelligence to information retrieval, such as Tou *et al.* (1982) and Tong *et al.* (1983), has either applied heuristic approaches to the search of raw text or involved search through carefully prepared knowledge bases. Understanding the text greatly widens the possibilities. In our own research, the generalization of hierarchical representations allows the system to learn about a wide range of complex objects and build up a rich memory. This memory is used extensively in test processing, primarily for disambiguation, to achieve robust performance. Finally, awareness of the expertise level of a user will allow RESEARCHER to tailor its answers to each user. The sum of these three related areas of investigation should lead towards the development of powerful intelligent information systems that can make better use of huge amounts of varying sorts of information than can purely text-based systems.

REFERENCES

Abelson, R. P. (1973) The structure of belief systems. In: Schank, R. C. and Colby, K. (eds), *Computer models of thought and language*. San Fransico, W. H. Freeman Co.

Barr, A., Cohen, P. R. and Feigenbaum, E. A. (eds) (1982) *The handbook of artificial intelligence*, Vol. 1–3. Los Altos, California William Kaufman, Inc.

Birnbaum, L. and Selfridge, M. (1981) Conceptual analysis of natural language. In: Schank, R. C. and Riesbeck, C. K. (eds), *Inside computer understanding*, Hillsdale, N.J., Lawrence Erlbaum Associates, pp. 318–353.

Carbonell, J. G. (1981) *Subjective understanding: computer models of belief systems*. Ann Arbor, Michigan, UMI Research Press.

DeJong, G. F. (1979) Prediction and substantiation: a new approach to natural language processing. *Cognitive Science* 3 251–273.

DeJong, G. F. (1983) Artificial intelligence implications for information retrieval. Proceedings of the Sixth International ACM SIGIR Conference, ACM SIGIR, Washington, DC. 1983.

Evans, T. G. (1968) A heuristic program to solve geometric analogy problems. In: Minsky, M. (ed), *Sematic information processing*, Cambridge, MA, MIT Press.

Finin, T. W. (1982) The interpretation of nominal compounds in discourse.

Technical Report MS-CIS-82-3, Moore School of Engineering, University of Pennsylvania.

Harris, L. R. (1978) Natural language processing applied to data base query. Proceedings of the 1978 ACM Annual Conference, Association for Computer machinery, Washington, DC, 1978.

Heaps, H. S. (1978) *Information retrieval: computational and theroetical aspects.* New York, Academic Press.

Hirst, G. (1983) *Semantic interpretation against ambiguity.* Ph.D. thesis, Department of Computer Science, Brown University.

Kay, M. (1979) Functional grammar. Proceedings of the Fifth Meeting of the Berkeley Linguistics Society, Berkeley, CA, 1979.

Kolodner, J. L. (1984) *Retrieval and organizational strategies in conceptual memory: a computer model.* Hillsdale, New Jersey, Lawrence Erlbaum Associates.

Lebowitz, M. (1981) Cancelled due to lack of interest. Proceedings of the Seventh International Joint Conference on Artifical Intelligence, Vancouver, Canada, 1981.

Lebowitz, M. (1982) Correcting erroneous generalizations. Cognition and brain Theory **5** (4) 367–381.

Lebowitz, M. (1983a) Intelligent information systems. Proceedings of the Sixth International ACM SIGIR Conference, ACM SIGIR, Washington, DC, 1983, pp. 25–30.

Lebowitz, M. (1983b) RESEARCHER: An overview. Proceedings of the Third National Conference on Artificial Intelligence, Washington, DC, 1983, pp. 232–235.

Lebowitz, M. (1983c) Generalization from natural language text. *Cognitive Science* **7** (1) 1–40.

Lebowitz, M. (1983d) Concept learning in a rich input domain. Proceedings of the 1983 International Machine Learning Workshop, Champaign-Urbana, Illinois, 1983, pp. 177–182. To appear in *Machine learning: an artificial intelligence approach*, Vol II.

Lebowitz, M. (1983e) Memory-based parsing, *Artificial Intelligence* **21** (4) 363–404.

Lebowitz, M. (1984) Using memory in text understanding. Proceedings of ECAI-84, Pisa, Italy, 1984.

Levi, J. N. (1978) *The syntax and semantics of complex nominals.* New York, McGraw-Hill.

McKeown, K. R. (1982) *Generating natural language text in response to questions about database structure.* Ph.D. thesis, University of Pennsylnavia.

Michalski, R. S. (1980) Pattern recognition as rule-guided inductive inference. *IEEE Transactions on Pattern Analysis and Machine Intelligence* **2** (4) 349–361.

Paris, C. L. (1984) Determining the level of expertise. Proceedings of the First Annual Workshop on Theoretical Issues in Conceptual Information Processing, Atlanta, Georgia, 1984.

Paris, C. L. (1985) Description strategies for naive and expert users.

Proceedings of the 23rd Annual Meeting of the Association for Computational Linguistics, Chicago, 1985.

Salton, G. and McGill, M. J. (1983) *Introduction to modern information retrieval*. New York, McGraw-Hill.

Schank, R. C. (1979) Interestingness: Controlling inference. *Artifical Intelligence* **12** (3) 273–297.

Schank, R.C., Kolodner, J. L. and DeJong, G. F. (1980) Conceptual information retrieval. Technical Report 190, Yale University Department of Computer Science.

Small, S. (1980) Word expert parsing: A theory of distributed word-based natural language understanding. Technical Report TR-954, University of Maryland, Department of Computer Science.

Tong, R. M., Shapiro, D. G., McCune, B. P. and Dean, J. S. (1983) A rule-based approach to information retrieval: Some results and comments. Proceedings of the Third National Conference on Artificial Intelligence, Washington, DC, 1983.

Tou, F. N., Williams, M. D., Fikes, R., Henderson, A., and Malone, T. (1982) RABBIT: An intelligent database assistant. Proceedings of the Second National Conference on Artificial Intelligence, Pittsburgh, PA, 1982, pp. 314–318.

Wasserman, K. (1984) Understanding hierarchically structured objects. Columbia University Department of Computer Science.

Wasserman, K. (1985) *Unifying represenatation and generalization: Understanding hierarchically structured objects*. Ph.D. thesis, Columbia University Department of Computer Science.

Wasserman, K. and Lebowitz, M. (1983) Representing complex physical objects *Cognition and Brian Theory* **6** (3) 333–352.

Winston, P. H. (1972) Learning structural descriptions from examples. In: Winston, P. H. (ed), *The psychology of computer vision*. New York, McGraw-Hill.

Winston, P. H. (1980) Learning and reasoning by analogy. *Communications of the ACM* **23** 689–702.

Part III

Referral and user modelling

> Knowledge is of two kinds. We know a subject ourselves or we know where we can find information upon it.
>
> (Samuel Johnson, quoted in Boswell 1791)

In information retrieval, the emphasis has been firmly on the second kind of knowledge, but the balance is shifting slowly. Addis (1982) has described expert systems as an evolutionary (not revolutionary) step in information retrieval, and in most cases their knowledge bases belong to the first of Johnson's categories. Even so, these developments are unlikely to decrease the importance of knowledge about finding information. The scope of existing expert systems is limited, and as their numbers increase so knowledge of what systems are available will be required.

Referral is concerned exclusively with the provision of Johnson's second type of knowledge. It may involve use of a catalogue or bibliographic database but would not stop there. Suppose an enquirer wanted a description of some standard manufacturing process used in the chemical industry. A catalogue would show what books a library had on chemical engineering and possibly, depending on the specificity of the indexing, which ones were mainly concerned with manufacturing processes, but would give no guidance as to the order in which these works should be consulted. A librarian, before even looking at the catalogue, would probably recommend checking the Kirk Othmer *Encyclopedia of Chemical Technology* or a similar reference work first. Referral demands a knowledge not only of the topics of particular works but also their functions and the sort of queries they are meant to satisfy.

In many cases the best source of information may be individuals or organizations with relevant expertise, and details of these as well as of printed publications would have to be possessed by a referral system. A truly intelligent, insightful information system with comprehensive coverage of information sources, knowledge of different types of query, and of its users, would be capable of both information retrieval and referral: there would be no sharp distinction between the two functions. However, progress towards that goal can be assured by a policy of divide and conquer and therefore these two tasks are best considered in separate sections of this book.

Avron Barr, one of the editors of the *Handbook of Artificial Intelligence* (Barr & Feigenbaum 1982), has given a succinct account of the difficulty of automating tasks of the referral type:

Enabling an individual to know something about what another knows, without actually knowing it, involves defining the nature of what is known elsewhere — who are the experts on what kinds of problems and what might they know that could be useful. This is related directly to the kind of categorization of knowledge that is the essence of library science. But instead of dealing with categories in which static books will be filed, AI must consider the dynamic aspect of systems that know and learn. The relation then between AI and disciplines like psychology, linguistics, sociology, brain science, and library science is a complex one. (Barr 1983, p. 252).

Any attempt to accomplish a task with such widespread ramifications should be worthy of careful study. The chapter by Vickery, Brooks and Vickery gives a detailed account of how diverse kinds of knowledge, represented by different means, were used in the production of the first expert system for referral, PLEXUS. This achievement required considerable ingenuity, as, apart from the intrinsic difficulty of the domain, there was the added requirement that the system should use hardware readily affordable by libraries. The chapter describes the design of PLEXUS, indicates what has been achieved so far, and points the way to further progress. As well as demonstrating to librarians what AI can contribute to automating the referral process, the chapter will also give those readers whose interest is primarily in AI some indication of the part that librarianship can play in contributing to an understanding of the problems referred to by Barr.

A proper understanding of an enquiry requires some knowledge about the enquirer. Often, in information retrieval, it is assumed that the relevance of a publication depends purely on its topic; but a layman and an astonomer seeking information on Halley's comet would probably not be satisfied with the same documents. The chapter on PLEXUS makes clear the importance of taking the characteristics of the user into account, and that task will be investigated more comprehensively in the next stage of the system's development. Elaine Rich has demonstrated how user models can be created. In her experimental system for recommending novels, GRUNDY, the probable literary tastes of enquirers are assessed with the aid of stereotypes of readers. GRUNDY is able to modify these stereotypes on the basis of experience and therefore has a learning capability. From a librarian's point of view, Rich's work could be regarded as complementary to that of Pejtersen (1984) who has created a classification scheme which is fully intended to be compatible with users' need criteria. With its emphasis on psychological factors, Rich's chapter helps to form a bridge between the information retrieval and the cognitive sections of this book.

REFERENCES

Addis, T. R. (1982) Expert systems: an evolution in information retrieval. *Information Technology: Research and Development* 1 (4) 275–283.
Barr, A. (1983) Artificial intelligence: cognition as computation. In: Mach-

lup, F. & Mansfield, U. (eds), *The study of information: interdisciplinary messages*. New York, Wiley, pp. 237–262.

Barr, A. & Feigenbaum, E. A. (eds) (1982) *The handbook of artificial intelligence*. London, Pitman.

Boswell, J. (1791) *The life of Samuel Johnson,* London.

Pejtersen, A. M. (1984) Design of a computer-aided user-system dialogue based on analysis of users' search behaviour. *Social Science Information Studies* **4** 167–183.

6

An expert system for referral: the PLEXUS project

A. Vickery, **H. M. Brooks** and **B. C. Vickery**, Central Information Service, University of London

1. AIMS AND OBJECTIVES

In 1984, CIS was awarded a grant by the British Library Research and Development Department to develop an expert system as a referral tool for use in libraries.

The Central Information Service of the University of London (CIS) is a unit within the Library Resources Coordinating Committee (LRCC), which is responsible for coordinating the libraries of the 65 colleges and institutions of the University of London. CIS has been in operation since 1974 and its primary responsibility is the organization of online computer information services. CIS has also carried out various research projects for institutions such as the British Library, FAO and UNESCO. The projects have ranged widely, from bibliographic surveys and reviews of the literature, to a travelling workshop to university libraries and departments to increase online awareness, to a referral project for the University. From 1978, CIS started to explore the use of microcomputers in library and information work, developing its own software for these applications. In recent years, CIS has become involved in the application of artificial intelligence techniques to information systems.

The objects of the project were as follows:

(1) to develop a generalized computer-based subject referral system that could be used to provide referral facilities to various types of information source;
(2) to use the system to implement a particular referral system that could be of value to libraries;
(3) to demonstrate to librarians the nature and potentialities of expert systems.

The aim, therefore, was to develop an expert system which would assist both librarians and end users in a referral situation. The system should be able to carry out the same kinds of task as the human reference librarian does in the situation, and should do it in a way which, if done by a human, would be described as intelligent. That is, the system would attempt to ascertain the user's problem, asking additional questions to supplement the user's original statement, if necessary. This problem description can then be transformed into a search strategy which can be applied to a database of referral resources. Should the initial strategy produce unsatisfactory results, it would be gradually reformulated until a satisfactory outcome is achieved. The information about the referral resources found by the search could then be presented to the user in an informative and helpful manner.

At a more specific level, it was felt that the following areas should be investigated:

(1) user–system interfacing for library environments;
(2) methods of knowledge acquisition suitable for this type of application;
(3) types of knowledge used by human experts to solve referral problems;
(4) specifications of the knowledge used to solve referral problems;
(5) methods of representation of these types of knowledge;
(6) tools for developing an expert system in this specific area;
(7) use of a world knowledge classification system;
(8) suitable architectures for the system.

One of the intentions of the project was to try to ascertain the problems of developing expert systems for library and information application. We therefore consider that our experiences with the actual construction process are as important as the prototype itself.

2. BACKGROUND

2.1 Referral

It is important to define what we understand by the term 'referral' before going on to describe the expert system itself.

Referral, according to the *Handbook of Special Librarianship and Information Work,* is the act of connecting a searcher for specialized information with an appropriate personal or organizational source. The 'Handbook' implies that the term only applies to interpersonal contacts, but, in practice, referral is usually taken to include also the referring of an enquirer to a specialist collection of documents, such as a specialist library. A different description of the function of referral is given in a Management/ Franklin Institute report which considers referral centres as not only responding to enquires concerning information resources and services, but also providing regular 'resources awareness' information. SDI (selective dissemination of information) service subscribers would be kept aware, on a periodic basis, of new information resources or changes in the content, cost or accessibility, of those already listed.

Finer (1977) point out that there are several definitions of a 'referral centre'. Some of the definitions exclude conventional information work. In this narrow sense, there are very few pure referral centres anywhere, and probably none in the United Kingdom, because even those query-answering organizations with very little literature support, such as Citizens' Advice Bureaux, give some advice and information as well as providing referrals. On the other hand, virtually every library or information centre gives referrals to specialized sources of information, as well as, or instead of, providing documents and substantive information, when such a response seems appropriate.

In their paper 'Aspects of referrral' (1984) John Martyn and Glenda Rousseau describe their study of referral processes. They conclude that referral cannot be considered as a separate activity. When a library or an information department answers an enquiry, the answer may be made up of locally-held information, documents containing relevant information, references to other documents and suggestions of other persons or institutions likely to be able to help. The librarian's first response to an enquiry will usually be to search printed sources. Referral will be used if printed sources fail, or if a referral source is likely to complement or supplement a document-based answer. It is in general the case, that referral is a component of an answer, and rarely the whole.

Most librarians have their own network of personal contacts, which is their principal tool in identifying potential sources of information. Their informal lists of sources include other librarians, many of whom will be former colleagues, and institutions and organizations which they have used as sources of information before. Maintenance of formal 'indexes of expertise' does not appear to be very common, and in some cases, where such indexes have been maintained in the past, they have been now abandoned, for reasons of cost, and because of the difficulty of keeping them up-to-date.

The value or effectiveness of referral is virtually entirely dependent on the performance of a referral source when it receives an enquiry. In comparison with other methods of information supply, referral has some obvious deficiencies, in that it is inherently slower than, for example, online search, and demands more effort from the user because the enquiry must be resubmitted to the referral source. It is also likely to be less precise than other methods of information acquisition. It is also apparent that the referral function can rarely be separated from the kind of service that directs the enquirer to documentary reference sources.

2.2   Natural language interfaces
The referral task involves interaction between the human librarian and the human user; and this interaction is a key component in the referral task. If we wish to develop an expert system for referral, then it is necessary to consider carefully the human–computer interaction and in particular facilitating easy communication in natural language.

A good deal of work has already been done on the development of natural language interfaces. A 1982 questionnaire yielded over one hundred summaries of natural language understanding systems, of which a considerable proportion represented natural language interfaces (Kaplan 1982).

The best mode of communication between the user and the machine, in either direction, would be a natural language interface. Each user would find it much easier to work in his own language than to learn an artificial language. A full natural language interface would support deeper systems operations effectively, i.e. allow proper access to the system's motivation and behaviour' (Sparck Jones 1984).

When a natural language interface is envisaged for an information system, this interface must be able to translate the natural language statements (e.g. English) into appropriate actions of the system. Speaking about natural language, we should realize that we mean just a subset of a natural language, a subset which will closely correspond to the domain covered by the information system. To identify the right language subset is difficult, and this is only one of the problems in building natural language interfaces.

The current computer systems capable of engaging in a dialogue with a human usually respond accurately only to simple requests, and even in the case of a simple dialogue the computer system cannot respond reasonably to the user's input without conforming to a rigid grammar. It can ask for simple clarification, but it will not understand this clarification if the user's input is unclear. Hayes and Reddy urge the construction of systems which can interact gracefully with their users (Hayes & Reddy 1979). They consider a graceful interaction not as a single monolithic skill, but as a number of diverse abilities, including:

(1) Flexible parsing: the ability to deal with natural language with all the ellipses, idioms, grammatical errors and fragmentary utterances it can contain.
(2) Robust communication: the set of strategies needed to ensure that a listener (or reader) receives a speaker's (or writer's) utterance, and interprets it correctly.
(3) Focus mechanisms: the ability to keep track of what the conversation is about.
(4) Explanation facility: the ability to explain what the system can and cannot do, what it has done, what it is trying to do, and why, both for the response to direct questions, and as a fallback when communication breaks down.
(5) Identification from descriptions: the ability to recognize an object from a description; including the ability to pursue a clarifying dialogue if the original description is unclear.

Vickery (1984) added six more points to the list:

(6) The learning mechanism: the ability of the system to acquire facts, new

skills and more abstract concepts from experience, and the ability to learn from its mistakes. This ability is one of the areas being currently investigated by artificial intelligence. For example AM — a computer program which develops new mathematical concepts.

(7) Knowledge of the user: the system should have the ability to diagnose the level of the user and create a model. Sparck Jones (1984) refers to the need of natural language interfaces to create user models to increase effectiveness, efficiency and acceptability of a system, especially of expert systems.

(8) Correction of errors: the users have to be provided with an opportunity to correct their errors (e.g. in input) or the sysem needs to be able to judge the validity of the input.

(9) User friendliness: the system should be user-friendly and easy to use.

(10) Tutorial aids for users: the system should be equipped with tutorial modules (help routines).

(11) Response time: the response time of the system should be adequate and the variance in response time should be minimized.

The task of a natural langugage interface to an information system is the reformulation of natural language questions as formal search specifications (Sparck Jones 1982). The process employed in such situations consists of analysis of the input questions, i.e. a representation of their meaning. Rich (1984) describes three approaches that combine all components of a natural language understanding program. These are: language through window, semantic grammars (e.g. Waltz 1978) and syntactic grammars (e.g. Sager 1981).

The most developed area of natural language processing is in database query. These systems demonstrate an effective use of necessary components of natural language understanding systems, namely syntax, semantics and pragmatics, through in most cases only the for handling inputs. But even those interfaces (which operate using a subset of English) can fail, unless the demands made on them are modest. These natural language interfaces would be of very limited value to expert systems because database systems have little call for discourse knowledge and procedures required to interpret and respond to larger texts and dialogues.

The interfaces needed for expert systems require solutions for treatment of 'ill-formed' input, of discourse and dialogue structure, and of language user's beliefs, goals, plans, etc. In order to achieve a properly functioning natural language interface, the functional expectations of the interface need to be combined with the much greater behavioural richness of a sophisticated expert system, a much closer coupling between front and back ends (Sparck Jones 1984). Natural language interfaces, even when meant to serve user convenience, are likely to have unfortunate repercussions because the user's expectations are raised. In these situations, the user, without realizing it, is able to produce inputs demanding new system resources. The new and more demanding needs can require not merely simple additions to, but substantial modifications of, the expert system itself.

3. PLEXUS — OVERVIEW

Goal of the project

To create a prototype of a tool to be used in public and academic libraries which will assist the reference librarian in answering user queries or will deal with the user directly. The system should be sufficiently 'user-friendly' for library users to operate the system by themselves. The system refers inquirers, where possible, to resources such as those found in *Walford Guide to Reference Sources* or in directories of online databases. *PLEXUS is neither a question-answering system nor a library catalogue system.*

Domain of the system

The prototype system is restricted to Gardening and related aspects of the subject. The subject domain will be expanded in later versions of the system. The domain was chosen because it was assumed to be of general appeal to the users of a public library.

Task of the system

To provide the user at all times with appropriate help and advice comparable to that given by a reference librarian. The system interacts with the user to develop an effective search strategy, searches the database and evaluates, together with the user, the search result. The outcome of a search is an annotated list of reference sources.

Paradigm

The framework of PLEXUS is that of an intelligent knowledge-based system. That is to say, it carries out conceptual problem-solving using various types of knowledge represented by a variety of methods including frames, production rules, semantic nets.

Stages in system development

(1) Defining the domain.
(2) Defining the knowledge needed by the system.
(3) Knowledge acquisition. The knowledge incorporated in the system has been extracted from reference librarians and information scientists with library background.
(4) Determining the form of knowledge representation. Rather than uniform knowledge representation, the nature of the referral problem determined that some knowledge should be represented as a semantic network (the knowledge classification), other knowledge by frames (problem statements) and the remainder as a hierarchy of production rules.
(5) System implementation and testing.
(6) Prototype evaluation and revision.

Knowledge base

The aim of the system was to embody some of the expertise of a reference librarian. The expert knowledge is concerned not so much with a particular subject domain but rather with how to elicit appropriate and sufficient information from a user to carry out a search for information sources in a subject domain. To construct an expert referral system one needs to embody a variety of different types of knowledge. One of the main issues then becomes how these different knowledge structures interact with each other in the problem-solving process. PLEXUS has neither a completely hierarchical nor a distributed architecture; it is rather a highly interactive body of elements.

The knowledge embodied in PLEXUS is of seven kinds:

(1) Librarianship and library knowledge.
(2) Knowledge of information retrieval techniques.
(3) Knowledge of the subject area.
(4) Knowledge of the subject literature.
(5) Knowledge of the structure of world knowledge.
(6) Knowledge of library users.
(7) Knowledge of problem-statement development.

Knowledge is represented in PLEXUS in four ways.

1. The BSO (Broad Subject Ordering) which provides the world knowledge framework. BSO was originated by UNESCO in 1971. It is a faceted classification scheme which is not only a subject code but also an ordering system. Implicit in the concept of an ordering system is the view that a coherently ordered listing of subjects is in itself an asset. In PLEXUS the horticulture sections from BSO are used. These have been extended and the notation modified. BSO has an implicit structure of semantic categories or facets, and each individual class within it is assigned to one of these facets. Each term of the dictionary is humanly assigned to at least one BSO entry.

2. The production rule sets which direct problem-statement development, search strategy development, search strategy modification and evaluation of output. PLEXUS embodies around one thousand rules which are specific to particular subtasks. This is the task-oriented rule knowledge. This knowledge is at various levels, concerned with tasks which must be accomplished to achieve problem development. At the highest level, they are concerned with the selection of an appropriate strategy for modelling the problem. For example,

> IF   none of the words in the user's statement are known (i.e.
>   occur in the dictionary)
> AND   STRATS has not been tried before
> THEN   use STRAT3 to try and develop a problem development.

Other, lower level, rules are concerned with how to interpret a term if that term can have more than one interpretation. For example,

> BLOSSOM in PLEXUS dictionary could mean:
> either to blossom......a process
> or the blossom......a part

The rules to decide on an interpretation can be phrased as follows:

> IF   there is another process concept present
> THEN assume blossom is a part
> ELSE if there is an operation concept present
> THEN assume blossom is a part
> ELSE if there is an object7 or object1
>   present (i.e. general term like plant or tree
>   or a specific plant name)
> THEN assume blossom is a process
> ELSE assume blossom is a part

Yet more rules are involved with specifying whether or not a particular set of frames constitutes a complete problem development and if not, what should be done to achieve this. For example,

> IF   the iframe has category OPER1
> AND   the context is 0 or 1 or 2
> AND   the object slot is not empty
> AND   the ENTITY slot is not empty
> AND   the ENVMNT slot is not empty
> AND   the ENVATT slot is not empty
> AND   the INSTR slot is not empty
> AND   the USEPRP slot is not empty
> AND   the TIMESLOT is not empty
> THEN the iframe is complete

The system will attempt to check the status of each specified slot and fill if necessary, using rules such as the one below:

> IF   the iframe has category OPER1
> AND   the ENTITY slot is [EMPTY]
> AND   the object slot term contains [TERM]
> AND   object slot term has category PART
> THEN GET ENTITY1

3. The content of the referral resources contained within the database and indicators of their literary form, etc. The original plan was to construct a database of referral resources from entries in the *Walford Guide to Refer-*

ence Sources. Unfortunately, the number of sources in Walford relating to gardening was insufficient. The basic core of Walford entries has therefore been supplemented by additional materials:

(a) gardening societies and institutions from the *Directory of British Associations;*
(b) references to printed works on gardening — mostly handbooks, encyclopaedias, glossaries, and dictionaries; directories of people, institutions and botanical gardens were also included;
(c) individual experts within the University of London.

The PLEXUS database was created using MIRABILIS software developed by CIS (to handle bibliographic information). There are currently 450 records in the database. Each record in the database consists of 15 fields, some of which are indexed. MIRABILIS constructs an inverted index to the database from terms in the indexed fields and this inverted index is used when carrying out Boolean search operations.

4. The semantic context of each dictionary term represented as the associated semantic category and its related frame structure, pointers to BSO classes and semantic nets which indicate synonymity between terms. This is the term-oriented factual knowledge of PLEXUS.

The PLEXUS dictionary holds the list of all words known to the system (at present about 1000). The basis for the dictionary is the set of terms extracted from the BSO schedule, from horticultural dictionaries and glossaries, and from the database index. A facility is provided for incorporating new terms that have arisen during a session. Each dictionary entry comprises the following elements: Term name (stemmed), a semantic category, BSO pointer and semantic net number. The semantic net number is used to group together synonyms.

PLEXUS uses a system of semantic categorization which consists of eleven categories, each of which can be divided into a number of subcategories. The categories are:

CATEGORY NAME	EXAMPLE
OBJECT	rose, aphids
PART (OF OBJECT)	seeds, cuttings
OPERATIONS	pruning, digging
PROCESS	die, flowering
INTERACTION	X infesting Y
INSTRUMENT	spade, weedkiller
ATTRIBUTE	herbaceous, silver
ENVIRONMENT	garden, greenhouse
USE	agriculture, domestic
TIME	Winter, May
LOCATION	London, tropics

An example of the subcategories for one of these, OBJECT, is given below:

OBJECT — entities within the domain

OBJECT1	plant names
OBJECT2	animal names (includes insects)
OBJECT3	micro-organism names
OBJECT4	disease and symptom names
OBJECT5	soil and rocks
OBJECT6	collective plant entities, e.g. lawn, orchard
OBJECT7	general names for entities in the domain, e.g. tree, plant
OBJECT8	biological concepts

Every term in the dictionary is assigned to one of these categories, e.g. daisy is an OBJECT1, dig is an OPERATION1, lime is an OBJECT5, greenhouse is an ENVIRONMENT4. Of course, some terms may have more than one meaning and therefore will have more than one category assigned. Associated with each category/subcategory is a frame structure. The frames define what other concepts may be associated with the frame concept in a well-framed problem statement. For example,

OPERATION1	(Action taken by human on plant or tree)
ACTATT —	attribute of action
INSTR —	instrument carrying out action
OBJECT —	object affected by action
OBJECTATT —	attribute of object
USERPRP —	use to which object will be put
ENTITY —	larger body to which object belongs if object is a part
ENVMNT —	environment in which plant or tree grows
ENVATT —	attribute of this environment
TIMESLOT —	time at which operation occurs

The set of frames instantiated by the user statement together forms the problem development.

Architecture
Consideration of the problem domain is needed in order to develop a system architecture which will tackle this problem successfully. The problem characteristics which most affect the choice of architecture are: the size of search space, the reliability of the data and the reliability of the knowledge base.

The search space in a referral system is a large one. This is further complicated by the fact that even in cases where the query lies within the subject domain of the system, retrieving no items at all might be the correct problem solution.

The data supplied by the user could be unreliable in a number of ways. The most common problem will be that of mis-spellings. There may also be, however, conceptual errors, as when the user provides an erroneous plant name, etc. A further critical problem is that the data, however correct, may be incomplete.

The knowledge used in a referral process is of several different types and is therefore represented in PLEXUS in different ways. We view a knowledge base as an incomplete model of the world which can always be improved but never be complete. The knowledge base is developed over a period of time using different knowledge acquisition processes. Insofar as the knowledge base is an incomplete representation of the expert's knowledge, there will always be an element of unreliability, although this should diminish as the knowledge base progresses. Additional factors contributing to the unreliability of the knowledge are the current lack of understanding and formalization of human expert problem-solving in a referral situation.

The particular set of problems presented by a referral situation is very different from those found in existing applications of expert systems outside the library and information field. Therefore it is not possible to employ directly a standard architecture. The design of PLEXUS nevertheless incorporates architectural features of a number of expert system models. The architecture we have evolved reflects a pragramatic attempt to tackle the problems presented by the application area and the constraints of implementation.

To overcome the problem of large search space, PLEXUS divides the referral task into four sub-tasks. These sub-tasks correspond to the functions GETUM, GETSTAT, SEARCH and EVALUATE. The functions have been implemented as separate modules. Each of these sub-tasks can interact with one or more knowledge structures and with one or more of the system resources.

In the prototype a more or less linear sequencing of functions is assumed. Processing proceeds from GETUM to GETSTAT to SEARCH and finally EVALUATE. However, there is some provision for some backtracking through the sub-tasks. If the search cannot proceed owing to poor retrieval results, or if the user is not satisfied with the outcome of the search, the system can repeat the GETSTAT and SEARCH elements.

The flow of control between sub-tasks is organized by the higher level production rule sets. It was felt that explicit representation of control stategies would allow more elaborate and sophisticated structures to be developed in future systems.

PLEXUS is largely data-driven. The information supplied by the user in response to the system questions determines the pattern and sequence of activation of the rules. The system can also be regarded as expectation-driven. The frames used to develop the problem model set up expectations of the data required by the system in order to formulate an effective search strategy.

Resources
The main system resources are:

(a) the database of referral resources,
(b) the dictionary of terms, and
(c) the BSO classification scheme.

Input
The input of the system consists of information acquired from the user during the user–system interaction. The user types in the description of his/her problem in natural language (English). The input is analysed into individual words. These are each matched against an extensive stoplist, which screens out general words not significant for the PLEXUS domain. The remaining words are then stripped of common suffices by a stemming algorithm. The final product is a set of stems, the only syntactic information preserved being the word sequence in the original input. This procedure can therefore handle any input, grammatical or not, but necessitates that PLEXUS then interpret the set of stems to produce a well-formed statement of the user problem.

Throughput
The system is able to infer whether or not it has received information from the user about his/her problem which is both appropriate and sufficient to carry out a search. In the event of this not being the case, the system will decide what actions to take to acquire the necessary information. The problem statement constructed by the system will be transformed into a search strategy which can be processed against the database. The results of a search are evaluated both by the system and the user. If too many or too few outputs are obtained, the system can infer an appropriate course of action; otherwise, the system presents the results to the user for assessment. Should this assessment be largely negative, the system will ask the user to restate the problem.

Output
The output from the system consists of descriptions of information resources stored in the database. The way in which information may be usefully organized within a database record and the way in which it is most helpful for the user to view this information are not always the same, however. One task carried out by the human librarian is that of explaining to the user how and why a referral resource might be of use, what the resource might be able to offer and how to locate it. This explanatory function is performed by PLEXUS by combining its knowledge of the user with its knowledge of the structure of the database of referral resources.

Evaluation
The prototype of the expert system will be evaluated during the second phase of the project over the following dimensions:

(1) Definition of system power. Does the system display intelligent behaviour especially on complex tasks? How?
(2) Robustness of the system. Can the system deal with incomplete or imprecise input data? How?
(3) Flexibility of the system. Can the system cope with an incomplete knowledge base? How?
(4) Response of the system. Can the system provide output in an acceptable time?
(5) Transparency of the system. Does the system adequately explain its reasoning and justify its conclusions?
(6) Performance of the system. Does the system provide output comparable to what would be provided by an experienced reference librarian?
(7) Efficiency of software and reliability of the underlying algorithms.
(8) Efficiency of the current hardware (SIRIUS 1 microcomputer).
(9) Evaluation of system components, such as the human–machine communication interface, the knowledge base and the control mechanisms.

Software
The software of PLEXUS is mainly written in PASCAL. It handles a knowledge base, user interface, database management system, production rules, etc.

Hardware
At present, the system is implemented on a SIRIUS 1 microcomputer with 850K RAM memory and a 20 Mbyte hard disk.

4.   A PLEXUS SESSION
A sample session with PLEXUS is given in the Appendix. In a normal session, the user is first presented with a brief explanation of the capabilities and scope of PLEXUS and is then led through a series of questions which enable the system to build a very simple model of the user in terms of the user's probable level of expertise in the subject domain, the user's familiarity with PLEXUS, his/her location and what attempts have been made to solve the problem so far. This module, GETUM, 'knows' which user characteristics are of importance to the referral process. At the end of this question–answer session a confirmatory message is displayed for the user's approval. If the user feels that there is a misunderstanding or mistake, the GETUM function can be repeated.

PLEXUS then attempts to develop a description of the user's problem. The user is asked to type a statement of the problem. There is no constraint on the form or manner in which this statement can be entered. The user is allowed complete freedom of expression. A single term, list of terms, phrase, or complete grammatical sentence are all equally acceptable. The knowledge resources associated with the problem description modelling function, GETSTAT, enable PLEXUS to determine whether the information provided in the user's initial statement is coherent, i.e. makes sense, and whether it is sufficient for an effective search stategy to be formulated.

What happens next depends on how much of the user's statement PLEXUS has 'understood', i.e. how many significant terms have been found in the dictionary. If the overall level is high, then PLEXUS calls the subfunction STRAT1, whose task is to assess how complete the description of the user's problem is, and to select questions which will elicit the missing information from the query. The questions PLEXUS asks the user are the bare minimum needed to achieve completeness. Using an intelligent knowledge-based system to drive this question-asking means that the system need only ask those questions necessary to acquire the information needed to achieve its goal and the generation of a routine set of questions can be avoided. That is, it allows irrelevant questions to be skipped.

If PLEXUS 'understands' nothing, i.e. none of the significant terms in the user's statment could be identified, the STRAT3 subfunction is called and this presents a display of the concepts in the domain to the user. The user is able to browse through this display, selecting any terms the user thinks appropriate. This serves to assist users who may have difficulties with standard methods of data entry. It also serves the purpose of outlining to the user the subjet scope of PLEXUS. If the user is unable to find suitable terms from this display, PLEXUS informs the user it is unable to help and terminates the session.

If the user's statement was partially 'understood' then STRAT2 is called. This subfunction 'knows' what concepts to expect in problems associated with its subject domain and attempts to ascertain into which of these concept categories an unknown term belongs. It tries to identify an unknown term by asking the user a series of closed questions which, in effect, get the user to classify that term according to the scheme employed in PLEXUS. Once the term has been categorized and its 'meaning' known, PLEXUS is able to treat that term as it would any other recognized term. Since it is possible, at a later stage, to incorporate such terms into the dictionary (or word memory), PLEXUS can be said to have a 'learning' capability, albeit of a limited nature.

The flexibility afforded by this multi-strategy approach means that only in a very few cases will the system be unable to obtain an adequate problem description, no matter what the user's initial input. Moreover the need for error messages is greatly reduced, thus 'saving face' for less adept users. It is important to underline that the GETSTAT function does not merely act as a natural language interface for the referral database. It does allow the user to describe his/her problem in English but is able to match this statement against its knowledge of an ideal problem description and it 'knows' a variety of methods for intelligently acquiring missing information or dealing with concepts it does not recognize.

Once PLEXUS has obtained a sufficiently 'complete' description of the user's problem the SEARCH function then transforms this description into a search strategy. SEARCH 'knows' how the elements of the problem description may be mapped into the syntax of the database management system's query language. The database management system used by PLEX-US is a standard DBMS/IR system and the search procedures use Boolean queries. It is important to note that the DBMS and the database of referral resources are in no way specially modified or adapted for PLEXUS. They are standard systems which could be replaced by some other system with comparable facilities.

The DBMS search procedures apply the strategy to the database. The outcome is evaluated initially in terms of the number of postings retrieved. If this is unsatisfactory, the search strategy is reformulated, employing knowledge of search tactics (in this case for small databases). Too few postings and the SEARCH function is then able to employ tactics for broadening the search. Too many postings and the SEARCH function will attempt to narrow the search. The tactics employed are essentially those used by human reference workers/search analysts. (Bates 1979; Fidel 1984, 1985). For example, if there are too few postings, the strategy may be reformulated by:

— entering a broader descriptor:
A thesaurus, BSO, is used as a resource. A pointer to a BSO entry is included in the dictionary information for most terms. This enables PLEX-US to retrieve the broader or narrower term given a particular word.

— excluding concepts from the query:
PLEXUS employs knowledge about which are the most crucial categories of concepts when searching in this domain, to decide which concepts to exclude first.

— adding equivalent terms or synonyms:
Many dictionary entries have an associated synonym net number so that PLEXUS 'knows' the synonyms of many terms and can make use of this information to broaden the search.

Knowledge about reformulation tactics and when to employ them is incorporated into the knowledge resources of the SEARCH function. Knowledge about the broader and narrower descriptors related to a search term is represented in thesaural form in BSO.

A search statement consists of a Boolean combination of individual seach terms. It can be modified by removing, adding or replacing terms, or by altering Boolean operators. If there is more than one term in the search statement (as is usually the case), PLEXUS must adopt some criteria to decide the sequence in which terms are to be removed or replaced. Criteria that could be used are:

(a) user assessment of the relative importance or significance of terms to the query problem;
(b) number of postings in the database index — the more heavily posted a term, the less discriminating is it in search;

(c)   criteria based on semantic categories.

User assessment of relative importance could be the optimum, but there is some reluctance to ask the user to provide this further input, and some doubt as to whether all users would be able to provide a suitable assessment. In the PLEXUS prototype, assessed significance of terms has not been used as a criterion, but it is intended to introduce an implicit assessment — the terms in the initial query will be given greater prominence in search.

In a large database, the number of postings of a term is a reliable guide to its discrimination in search, but in a relatively small database the number of postings can be randomly distributed, so this criterion has not been adopted. However, the existence of postings for particular types of term is relevant, as is explained below.

In the statement of a subject, terms depend on one another. A term that represents a part, a process, an attribute or a use is in a semantic sense subsidiary to the parent object; an instrument relates to the operation employing it; time and location are general contextual categories, and environment might be considered in the same light. Such relations between semantic categories have been extensively considered in the context of faceted classification (Vickery 1975; Ranganathan 1967). Chains of dependence among categories may be constructed, such that each member of a chain is dependent on its predecessor. In terms of the categories used in PLEXUS, a branching chain such as the following can be envisaged.

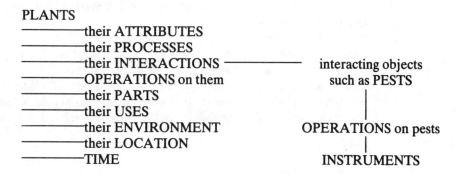

A dependence chain of this kind can form the basis of criteria to decide on the sequence of terms to be removed from or replaced in a search statement — terms at the ends of chains being the first to be modified. Such criteria, however, must be combined with factors mentioned earlier, and in particular with the existence in the database index of postings for terms in particular categories. In deciding the sequence of categories to be modified, categories more likely to figure among index terms should not be removed or replaced early in the process. To sum up, production rules embodying these criteria provide PLEXUS with the knowledge needed to drop terms in sequence.

The first strategy of search reformulation is thus to drop some search terms. If this is unsuccessful, PLEXUS proceeds to a second strategy — term replacement. For this purpose, PLEXUS consults the BSO classification schedule that it incorporates. As previously described, this is in the form of a hierarchical tree. A term X could be replaced by its parent node, collateral nodes, or subsidiary nodes. The application of all these criteria would produce a more comprehensive search. But the purpose of modification in PLEXUS is rather to produce a search statement that has a greater chance of successfully matching appropriate index terms. In most cases, if the original term does not provide a match, neither will a search on collateral or more specific terms. The criterion chosen in the prototype is to move to the parent term.

The reformulated query is presented to the DBMS search procedures for processing again, the outcome is re-assessed and further modification undertaken if necessary.

Finally, when an acceptable number of items has been retrieved, these are presented to the user in an informative manner by the EVALUAT function. This uses knowledge about the user, obtained from the user model, to determine the order in which items are displayed. Institutions, for example, which are located near to the user are presented before those which are located some distance away.

The task of the EVALUAT function is to:

(a) relate to the user any previous search formulations that have been tried and their outcomes.
(b) display the retrieved information about the referral resources to the user in an informative and explanatory way. It should be clear to the user how to locate the resource and what the resource offers.
(c) obtain an assessment from the user of the potential value of the resources for which information has been retrieved and to obtain the user's evaluation of the usefulness of the PLEXUS session as a whole.

5. DISCUSSION

5.1 Design issues

There are number of issues which crucially affected the design of PLEXUS and which are therefore worthwhile to emphasize. These include:

(1) user interface;
(2) error trapping;
(3) terminology;
(4) ill-formed queries.

1.   User interface

Of particular concern was the user interface, that is, means by which the user communicates with the system and vice versa. Our analysis of the environment in which PLEXUS would operate suggested that it would be esential to have an interface which would cope with an extremely heterogeneous user population, i.e. an average sample of library users. No assumption can be made about the background, educational level, computer literacy, familiarity with the subject. Such a situation is probably best handled by employing sophisticated user modelling capabilities. However, given the limited time available for the probject, it was decided to leave this function for phase II and instead to implement an extremely flexible robust interface. This interface should be able to handle a wide variety of input styles and be able to make maximum use of the information available.

The design criteria for the user interface were as follows:

(a) The user should be able to operate the system without recourse to a manual or human adviser. Input should be through natural language statements, menu-driven or closed questions.
(b) The system should degrade gracefully, i.e. it should not crash or present the user with a failed message after the first attempt.
(c) PLEXUS should not display explicit error messages. It has been found that users are discouraged from using systems in public places if they feel their errors in handling the system would be visible to others.
(d) Users should be able to enter statements in any form, a single word, list of words, phrases or grammatical sentences.
(e) The interface must be able to deal intelligently with terms it cannot recognize.

2.   Error trapping

Consultations with librarians suggested that it was important to take into account users who would try to fool the system with queries which are totally outside the system capabilities or with nonsense queries. Attention has been paid to developing trapping routines which would reject inappropriate queries at an early stage.

3.   Terminology

One consequence of the heterogeneous nature of PLEXUS's intended user population is that it is not possible to assume a standard usage or accepted meanings for terminology. There is often a large difference in the usage of terms depending on the educational level and subject expertise of the person. This is particularly the case in subject domains which cut across all levels of society, e.g. law, medicine, gardening. A sophisticated user modelling capability might allow predictions to be made about the way in which a particular user would make use of certain terms or phrases. For the purpose of phase I of this project, it was decided to select the broadest use of terms in the domain. This has the disadvantage that the usage may strike some users as being technically incorrect but should be acceptable to the majority.

4.   Ill-formed queries

Users are often unable to specify the kind of information they require. It was necessary therefore to develop more than one method for the user to express his/her problem.

5.2   Hardware and software considerations

Another important aspect of the PLEXUS project was the decision to implement the system on a microcomputer. This decision was influenced by the need to develop a comparatively cheap system. Dedicated artificial intelligence workstations are relatively expensive and certainly beyond the means of the majority of libraries. The same is true for the other computers favoured by AI researchers, the DEC10 and DEC20 series and VAX series. In addition, there would be problems of portability had the system been developed on a mainframe. At the time the project commenced, the most reasonable microcomputer system in terms of cost, processing power and availability was the SIRIUS 1 microcomputer. Accordingly PLEXUS has been implemented on a SIRIUS 1 with an extended internal memory and with 20 Mbyte external hard disk storage.

Software selection was partly constrained by hardware choice and partly by the application area of the system. Software tools for expert system construction can be divided into three main groups:

(1) AI programming languges, e.g. LISP and PROLOG;
(2) general-purpose representation langugaes, e.g. ROSIE, KRL and OPS5;
(3) expert system shells or skeletal systems, e.g. EMYCIN, SAGE, EXPERTEASE.

The general-purpose representation languages could be immediately ruled out because none were available for microcomputers. Serious consideration was given to acquiring an expert system shell or skeletal system. The advantage of using a shell is that it makes it possible to build an expert system for some new applications relatively quickly. However, to be successful, the new task must bear sufficient resemblance to the task for which the shell system was originally constructed.

An initial analysis of the referral task suggested that it would be useful, and probably necessary, to have multiple knowledge resources employing different methods of representation. While work is underway to develop shells which permit such a flexibility in knowledge base structuring, existing shells on the whole do not. Those available for microcomputers are even more limited in the scope they afford for knowledge base design.

Our choice of control mechanism was originally that of a blackboard model, since this is the architecture that recent studies have suggested is most appropriate for information provision mechanisms (Belkin *et al.* 1984). Few of the existing shells offer such an architecture. Those that do, for example AGE and HEARSAY-III, have limited availability and are restricted to mainframes or minicomputers. Most other shells are based on the MYCIN backward-chaining control mechanisms. Such goal-driven behaviour is appropriate for diagnostic systems, but seems unsuitable for the current application which is more data-driven.

Finally, a survey of shells available for microcomputers at the time the project was initiated indicated that none had user interface features or natural language handling capabilities that we felt this application required. Reluctantly, since a shell would have provided a speedier developmental path, we decided not to use a shell, but to implement the inference engine and knowledge base construction systems from scratch. It is difficult to say whether or not this would be our conclusion were the project to be initiated now. There have been advances in the range and sophistication of the shells available for microcomputers but little has been done in the areas of concern to us.

The two remaining options were to use an AI or a conventional programming language. In principle, anything that can be processed by a computer can be implemented in a conventional programming language, but in practice some languages are more convenient for handling particular applications than others. Artificial intelligence languages have been devised to permit the easy expression in symbolic form of objects and the relations between them and to allow the relatively easy implementation of complex reasoning chains. The two best known AI languages are LISP and Prolog.

Both LISP and Prolog are available on microcomputers. The LISP interpreters available for use on a microcomputer are greatly scaled down from the mainframe originals. They are only available in interpreted form, they run extremely slowly and there seem to be problems with memory allocation and garbage collection. MicroPROLOG is, on the other hand, a relatively sophisticated product. It permits the use of most PROLOG facilities and possesses input/output capabilities. At the time the project began, microPROLOG was only available as an interpreted language, which meant that run–time–speeds were slow. The declarative nature of PROLOG meant that the procedural aspect of the system would be difficult to implement, and in addition, it embodies an essentially goal-driven control structure, which we wished to avoid using for the overall system.

it was decided to implement part of the knowledge-base construction software in PROLOG and to implement the remainder of the system in

PASCAL. This would allow most of the programs to be run in compiled form, thereby speeding up operating time, and would enable us to develop the control mechanisms this application requires.

6. CONCLUSIONS

The construction of the prototype system took 20 months. A full-time senior programmer and a part-time system analyst were employed. Additional contributions were made by outside consultants. At the moment, we approach the second phase of the project, namely the evaluation period. This will last a further 18 months and is again supported by the British Library. The main aim of the second phase will be assessment of the prototype by professional reference librarians and the testing of the system in an operational environment. Feedback from these tests will also enable a more robust sytem to be produced.

Finally, we hope that the outcome of the Expert System for Referral project will not be 'merely' an operational system but will also further the use of artificial intelligence techniques in library and information systems.

APPENDIX — SESSION WITH PLEXUS

PLEXUS
PUBLIC LIBRARY SYSTEM FOR RETRIEVAL

PLEXUS is here to help you with any GARDENING problems you may have. PLEXUS will try to find places, people, books, institutions or societies which may be able to help you to find an answer to your gardening problem.

PLEXUS won't be able to give you an answer as such, but it will put you in touch with resources that will help you solve your problem.

PLEXUS only handles gardening problems, so if you ask it anything else, it won't be able to help you.

Press any key to go on, or
Press the ESC key to end the enquiry (1)

Before telling me about your problem. please answer the following six short questions about yourself.

Your answers will help me in deciding how best to help you. O.K.?

Press any key to go on, or
Press the ESC key to end the enquiry. (2)

Figs. 1 and 2 — Explanation of PLEXUS to a new user.

Have you ever used PLEXUS before?

Please answer Yes or No.
You should end your answer by pressing the RETURN key.

Your answer is..........NO   (3)

Is gardening your job?

Please answer Yes or NO.
You should end your answer by Pressing the RETURN key.

Your answer is..........NO   (4)

How long have you been gardening?

Please choose the option that best describes you:

    1. I have just started gardening.
    2. I have been gardening for a few years.
    3. I have been gardening for many years.

Please enter the option number.... 1 or 2 or 3

Your answer is.......1   (5)

Figs. 3–5 — Development of user model.

If you had a gardening problem before, have you...

    1...asked friends or relatives.
    2...asked at a garden centre or nursery.
    3...asked at your local library.
    4...asked a gardening society or institution.
    5...asked experts on TV or radio phone-in shows or written to magazines or
       newsletters.
    6...looked up information in books or encyclopaedias.
    7...You haven't had a gardening problem before.
    8...None of these.

Choose one or more options by entering the option numbers separated by
blanks.

Your answer is.......36   (6)

Is this the first time you've asked anyone about the gardening problem you've got at the moment?

Please answer Yes or No.

You should end your answer by pressing the RETURN key.

Your answer is.......Yes   (7)

Where do you live?

1. Greater LONDON
2. Scotland
3. Wales
4. Other parts of the British Isles

Your answer is.......1   (8)

Figs. 6–8 — Further development of user model.

So let me see if i've got it right.......

You haven't used PLEXUS before.
You have just started gradening.
When you've had a gardening problem before you have asked about it at your
        local library.
You haven't asked anyone about our current gardening problem until now.
You live in LONDON.

Is this O.K.?

Please answer Yes or No.
You should end your answer by pressing the RETURN key.

Your answer is.......Yes.   (9)

Fig. 9 — Summary of user's answers.

Please tell me a little about your problem of interest.

I am interested in CACTI

(Searching the stoplist and stemming text.)
(Searching the dictionary)
(CACTI was found)

(1 term recognised out of 1)

(Entering strategy 1)
(Entering ruleset 2.21; assigning the context.)
(Assigning context 0.)
(Instantiating frames for:)
(CACTI of category 8.)
(Entering ruleset 2.3: attempting to fill empty slots by asking questions.)

(10)

Fig. 10 — Input of problem statement.

Is the kind of CACTI important?

Please answer Yes or No
You should end your answer by pressing the RETURN key.

Your answer is.......No   (11)

Did you want to do something to the CACTI?
e.g. prune, fertilise, spray, thin out?

Please answer Yes or No.
You should end your answer by pressing the RETURN key.

Your answer is.......Yes

What did you want to do?
Enter a single term.......PROPAGATE   (12a)

Figs. 11 and 12a — Clarification of the enquiry.

(Preparing to search the dictionary)
(Searching the stoplist and stemming text)
(Searching the dictionary)
PROPAG was found)

Press any key to go on   (12b)

Fig. 12b — Searching the dictionary.

Where are the CACTI growing?

1. in the graden
2. on the lawn
3. in an orchard
4. in a nursery
5. in a greenhouse
6. in a window box
7. in the house
8. in water
9. in a field
10. in a wood
11. somewhere else

Select one and enter its number.......5   (13a)

Fig. 13a — Filling in the slots.

(Preparing to search the dictionary)
(Searching the stoplist and stemming text)
(Searching the dictionary)
(GREENHOUS was found)

Press any key to go on   (13b)

Fig. 13b — Searching the dictionary.

Is a particular tool or method to be used for PROPAG the plant? e.g. a spade, a
fertiliser.

Please answer Yes or NO
You should end your answer by pressing the RETURN key.

Your answer is.......NO   (14)

Fig. 14 — Filling in the slots.

Searching the database for.....

CACTI AND PROPAG AND GREENHOUS

The search has found 0 items
This is too few.   (15)

Fig. 15 — Initial search strategy.

(Dropping 'ANDED' terms from the search list to widen search: stage 1)
(Category 8 is on the search list at this stage)
(Category 21 is on the search list at this stage)
(Category 29 is on the search list at this stage)
(Unable to find a further category to drop at this stage)
Searching the database for.....

CACTI AND PROPAG AND GREENHOUS

The search has found 0 items
This is too few   (16)

Fig. 16 — Checking possible terms for dropping.

Searching the database for . . .

(CACTI OR SUCCULENT) AND (PROPAG OR HORTICULTURE) AND
(GREENHOUS OR ENVIRONMENT)

The search has found 0 items
This is too few   (17)

Fig. 17 — Climbing the BSO.

(Dropping 'ANDED' terms from the search list to widen search: stage 1)
(Category 8 is on the search list at this stage)
(Category 21 is on the search list at this stage)
(Category 29 is on the search list at this stage)
(Dropping term PROPAG from the search list)
(Dropping term HORTICULTURE from the search list)
Searching the database for...
(CACTI OR SUCCULENT) AND (GREENHOUS OR ENVIRONMENT)

The search has found 0 items
This is too few.......   (18)

Fig. 18 — Dropping the terms PROPAG and HORTICULTURE.

(Dropping 'ANDED' terms from the search list to widen search: stage 2)
(Category 8 is on the search list at this stage)
(Category 29 is on the search list at this stage)
(Dropping the term GREENHOUS from the search list)
(Dropping the term ENVIRONMENT from the search list)
Searching the database for......
(CACTI OR SUCCULENT)

The search has found 6 items
This is about the right number   (19)

Fig. 19 — Dropping the terms GREENHOUS and ENVIRONMENT.

Unfortunately there is nothing on file which deals specifically with

CACTI AND PROPAG AND GREENHOUS

However there are 6 items which deal with

(CACTI AND SUCCULENT)

Press RETURN to continue   (20)

Fig. 20 — The EVALUAT module.

6 items have been found altogether

4 publication(s) have been found
2 organization(s)

Which from these would you like to see. Choose from the following:

1. All of the items found
2. Publications only
3. Organisations only
4. NONE of the items found

Enter the number of your choice.......1

Fig. 21 — Conclusion of search.

4 publications
Item 1
This is *an encyclopaedia*
called *The illustrated reference on cacti and other succulents*
by *Lamb E and Lamb B*

Would you like some more information — Yes/No? Y

The publisher is Pan Britannica Industries Ltd, 1973.
It is about choosing indoor plants, arranging plants, foliage house plants,
flowering house plants, warmth, air, light, water, cleaning, pruning, pots
and potting, what went wrong, pests, diseases, cacti, succulents, miniature
trees. Other features:
Handbook, 35pp, price 15p.

Does this publication seem useful — Yes/No? Y
Would you like to print out the details — Yes/No? N

Item 2
This is *a textbook*
called *The Collingridge book of cacti and other succulents*
by *Rochford T. C, Christopher T*

Would you like some more information — Yes/No? N
Does this publication seem useful — Yes/No? Y
Would you like to print out the details — Yes/NO? N

Item 3
This is *a textbook*
called *Cacti and succulents*
by *Andersen G.*

Would you like some more information — Yes/No? N
Does this publication seem useful — Yes/No? Y
Would you like to print out the details — Yes/No? N

Item 4
This is *my handbook*
called *Be your own house plant expert*
by *Hessayon D. G. (Dr)*

Would you like some more information — Yes/No? N
Does this publication seem useful — Yes/No? Y
Would you like to print out the details — Yes/No? N

2 organizations

Item 1
The organization is called *Cactus and Succulent Society of Great Britain*

It is located in: B

Would you like some more information — Yes/No? N
Does this publication seem useful — Yes/No? Y
Would you like to print out the details — Yes/No? N

Item 2
The organization is called *The National Cactus and Succlent Society*

It is involved with: *Study of different genera of succulent plants*

It is located in: M

Would you like some more information — Yes/No? N
Does this publication seem useful — Yes/No? Y
Would you like to print out the details — Yes/No? N

House useful did you find this session?

1. Very useful
2. Fairly useful
3. Not useful
4. A waste of time

Enter the number of your choice.....1

REFERENCES

Bates, M. J. (1979) Information search tactics. *JASIS* **30** 205–214.
Belkin, N. J., Hennings, R. D. & Seeger, T. (1984) Simulation of a distributed expert-based information provision mechanism. *Information Technology, Research and Development* **3** 122–141.
Card, S. K., Moran, T. P. & Newell, A. (1983) *Applied information processing psychology: the human–computer interface*. Hillsdale, N. J., Erlbaum.
Damereau, F. J. (1981) Operating statistics for the transformational question answering system. *Amer. J. Computational Lingustics* **7** 30–42.
Fidel, R. (1984) Online searching styles: a case-study based model of searching behaviour. *Journal of the American Society for Information Science* **35** 4 211–221.
Fidel, R. (1985) Moves in online searching. *Online Review* **9** 1 61–74.
Fillmore, C. (1968) The case for case. In: Bach & Harms (eds), *Universals in linguistic theory*. New York, Holt, pp. 1–88.
Finer, R. (1977) Referral centres and services: a review. Aslib Occasional Publication no. 22. London, ASLIB.
Handbook of Special Librarianship and Information Work, 4th edn. (1979) London, ASLIB.
Hayes, P. & Reddy, R. (1979) Graceful interaction in man–machine communication. *Proc. 6th Internat. Joint Conference on Artificial Intelligence,* pp. 372–374.

Hayes, P. G. & Mouradian, G. V. (1981) Flexible parsing. *Am. J. Computational Linguistics,* **7** 4 pp. 232–242.

Kaplan, S. G. (1982) Special section — Natural language. *ACM SIGART Newsletter* January 27–109.

Martyn, J. & Rousseau, G. (1984) Aspects of referral. *ASLIB Proceedings* **36** 6. 253–267.

Ranganathan, S. R. (1967) *Prolegomena to library classification,* 3rd edn. London, Asia Publishing House.

Rich, E. (1984) Natural language interfaces. *Computer* **17** 39–47.

Sager, N. (1981) *Natural langugage information processing.* Reading, Mass., Addison-Wesley.

Sager, N. and others. Natural language information formatting. *Advances in Computers* **17** 89–162.

Schank, R. C. (1975) *Conceptual information processing,* Amsterdam, North-Holland.

Shapiro, S. C. & Kwasny, S. C. (1975) Interactive consulting via natural language. *Comm. ACM,* **18** 8. 459–462.

Sparck Jones, K. (1982) Natural language access to databases: some questions and a specific approach. *J. Inf. Sci.* **4** 41–48.

Sparck Jones, K. (1984) Natural language interfaces for expert systems: an introductory note. In: *Research and Development in Expert Systems, Proc. of the Fourth Technical Conference of the British Computer Society Specialist Group on Expert Systems, Univ. of Warwick, 18–20 December 1984,* pp. 85–94.

Stearns, J. F. (1964) Referral relationships. *Library Journal* March 1011–1014, 1060.

Vickery, A. (1984) An intelligent interface for online interaction. *J. Information Science* **9** 7–18.

Vickery, B. C. (1975) *Classification and indexing in science,* 3rd edn. London, Butterworths.

Waltz, D. L. (1978) An English language question-answering system for a large relational data-base. *Comm. ACM* **21** 7. 526–539.

Woods, W. A. (1970) Transition network grammars for natural language analysis. *Comm. ACM* **13** 591–606.

7

Users are individuals: individualizing user models

Elaine Rich, Microelectronics and Computer Technology Corporation, Austin, Texas, USA

1. INTRODUCTION

It has been recognized that in order to build a good system in which a person and a machine cooperate to perform a task it is important to take into account some significant characteristics of people. The system can then be designed to take advantage of those characteristics, rather than to fight against them.

Traditionally, this has been done by collecting data on an average person's performance on various tasks in various environments. For example, Fitts' law (Fitts & Peterson 1964) says that the time it takes for a person to move an object in his hand to a particular target position is proportional to log 2(2A/w) where A is the distance to be moved and w is the width of the target. This result suggests how the spped with which a person can operate a machine can be increased by increasing the size of the targets (such things as buttons and switches) that the operator must hit. As another example of this class of work, consider the large body of data on the relationship between the size of letters and their legibility (Smith 1979). These results are important in the design not only of a wide variety of machines but also of other artifacts such as traffic signs.

The major weakness of these studies is that they make the assumption that the people who are involved constitute a homogeneous set. Under this assumption, the values that are determined to characterize a 'typical' person can be used to design a system to be used by everyone. Although in most cases it is true that for at least the majority of the people, the system is better adapted to them than it would have been without those studies, it is not true that such a system is likely to be the best that could be produced. A much better system would be one in which the interface presented to each person was tailored to his own characteristics rather then to those of some abstract 'typical' person. Although discussions of individual differences among users are rare in the human factors literature, they are not altogether absent. For example, Hudgens & Billingsley (1978) argue that sex is an important variable in human factors research. Another study, by Loo (1978), discusses individual differences in the perception of traffic signs. One reason that such studies have been rare is that it is often either too expensive or impossible to provide in physical devices the level of flexibility that they suggest. However, as we begin to see more and more of people's interactions with machines being mediated by computers under software control, it becomes possible to provide the flexibility necessary for truly personalized systems.

As a simple example, consider again the issue of letter size and legibility. If the letters of a display are being produced using a standard LED display, they will be the same size for all readers. But suppose the letters are being displayed on a CRT controlled by a computer. Now lines can be drawn wherever necessary to produce a wide variety of letter sizes as requested by individual users.

Recently, designers of user–computer interfaces have begun to focus attention on the needs of particular types of users. One group that has been frequently discussed is the class of 'casual' users, who cannot be expected ever to use the system with a great deal of regularity (see, for example, Codd (1974) and Cuff (1980)). This group must then be contrasted with the less well studied species, the regular, experienced user. Unfortunately, few systems will be used exclusively by people of a single class. And it appears that system features that make life easy for one type of user make it correspondingly more difficult for another. For example, one study of the performance of expert users at a text editing task (Card *et al.* 1980) suggests that the number of keystrokes required to perform an operation should be minimized. Another study of people just learning to use an editor (Ledgard *et al.* 1980) suggests that English-like, full word commands should be used. These different requirements point to the need for a system that can appear differently to different users.

It is fortunate that the computer provides the means to increased personalization since it also produces a greater need for it by increasing the range of tasks for which people can hope to profit by dealing with machines. Tasks that were previously performed by people, such as collecting desired information from some kind of database, are now being done by computers. People who performed those tasks were able to accommodate the diverse needs of the other people with whom they dealt. For machines to assume those tasks and handle them satisfactorily, they too will have to be capable of accommodation to individual needs. In order to do that, they will have to exploit models of the individual users they encounter. This will require an expansion of the traditional notion of a 'user model'.

In the rest of this article, we will explore the issue of user modeling specifically in the context of computer software systems, both because of the increasing use of such systems by large groups of people and because of the inherent flexibility of such systems that makes effective modeling possible.

2.   THE SPACE OF USER MODELS

The term 'user model' can be used to describe a wide variety of knowledge about people. The uses of user models span an equally-wide domain. The relationships among these diverse structures can be seen fairly easily if the universe of 'user models' is characterized as a three-dimensional space. The dimensions, each of which will be discussed in more detail below, are:

(1) one model of a single, canonical user vs a collection of models of individual users.
(2) models specified explicitly either by the system designer or by the users themselves vs models inferred by the system on the basis of users' behavior.
(3) models of fairly long-term user characteristics such as areas of interest or expertise vs model or relatively short-term user characteristics such as the problem the user is currently trying to solve.

There are other significant differences among the systems using these various types of user models, but they follow from these major differences. Systems with a single model of a canonical user can have that model permanently embedded within themselves, whereas systems with models of individual users must build the model on the fly, and so must make explicit the ways in which the model influences the performance of the overall system. Systems that extract the user model from the user's behavior must grapple seriously with the issues of incorrect or conflicting information arising from the inferences that led to the model. Systems with explicitly stated user information can, on the other hand, avoid many of those issues. Systems that deal with short-term knowledge must deal successfully with the problem of detecting when things change, while longer-term systems may be able to finesse that issue. But as these differences reduce to the three outlined above, they do not need to be focussed on explicitly.

The next three sections briefly discuss how one might choose the best position in this three-dimensional space.

2.1   Canonical vs individual models

This dimension characterizes the major difference between 'classical' human factors work and the more flexible models needed to provide the individual interfaces that software control allows. A variety of computer systems have been designed around a canonical user model. For example, ZOG (Robertson *et al.* 1981) is a frame-based system that facilitates user–computer communication. Its design was heavily influenced by such factors as the response speed necessary to prevent user frustration. Another example of a system built around a model of a canonical user is Genesereth's automated consultant for MACSYMA, a symbolic mathematics package (Genesereth 1978). The consultant exploits an explicit model of the problem-solving strategy used by MACSYMA users. But, as suggested above, there is limit to the usefulness of these canonical models to a system with a heterogeneous user community. Individual models can enable such systems to provide each user an interface more appropriate to his needs than could be provided using a canonical model. Of course, it is necessary to demonstrate that there exist techniques for implementing such models so that they actually do improve the performance of the system. A variety of such techniques will be presented in section 3.

The decision to exploit individual user models has a profound impact on the other aspects of user modeling. If a system possesses only a single model of a canonical user, that model can be designed once and then directly incorporated into the overall system structure. If, on the other hand, the system is ultimately to possess a large array of models corresponding to each of its users, the question of how and by whome those models are to be contructed arises. This leads to the second dimension in the space of user models.

2.2   Explicit vs implicit models

There are two ways to make systems different for different users. One is to allow users to modify the system to suit themselves. This is the approach taken by many systems that allow users to create explicitly their own environments within the system. Consider, for example, a computer program that enables system users to communicate with each other by sending mail messages back and forth. The program stores the messages in a set of files and provides functions by which users can read messages, answer them, and so forth. Such systems often allow users to set system parameters to determine such things as which message fields will be displayed when a message is printed. A much greater degree of personalization is provided by systems such as most implementations of the programming language LISP that allow users to specify an arbitrarily complex program that will automatically be executed whenever the user enters the system. With this facility, a user can create his own procedures, alter system variables, or define his own symbols. This same approach can be seen in many 'personalized database' systems (Mittman & Borman 1975). In these systems, the personalization comes from the fact that each user can explicitly select documents and information of interest to him and store them in a private database.

But this approach leaves quite a lot of responsibility in the hands of the user and is probably not appropriate for systems that expect truly naive users, i.e. people who will use the system only once or maybe two or three times, since a non-trivial amount of expertise is required in order to be able to know what one wants to specify and how to specify it.

The other way to approach the problem of personalization is to provide the system with enough information about users that it can take charge of its own personalization. This can be done either trivially or in an intelligent way. A trivial example is a program that asks the user to rate his level of expertise with the system. The program then uses that level to determine how much information to provide in error messages. The program essentially contains models of how much information people at each level already possess.

A more sophisticated approach to automatic user modeling is needed in many systems on order to deal with both the need for more information about each user and the problem that users cannot always tell the system what it needs to know. Examples of this latter problem occur often in the domain of Computer Aided Instruction (CAI). A CAI system needs to know what each individual student knows, doesn't know, and knows incorrectly. The student, unfortunately, does not always know what he doesn't know, much less what he knows incrorrectly.

Of course, students are not alone in their lack of knowledge about themselves. There is a lot of evidence in the psychological literature to support the assertion that people are not reliable sources of information about themselves (see, for example, Nisbett & Wilson (1977) and McGuire & Padawer-Singer (1976)).

In addition to the lack of accuracy inherent in explicit models, there is yet another consideration that argues for allowing the system to build its user models itself. People do not want to stop and answer a large number of questions before they can get on with whatever they are trying to use the system to do. This is particularly true of people who intend to use the system only a few times, and for only brIef periods. To best serve these users, the system should form as good an initial model as it can and let the user immediately begin to use the system. This initial model can be based on the known characteristics of the system's overall user community, whatever additional information the system already has about each individual user (for example, his job title), and a set of facts characterizing a new user of the system. As the person interacts with the system, he provides it with additional information about himself. As it acquires this information, the system can gradually update its model of the user until eventually it comes to be a model of that individual as distinct from the canonical user. Using this approach, the greatest effort will be expended on the contruction of models of frequent users, while much less effort will be expended on models of extremely infrequent users, models that would have little payoff in overall user satisfaction.

The most important implication of choosing to let the system build its own model of the user, based on the interactions between them, is that most of the information contained in the model will be guesses. Thus the system must have some way of representing how sure it is of each fact, in addition to a way of resolving conflicts and updating the model as new information becomes available. Section 3 will suggest some ways of doing this.

2.3   Long-term vs short-term models
In discussing the first two of these three dimensions, it was possible to argue that one form of user modeling would lead to a more habitable system than another. In discussing this third dimension, that is no longer the case. In order to interact reasonably with a user, a system must have access to a wide

variety of information about him, ranging from relatively long-term facts,-like his level of mathematical sophistication, to quite short-term facts, like the subject of the last sentence the user typed. Although all of this information can contribute to the habitability of a system, it is useful, at least at the beginning of an exploration into the topic of user modeling, to separate the problem of inferring long-term models from that of inferring short-term models because different techniques may be appropriate for the solution of the two problems.

It is probably reasonable to demand that the amount of effort spent to decide on a particular fact about a user be roughly proportional to the amount of time that fact will be able to be used. At one extreme, it is important that it not happen that so much time is spent trying to infer a fact that the fact is no longer relevant. At the other extreme, it may be reasonable to spend a lot of time, spread over many sessions to form an accurate model of some essentially permanent characteristics.

There have been efforts devoted to both long-term and short-term individual user modeling. Short-term modeling is important in understanding natural language dialogue. Consider, for example, the following interchange:

> Customer: How much is a ticket to New York?
> Clerk: One hundred dollars.
> Customer: When is the next plane?
> Clerk: The next plane is completely booked, but there's still room on one that leaves at 8.04.
> Customer: O.K., I'll take-it.

In order to make that response, the clerk had to refer to a model of the customer's current goal, getting to New York. It would have been inappropriate to have responded literally to the question and said simply 6:53. If computer systems are going to perform the task of the clerk in this example, then they will need to be able to build and use models of the goals of their users. But models of such things as current goals are of fairly short-term use. The same customer could appear tomorrow intending to meet someone coming from New York and thus expecting a different response. Thus extremely responsive methods must be developed to perceive such goals and to notice when they change. For some more extended discussions of these sorts of issues, see Perrault et al. (1978) and Mann et al. (1977).

But many systems could usefully exploit a large amount of much more stable knowledge about their users. These long-term models can be derived over the course of a series of interactions between the system and its users. The models can contain such information as the user's level of expertise with computer systems in general, his expertise with this system in particular, and his familiarity with the system's underlying task domain. In addition to these general things that could be of use in a wide variety of systems, the user models employed by a particular system will often need to contain specific information relevant to the system and its task domain. For example, in the librarian program to be discussed in section 4, each user model contains information about such things as a preference for books with fast-moving plots and a level of tolerance of descriptions of violence.

2.4   A review of the space

Fig. 1 shows the eight classes of user models generated by the three dichotomies we have just discussed, along with a few examples of each. The rest of this paper will focus on the lower right-hand corner.

	CANONICAL USER	INDIVIDUAL USER
EXPLICIT	it does not make sense for users to specify models of a canonical user, except possibly that users might describe themselves and the system might use many such descriptions to build a single model of a canonical user	SHORT-TERM If users specified short-term models, they would have time for little else LONG-TERM —Setting of parameters in systems such as a mail program —Systems, such as LISP, that allow arbitrary profile procedures ro be run —Personalized databases
IMPLICIT	SHORT-TERM Short-term data are so specific that they must be individual LONG-TERM —Game playing programs that assume opponent will play to win —ZOG —MACSYMA Advisor	SHORT-TERM —Conversational programs —CAI systems LONG-TERM —Grundy —Scribe helper

Fig. 1 — The space of user models.

3.   SOME TECHNIQUES FOR BUILDING USER MODELS

Having outlined both the need for user modeling and the kinds of approaches that can be taken toward it, some specific techniques that can be used for such modeling can now be presented. In this section, a variety of these techniques will be discussed:

— identification of the vocabulary and concepts employed by the user;

— gauging the responses with which the user seems satisfied;
— using stereotypes to generate many facts from a few.

These techniques fall into two broad groups: methods for inferring single facts at a time and methods for inferring whole clusters of facts at once. The next two sections dicuss these two kinds of techniques.

3.1   Inferring individual facts

One of the simplest ways to derive information about a user is to look at the way he uses the system. Someone who begins a session with a series of advanced commands is probably an expert. Someone whose first few attempts to form commands are rejected by the system is probably a novice and needs some help. An easy way to implement user modeling based on this sort of information is to construct a dictionary of system commands, options, and so forth, and to associate with each item an indication of what information the use of that item provides about its user. This information can be on a variety of dimensions, such as expertise with the system and expertise with the underlying task. Once acquired, this information can be used to help decipher user errors and to produce messages with the right level of description.

Another way that users provide information about themselves is via the patterns of their commands. Suppose a user asks a system for a particular piece of information. If he gets what he wants, he will either leave or get on with his next request. But if he does not get what he wants, he is likely to try to restructure his request in another attempt to get what he wanted. This attempt should signal to the system that it did not satisfy the user's need with its first response.

The use of both of these techniques can be illustrated by a brief examination of a system we are currently building, an interactive help facility for the document formatting system, Scribe (Reid, 1980). Users of this system can ask questions such as:

— How can I get an index generated?
— Why are the margins so wide?
— What is the difference between the itemize and the enumerate command?

The system stores its knowledge about Scribe as a set of condition–action rules. In their simplest form, these rules contain a single Scribe command as their condition, and the associated action describes the effect produced by the command. However, the way most commands operate is determined by the current values of some number of internal system variables, so these, too, must be mentioned as part of the rules' conditions. This often means that several rules, each with different conditions, all describe the operation of the same Scribe command. The description of the system's operation as given by these rules is hierarchical. The actions specified in many of the rules are not primitive actions, such as place a character at a particular spot on a page, but rather are higher-level actions, often other Scribe commands, whose effects are in turn described by additional rules. The action component of many rules is the setting of some system variable that will later affect the operation of other rules.

This hierarchical organization of the information in the system makes it possible for the system to answer questions at many different levels of detail. So, for example, if the system is asked a 'why' question, such as 'Why are the margins so wide?', it can respond either by stating the conditions that caused a particular rule to fire (e.g. 'The value of lmarg is 10 and the value of rmarg is 10') or it can chain back through the rules to determine how those conditions could have come to be true. The appropriate level at which to answer a particular question is a function of the level of the question itself and the level of knowledge of the user who asked the question. In order to be able to decide on the correct level, the system maintains a dictionary that contains an entry for each of the things that can occur in the rules — both as actions and as conditions. Associated with each entry is information that describes when it may be appropriate to mention the associated concept in an explanation. For example, each concept has a rating that describes how expert a person would have to be at Scribe to be able to understand an explanation in terms of it. Thus many of the internal system variables have very high ratings, while the simple user commands have very low ones. Each concept also has a separate rating that describes the level of sophistication with computer systems necessary to udnerstand it. For example, Scribe input files are block structures and Scribe's processing of them follows the standard block structure model. A programmer, even if he were a novice Scribe user, would understand an explanation in those terms, while a more Scribe-sophisticated typist might not. Whenever the help system tries to find an answer to a question, it first finds the rule (or rules) that apply to the particular situation. Then it looks at the concepts mentioned in those rules and compares what it knows about them to what it knows about the user who asked the question. If the levels match, a response is generated immediately. If they do not, the system chains through the rules, moving either up or down in the hierarchy as appropriate, until it finds an explanation at the correct level.

Of course, this method assumes that the help system has a model of the level of sophistication of the user. How can such a model be constructed? Fortunately, the same dictionary of concepts that was used when exploiting the model can also be used to construct it. When a user asks a question, he phrases it in terms of observed actions (such as where characters are on the page), Scribe commands, and Scribe parameters. The help system then matches this question to its rule base in its attempt to answer it. To do this, it looks up each of the elements of the question in its dictionary (which also serves as an index into the rules). People often refer to concepts simpler than the most complex ones they understand, but they do not talk about concepts more complex than the ones they understand. So the system can begin building its models of a new user by taking values associated with the first concepts he mentions. If more sophisticated concepts are mentioned later, the model of the user's level of expertise can be raised.

The model of the user can also be modified, as suggested above, by observing the patterns of the user's questions. Suppose the system misjudges the user's level and answers his first question by referring to a system parameter that means nothing to the user. The user's next question will almost certainly refer to that parameter in an attempt to figure out what it means. When the system sees this, it can conclude that its model is wrong and then modify it when it discovers the level of explanation with which the user is satisfied. Similarly, if the system underestimates the user's knowledge, it will give him fairly broad, general answers, he will ask for more specific information, and the system can then update its model.

This kind of user modeling is very simple. It makes the, almost certainly unjustified, assumption that there is a fixed order in which people learn things about a system. Although this assumption is probably false, it is not completely wrong. The alternative approach would be to construct, for each user, a detailed model of exactly what he knows. This approach is necessary in CAI systems, which must control the teaching sessions with such models (see, for example, Self (1977)). But this approach is very expensive, both in terms of the time it takes to construct the models and the space it takes to store them for a large number of users. The relationship between the user and the system is much looser in the context of a help system than it is in a CAI system. The user retains control of the interaction, and instead of being used in concentrated sessions to master ideas, help systems are normally used sporadically to solve particular problems. Thus the need for an exact model of the user's knowledge is less severe. Although there is, of course, no clear-cut line that can be drawn between these two types of systems, it does appear that in many situations, less than complete user models can be of use to a help system.

3.2   Using stereotypes to infer many things at a time

The techniques that have been discussed so far enable a system to infer individual facts about a user. But if a user model is to be very complex, the question of how to collect all the required information within a reasonable period of time arises. Possibly a user will have only a few interchanges with a system, so user modeling that requires many interactions to build an initial model will be of little use. Fortunately, in many situations it is possible to observe one or a small number of facts and from them to infer, with a fair degree of accuracy, a set of additional facts. Human traits are not distributed completely at random throughout the population. Rather they often occur in clusters. These clusters can arise for a variety of reasons, such as the existence of a single factor that causes several traits to be present at once, or the existence of a causal chain among the traits themselves. For example, a person who is wealthy is likely to have travelled more than another person who is very poor.

People represent such knowledge about co-occurring traits in a collection of stereotypes. Although the word stereotype has many negative associations, it is important to restrict its use here to the purely descriptive enumeration of a set of traits that often occur together. From this perspective, a stereotype is simply a way of capturing some of the structure that exists in the world around us. From the last couple of decades of work in artificial intelligence, we have come to understand the magnitude of the knowledge required to reason about the world. Fortunately, we have also discovered that the knowledge has a great deal of structure, which, if it can be captured, considerably constrains the things that must be considered at any one time. For example, events do not occur at random. Instead, common patterns of events, such as walking into a restaurant, getting a menu, ordering, eating, and paying, are observed. These event patterns have led to the development of scripts (Schank & Abelson 1977), which have proved extremely useful in the construction of programs to understand descriptions of events such as those found in newspaper stories. Stereotypes provide a similar structure for information about people. Just as scripts are useful for doing the kind of reasoning about events required to understand newspaper stories, stereotypes are useful for doing the kind of reasoning about people required to build user models. In particular, they provide a way of forming plausible inferences about yet unseen things on the basis of the things that have been observed.

A sterotype represents a collection of traits. It can be represented as a collection af attribute-value pairs. We will call each such attribute a *facet*. A model of an individual user can also be represented as a set of facets filled with values. The facets of the stereotypes used by a system should correspond to the facets of the user models built by the system. For example, one of the traits it might be useful to consider is the user's level of experience with a particular system. So models of individual users as well as the appropriate stereotypes would contain the facet 'expertise', which could take on values, say, from 1 to 10.

Some traits may be easily observable. They serve as *triggers* that cause the activation of the entire stereotype. Since the presence of a trait may only be suggestive of a particular stereotype rather than absolute evidence for it, each trigger has associated with it a rating that is a rough measure of the probability that the stereotype is appropriate given that the trigger was observed. Of course, it is not only the relationship between triggers and stereotypes that is at best suggestive. A stereotype says only that a collection of traits often occur together, not that they always do. So, associated with each facet in the stereotype must be a rating that estimates the probability of the corresponding trait given the appropriateness of the stereotype.

Stereotypes represent structure among traits. There is often additional structure that can be captured by representing a collection of stereotypes as a hierarchy. Information in very general stereotypes can be used unless conflicting information is suggested by more specific stereotypes. The most general stereotype available to a system built on stereotypes will do no worse than one built on the traditional built-in model of a canonical user.

One of the most important problems to be addressed in any user modeling system based on inferences from the user's behavior is how to detect and resolve conflicts between inferences. In order to facilitate this, ratings are attached both to triggers and to each prediction (facet) of each stereotype. In addition, each facet of an individual user model must contain not just a value, but also an estimate of the system's confidence in that value (which can be used to determine how much the value should be allowed to influence the performance of the overall system) and a list of reasons why the value is believed. This list of reasons is important. For example, suppose a stereotype is activated as a result of some observed trait of a user. That stereotype predicts a value for a particular facet, but the system's model of the user already contains a different value for that facet. If the system remembered where it got that value from, it may be possible to resolve the conflict fairly easily, as, for example, if the earlier value came from a stereotype more general than the one just being activated.

Sometimes, several different stereotypes may predict the same value rather than different ones for a facet. In this case, the system's level of confidence in the prediction can be higher than it would be if only one source of information were present. Since it is reasonable for stereotypes to predict other stereotypes and for particular facet–value pairs to predict stereotypes, the influx of new information may necessitate the propagation of rating changes throughout the user model. The exact extent to which it is effective to continue such propagation is an issue that needs to be determined empirically.

All of these methods of combining the inferences suggested by various stereotypes can be generalized to form the basis for integrating a wider variety of sources of knowledge about an individual user. Helpful as stereotypes can be at enabling the initial construction of a user model fairly quickly, they do not eliminate the need for other kinds of information, including both the answers to direct questions and the other indirect techniques discussed above in the context of the Scribe helper. But once each element of the user model is accompanied by a rating and a list of the evidence supporting it, it is easy to add arbitrary sources of knowledge. New information that supports old values causes the ratings attached to the values to increase. New information that conflicts with old values causes the conflict resolver to examine the credibility of the competing voices to produce as good an estimate of the truth as possible. The user's answers to direct questions can be given priority over simple inferences, which can in turn be given priority over the predictions of stereotypes.

The discussion so far of the use of stereotypes has been general and has avoided reference to particular systems or task domains. In the next section, a specific system that used stereotypes successfully to build models of its users will be discussed. The general points mentioned in this section will be illustrated with concrete examples.

4. GRUNDY: A CASE STUDY IN THE USE OF STEREOTYPES

In order to test many of the ideas outlined above, a pilot system called Grundy was built. Grundy recommends novels that people might like to read. To do this, it exploits two collections of data:

— Descriptions of individual books. Each description is a set of facets
  filled with appropriate values.
— Stereotypes that contain facets that relate to people's taste in books.
  Associated with each stereotype is a collection of triggers.

In addition, Grundy has some knowledge about each of the facets that
can occur in the stereotypes. This knowledge is used to help to resolve
conflicts between competing inferences and also to map from information in
the user model to information in the book descriptions. For a description of
Grundy more complete than the one presented here, see Rich (1979a,b).

When a new user begins a conversation with Grundy, he or she is aked to
provide a few words that (s)he thinks provide a good self-description.
Grundy uses those words as triggers for the appropriate stereotypes, and it
begins building its model of the user. Usually several stereotypes are
activated at this point and often there are conflicts among their predictions,
which Grundy resolves as well as it can. Grundy then estimates (using a
combination of the number of things it believes and how strongly it believes
them) whether it has enough information to begin recommending books. If
it does, then it goes ahead. If it does not, it asks the user for a few more
words.

Fig. 2 shows two of the stereotypes used by Grundy. Fig. 3 shows what
Grundy's model of a user would look like after being told the user's name
(and deducing from it that she is female) and after specifically activating the
WOMAN, FEMINIST, and INTELLECTUAL stereotypes. Whenever
Grundy activates a stereotype it also activates all of that stereotype's
generalizations, so the stereotypes EDUCATED-PERSON and ANY-
PERSON (the canonical user model) have also been activated. Notice that
each of the stereotypes contains only some of the facets contained in a
complete user model. This often occurs since many stereotypes involve only
one (or perhaps a few) significant aspects of a person.

After it accumulates enough information to get started, Grundy begins
recommending books one at a time until the user tells it to stop. The process
of choosing a book proceeds as follows.

(1) Select a salient facet in the user model. Salient facets are those with
    non-middle-of-the-road values and high ratings.
(2) Use an inverted index into the book database to select all the books
    suggested by this particular facet value.
(3) Compare each of the chosen books to the user model along all
    dimensions. Eliminate books that exceed certain thresholds (such as
    tolerance for violence).
(4) Of the books that have not been eliminated, choose the one that is
    the best match. If it is above a threshold of closeness of match,
    recommend it. Otherwise, go to step (1), choose a new facet, and try
    again.

FACET	VALUE	RATING
Activated-by	Atheletic-w-trig	
Genl	ANY-PERSON	
Motivations		
Excite	800	600
Interests		
Sport	900	800
Thrill	5	700
Tolerate-violence	4	600
Romance	−5	500
Education	−2	500
Strengths		
Physical-strength	900	900
Perseverance	800	600

SPORTS-PERSON

FACET	VALUE	RATING
Activated-by	Feminist-w-trig	
Genl	ANY-PERSON	
Genres		
Women	800	700
Politics	Liberal	700
Sex-open	5	900
Piety	−5	800
Political-causes		
Women	1000	1000
Conflicts		
Sex-roles	900	900
Upbringing	800	800
Tolerate-sex	5	700
Strengths		
Perseverance	800	600
Independence	800	600
Triggers	Fem-woman-trig	

FEMINIST

Fig. 2 — Some sample Grundy stereotypes.

Having selected a book, Grundy tells the user its author's name and the title, and then asks her whether she has read it before. If she has, Grundy knows that it is on the right track. It can now reinforce its belief in the things that led it to choose this book. (See section 5 for more discussion of the issue of modifying Grundy's database). If she did not like the book, Grundy needs to find out why. Ideally, it would simply say, 'Why not?', but far more knowledge than Grundy has would be required to interpret answers to such a question. For example, someone might say that she did not like the book because the main character reminded her of her dentist. So instead, Grundy tries to find out which of the beliefs that it has about the user and that it used to choose that book was wrong. To do so, it asks a few direct questions until

Gender	female	1000	inference-female name
			WOMAN
nationality	USA	100	ANY-PERSON
Education	5	900	INTELLECTUAL
Seriousness	5	800	INTELLECTUAL
Piety	−3	423	WOMAN
			FEMINIST
			INTELLECTUAL
Politics	Liberal	910	FEMINIST
			INTELLECTUAL
Tolerate-sex	5	700	FEMINIST
Tolerate-violence	−5	597	WOMAN
Tolerate-suffering	−5	597	WOMAN
Sex-open	5	960	FEMINIST
			INTELLECTUAL
Personalities	4	646	WOMAN
Opt-pes	0	100	ANY-PERSON
Plot-intr	0	100	ANY-PERSON
Plot-speed	−2	475	EDUCATED-PERSON
Suspense	0	100	ANY-PERSON
Thrill	−4	839	WOMAN
			INTELLECTUAL
Romance	3	696	WOMAN
Confusion	3	570	EDUCATED-PERSON
Real-fant	0	100	ANY-PERSON
Comedy	0	100	ANY-PERSON
Genres			
Literature	900	700	INTELLECTUAL
Women	800	700	FEMINIST
Political-causes			
Woman	1000	1000	FEMINIST
Strengths			
Perceptiveness	700	570	EDUCATED-PERSON
Intelligence	900	800	INTELLECTUAL
Independence	800	600	FEMINIST
Perseverance	800	600	FEMINIST
Sympathy	700	497	WOMAN
Kindness	700	497	WOMAN
Weaknesses			
Reason	800	600	INTELLECTUAL
Conflicts			
Difference	800	600	INTELLECTUAL
Upbringing	800	800	FEMINIST
Sex-roles	900	900	FEMINIST
Propriety	700	497	WOMAN
Love	700	497	WOMAN
Motivations			
Learn	900	700	INTELLECTUAL
Interests			
Ideas	900	900	INTELLECTUAL

Fig. 3 — A sample Grundy user model.

it either locates the problem or is forced to give up. If it found the problem, then it can update both its model of the user and its database of stereotypes.

If the user tells Grundy that she has not read the book, then Grundy tells her some things it thinks would interest her about it. Grundy uses its model of the user to choose which of the book's characteristics to mention. Then it asks the user whether she thinks she would like the book. This time, if she says yes, Grundy does nothing, since the positive response is based only on the few facts the user has seen. But if the user says the book does not look interesting, Grundy uses its procedure described above to try to find out what went wrong, so that it can try to find something she will like better.

In order to test the usefulness of Grundy's user models, an experiment was conducted in which Grundy gave each of its users as many suggestions as they wanted. It also gave them each several suggestions chosen at random without the aid of the user model and asked them whether the suggestions looked good. These served as a control. Table 1 shows the percentage of suggestions that were described as good as opposed to those described as bad, both in controlled mode (where the user model determined the

Table 1 — The usefulness of Grundy's user models

	Controlled	Random
Good	72%	47%
Bad	28%	53%

selection) and in random mode. These numbers show that Grundy does significantly ($p<10^{-9}$) better with the user model than without it.

Although Grundy's model of its users do not come close to capturing all of the intricately connected factors that determine which novels a person will like, its rate of success at making suggestions indicates that less than complete user models can provide useful guidance to interactive systems.

5.   Learning in Grundy

Stereotypes are extremely useful in enabling a system to build quickly an initial model of a new user so that it can get on with whatever the real task is. But how can we develop accurate stereotypes for a system to use? Will all of the user modeling efforts be futile if the stereotypes are inaccurate? These are important questions that still need complete answers, but experience with Grundy suggests that they do not represent insurmountable obstacles. Grundy's initial stereotypes represented merely my intuitions about people and the books they read. No attempt was made to collect any hard data. Despite this, the stereotypes are very useful. But the more interesting thing that can be observed is that Grundy is able to modify its stereotypes on the basis of its experience when the experience contradicts the predictions of the stereotypes. Only fairly simple modifications can be made. Facets cannot be added to or deleted, but the value of a facet can change, as can its rating.

Grundy's initial stereotype for a typical male reader indicated that men like to read books with fast-moving plots and a lot of thrill and excitement.

This may be true of the male population of the USA. But the men Grundy actually saw were not a very broad cross-section of that population; they were all university faculty and graduate students. So they tended to like intellectual sorts of books, which tend to be stronger on philosophy than on plot. So Grundy gradually modified its MAN stereotype to reflect the tastes of the population of men it actually saw rather than some population I had imagined. The fact that it could do this suggests two encouraging things about the merits of the use of stereotypes in user modeling systems:

— It is not critical that exact data describing the user community be available in order to build an initial set of stereotypes.
— If a single system is used in a variety of communities its stereotypes can evolve separately in each of them so that each is characterized fairly accurately.

Other types of learning that Grundy does not do are, of course, possible. Grundy stores all of its user models so that when a user returns for later sessions, a new model need not be built from scratch. Thus it would be possible to construct entirely new stereotypes by observing patterns of traits that occur commonly among the users.

6. CONCLUSION

In this paper, I have argued that for many interactive computer systems, the user community is sufficiently heterogeneous that a single model of a canonical user is inadequate. Instead, the ability to form individual models of individual users is needed. And then I have shown that besides being necessary, such models are also possible, and a collection of ways in which they can be built and exploited has been presented. The thing all of these techniques have in common is that they involve guesses about the user. These guesses are made by the system on the basis of its interaction with the user. As a result, the possibility of error must always be considered. To handle this, the system must do two things:

— it must attach ratings and justifications to each of the things it believes.
— it must not regard the user model as fixed, but rather as something upon which it can continuously improve by collecting feedback from the user on each interaction.

REFERENCES

Card, S. K., Moran, T. P. & Newell, A. (1980) The keystroke-level model for use: performance time with interactive systems. *Communications of the Association for Computing Machinery* **23** 396–410.
Codd, E. F. (1974) Seven steps to rendezvous with the casual user. In:

Klimbie, J. W. & Koffeman, K. L. (eds), *Data Base Management*. Amsterdam: North-Holland.

Cuff, R. N. (1980) On casual users. *International Journal of Man–Machine Studies* **12** 163–187.

Fitts, P. M. & Peterson, J. R. (1964) Information capacity of discrete motor responses. *Journal of Experimental Psychology* **67** 103–112.

Genesereth, M. (1978) An automated user consultant for MACSYMA. *Ph.D. thesis*, Harvard University.

Hudgens, G. A. & Billingsley, P. A. (1978) Sex: the missing variable in human factors research. *Human Factors* **20** 245–250.

Ledgard, H., Whiteside, J. A., Singer, A & Seymour, W. (1980) The natural language of interactive systems. *Communications of the Association for Computing Machinery* **23** 566–563.

Loo, R. (1978) Individual differences and the perception of traffic signs. *Human factors* **20** 65–74.

Mann, W. C., Moore, J. A. & Levin, J. A. (1977) A comprehension model for human dialogue. In: *Proceedings International Joint Conference Artifical Intelligence* **5** 77–87.

McGuire, W. J. & Padawer–Singer, A. (1976) Trait salience in the spontaneous self-concept. *Journal of Personality and Social Psychology* **33** 743–754.

Mittman, B. & Borman, L. (1975) *Personalized data base systems.* Los Angeles, Melville Publishing Co.

Nisbett, R. E. & Wilson, T. D. (1977) Telling more than we can know: verbal reports on mental processes. *Psychology Review* **84** 231–259.

Perrault, C. R., Allen, J. F. & Cohen, P. R. (1978) Speech acts as a basis for understanding dialogue coherence. In: *Proceedings of the Second Conference on Theoretical Issues in Natural Language Processing.* Association for Computational Linguistics.

Reid, B. K. (1980) Scribe: a document specification language and its compiler. Ph.D. thesis, Carnegie–Mellon University.

Rich, E. A. (1979a) Building and exploiting user models. Ph.D. thesis, Carnegie-Mellon University.

Rich, E. A. (1979b) User modeling via stereotypes. *Cognitive Science* **3** 329–354.

Robertson, G., Newell, A. & Ramakrishna, K. (1981) The ZOG approach to man–machine communication. *International Journal of Man–Machine Studies* **14** (4) 461–488.

Schank, R. C. & Abelson, R. P. (1977) *Goals, plans, scripts and understanding: an enquiry into human knowledge structures.* Hillsdale, New Jersey, Erlbaum.

Self, J. A. (1977) Concept teaching. *Artificial Intelligence* **9** 197–221.

Smith, S. (1979) Letter size and legibility. *Human Factors* **21** 661–670.

Part IV

Cognitive science and information science

The motivation for the study of artificial intelligence is not purely utilitarian: it may help us to understand the human mind. Conversely, a deeper comprehension of natural intelligence may well assist us in extending the capabilities of computers. This section explains why we need to know more about natural intelligence to ensure further progress.

Mellon (1965), in the well-known guide to the literature of chemistry, quotes a remark by the crystallographer William L. Bragg on a fundamental prerequisite for use of libraries:

> Anyone who wants to use a library effectively must already have some knowledge of the same nature as that which he hopes to find there. If not, he does not know where or how to look; nor can he grasp fully what he finds even if he happens to hit upon the right book.

Analogous problems arise whenever anything new is learnt. Winston (1984) in a work on AI quotes 'Martin's law', which states 'you can't learn anything unless you almost know it already'. Like many ideas propounded in the literature of artificial intelligence this one is not really new. Plato held that all learning was basically recollection of inate knowledge because he could not account for it in any other way. That was a rather extreme position, but the importance of prior knowledge is quite evident and was the basis of the theory of apperception proposed by the German philosopher Johann Friedrich Herbart (1776–1841). He argued that in the course of mental development certain groups of concepts or 'presentation masses' acquire a lasting dominance which exercises a powerful selective influence upon the ideas struggling to enter or re-enter consciousness. Apperception is the means by which a presentation mass assimilates new material. Herbart's work had some influence on educational theory but, unfortunately, little on psychology. Consequently, psychology was insufficiently developed to be of much practical use when librarians attempted to create a science of 'biblio-psychology' in the early decades of this century.

An appreciation of the fact that the influence of authors on readers could not be accounted for by a straightforward transmission of contents was one of the cornerstones of bibliopsychology. This and four other laws were listed by Otlet (1934), but the outstanding figure in the movement was the Russian librarian Nicholas Rubakin (1862–1946). He conducted numerous experiments in which readers' reactions to individual words of text were recorded under various headings, and by means of a numerical scoring system, the effects of different books on readers were assessed. By such means, both readers and books could be classified (Simsova 1968).

Rubakin's work had little lasting influence on librarians and, in any case, was probably more relevant to fiction than to factual literature. When interest in psychological factors was renewed in the 1970s, the principal cause was a concern with barriers to progress in information retrieval. The tools of investigation were those of cognitive psychology rather than the stimulus–response techniques of bibliopsychology. The Royal School of Librarianship, Copenhagen, was, and is, one of the main centres for this work. In his chapter Ingwersen gives an account of what has been learnt about the role of the intermediary in information retrieval and considers the implications for the design of intelligent systems for access to information. Interfaces have been developed which can cope with some of the problems normally tackled by an intermediary: CANSEARCH described in Pollitt's Chapter 4 is a good example. However, Ingwersen's CIRCUS model makes it clear that a great deal of work remains to be done before all the remaining problems are solved.

Ingwersen ventures the hope that information science will come to be accepted as one of the cognitive sciences. Meredith (1966), a psychologist, did consider the role of information science in his major work on communication, but so far the study of the cognitive aspects of this subject has been left largely to librarians and computer scientists. The chapter by Shaw and Gaines presents an overview of cognitive science and its relevance to the development of intelligent computer systems. Two note-worthy themes of their earlier work (Gaines & Shaw 1984) reflected in this chapter are an emphasis on the role of the computer as a medium of communication and the importance attached to personal construct psychology, developed by George Kelly.

In contrast to the behaviourists, Kelly did not believe that human activity is determined completely by external stimuli. Instead the individual acts as a 'personal scientist' who attempts to anticipate what the future holds by imposing some sort of meaning on the events of life. 'Man looks at the world through transparent patterns or templates which he creates and then attempts to fit over the realities of which the world is composed' (Kelly 1955, pp. 8–9).

Kelly believed that the mind is made up of large but finite number of these templates or constructs. Each construct takes the form of a scale defined by two extremes. Thus an individual's opinion of a novel may be defined in terms of constructs such as good/bad plot, well-written/badly written, exiting/dull, etc. (Aleksander & Burnett 1984). In fact, personal construct theory has been used to analyse opinions of particular books (Keen & Bell 1980).

Gaines and Shaw (1984) have developed a decision-making system, PLANET, based on Kelly's theories. Practical uses of automated methods of eliciting personal constructs have been described in an earlier survey (Shaw 1980). One very recent application is the creation of expert systems. Prototype knowledge bases can be produced quite rapidly by such means (Boose 1985). A more ambitious proposition involving the theory itself, and not knowledge elicited through its use, has been considered by Aleksander and Burnett (1984). They criticized claims that expert systems exhibit intelligence and suggested that Kelly's theory could provide guidelines for the development of programs displaying some real intelligence.

If personal constant psychology is a reasonably accurate description of the way the mind works, then it is bound to exercise considerable influence on progress in artifical intelligence and information science. Shaw and Gaines take a bold look beyond the horizon of the fifth generation computer, and outline the characteristics of a hypothetical sixth generation machine. It is encouraging to think that even if the much heralded fifth generation machine becomes a reality and lives up to expectations, there will be no shortage of new challenges to face.

REFERENCES

Aleksander, I. & Burnett, P. (1984) *Reinventing man: the robot becomes reality*. Harmondsworth, Penguin.

Boose, J. H. (1985) A knowledge acquisition program for expert systems based on personal construct psychology. *International Journal of Man–Machine Studies* **23** (5) 495–526.

Gaines, B. R. & Shaw, M. L. G. (1984) *The art of computer conversation: a new medium for communication. Englewood Cliffs, Prentice-Hall.*

Keen, T. R. & Bell, R. C. (1980) *One thing leads to another: a new apporach to elicitation in the repertory grind technique. International Journal of Man–Machine Studies* **13** (1) 25–38.

Kelly, G. A. (1955) *The psychology of personal constructs*. New York, Norton.

Mellon, M. G. (1965) *Chemical publications: their nature and use*, 4th edn. New York, McGraw-Hill.

Meredith, P. (1966) *Instruments of communication: an essay on scientific writing*. Oxford, Pergamon.

Otlet, P. (1934) *Traité de documentation*. Brussels, Editiones Mundaneum.

Shaw, M. L. G. (1980) *On becoming a personal scientist*. London, Academic Press.

Simsova, S. (ed) (1968) *Nicholas Rubakin and bibliopsychology*. London, Clive Bingley.

Winston, P. H. (1984) *Artificial intelligence*, 2nd edn., Reading, Mass, Addison-Wesley.

8

Cognitive Analysis and the Role of the Intermediary in Information Retrieval

Peter Ingwersen, Royal School of Librarianship, Department of Design and Implementation of Specialized Information Services, Copenhagen, Denmark

1. INTRODUCTION

Today's intermediary, human or computerized, faces the complicated task of translating user statements and concepts into user requirements, which must then be restructred to correspond to the organization of documents or organization of data in documents. This results in the acquisition of information desired by the user.

This chapter is concerned with the contribution cognitive sciences and processes can make towards an understanding of the information retrieval (IR) processes, in particular when an intermediary mechanism is involved. This mechanism may be of human or computerized nature. The IR — or information searching processes concerned — include manual routines as well as printed and electronic sources and systems. All users — not only the scientist — and, in principle, all kinds of information requests are of interest. Thus, the aim of this chapter is to discuss and emphasize certain features and characteristics of the intermediary which ought to be taken seriously when one is supporting human mediators and end users or replacing human intermediaries with computerized mechanisms.

Belkin's (1978) definition of information science as, 'facilitating the effective communication of desired information between human generator and human user' illustrates, in my opinion, the most important aspect of this science. This aspect necessitates an interest in the following areas of information science and can be used as a framework for my presentation:

— information in human, cognitive communication systems;
— the idea of desired information;
— the effectiveness of information (systems) and the effectiveness of information transfer;
— the relationship between information and generators;
— the relationship between information and user.

The first four points are of major concern, whereas the last two only will be dealt with marginally.

Which are the cognitive sciences, and why are they important to information science and IR in particular?

People use information systems, i.e. libraries, online databases, information providers, books etc., because they seek solutions to problems or are looking for intellectual and cultural experiences. Each single step in the IR process, for the individuals involved, is concerned with problem-solving and learning situations. It is important not to overlook that the concept 'individuals' also includes system components and devices, such as database and indexing structures as well as output and feedback mechanisms.

Hence, the cognitive sciences — understood as an intersection of linguistics, artificial intelligence (AI) and psychology, as stated by Schank and Abelson (1977) — are of major importance since they deal with problem-solving, communication, perception, knowledge representation, and conceptualization. These fields also serve as an interdisciplinary source for the development of educational theory and didactics.

Fig. 1 outlines cognitive and other sciences closely related to information science. In fact, one may suggest treating information science as a cognitive science on a par with psychology, linguistics, AI and their interlinked disciplines.

The figure provides a scenario to which we can relate the further analysis and discussion of the nature of the IR process and the intermediary role in connection with different cognitive processes. Other fields shown in the figure, such as sociology and philosophy, are briefly touched upon.

The chapter begins with a brief description of the cognitive viewpoint and its relevance to IR in general and the intermediary in particular. This epistemological section includes references to cognitive psychology and psycho-linguistics as well as paradigm theory, and is followed by an outline of the major types of cognitive structures imbedded in IR systems and searchers.

The succeeding sections concentrate on the intermediary roles and functions exemplified by a cognitive model of the communication processes in IR. Characeristic elements of behavioural pattern and the search interview are discussed, based on empirical findings deriving from real-life investigations. Different, basic types of information requirements as well as levels of knowledge possessed by searchers during IR are analysed.

Finally, theoretical and empirical results are merged into a descriptive model of three major types of computerized intermediary mechanisms.

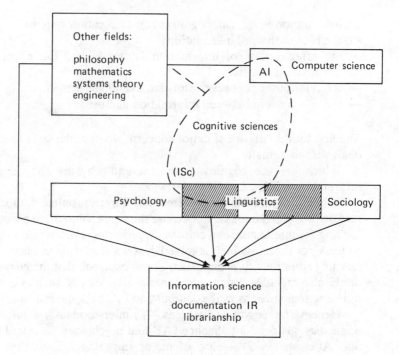

Fig. 1 — Scientific disciplines related to information science.

2. IR AND COGNITIVE SCIENCES

Possible links with recent approaches to the problems of representation of knowledge and other cognitive issues relevant to information retrieval have been explored by Belkin (1977).

Linguistics has traditionally contributed very valuable approaches to classification and indexing, for example with respect to the use of natural language and the representation of meaning. Linda C. Smith (1980) has produced a thorough review of AI applications in IR systems up to 1980, and has very recently (1986) outlined an AI taxonomy highlighting the potentials of AI and 'knowledge-based system' as tools for information use. In particular, she stresses the importance of human factors and the significant difference between human-controlled systems in which the computer assists humans and machine-controlled systems in which decisions are made by the system.

One of the fundamentals in the development of the cognitive sciences is the cognitive viewpoint which elucidates the role of knowledge structures in information processing and the meaning of information. This view is briefly outlined below, followed by an investigation into the nature of personal cognitive structures, exploring human processing of information, conceptualization and perception as major issues.

2.1   The cognitive viewpoint

The purpose of IR is essentially to correlate the contents of an information system — i.e. a printed, computerized or human source containing concepts — with the information-seeking human. A (human) intermediary component is often introduced to facilitate the IR process in terms of clarification of initial questions, terminology and search strategy.

What we, in fact, are dealing with in IR are a variety of different, individual knowledge structures generated and stored in systems and documents as well as present in individual users and intermediaries. 'Documents' are understood as physical entities containing symbols. The concept 'knowledge' structures' (KS) derives from the cognitive sciences and has been applied to information science, for example by Brookes (1977). Furthermore, the concept is essential to the cognitive viewpoint. Briefly, its main thesis is that '..any processing of information — whether perceptual or symbolic — is mediated by a system of categories or concepts, which, for the processing device, are a model of its world' (de Mey 1980).

The device may be human or machine, and 'the world model', often designated 'image' or 'world knowledge', consists of 'knowledge structures'. These are determined by the individual and social/collective experiences, education, training, etc. It is the individual knowledge structures of the information processing mechanism — the system of categories and concepts — which provide the basis for decisions on which ambiguities (or problems) should be eliminated.

The KS can be visualized as extensive series of multidimensional maps hanging from a classroom ceiling, as suggested by Ingwersen (1982, 1984a) — see Fig. 3. Different maps may cover the same material (e.g. 'vehicles' on the left-most and the right-most maps) ordered according to various overriding concepts. Some maps (in the mind of an individual) may contain 'blank' regions (e.g. the 'Moon map'), others being non-existent (e.g. a map containing 'car-trains—the Channel' relations). However, another person may indeed possess the latter one, or possess maps more dense or drawn up differently. In the course of dicussion or interaction, new maps may be pulled down and others up, as needed to follow conceptual developments, e.g. 'vehicles'→'cars' (left), followed by 'cars'→'Moon' (right). Blank regions may be filled out (=individual learning). A complete change of series of maps may occur in a sequence of mental operations or during conversations (serendipity effects).

'Information' is seen as supplementary to the conceptual system representing the mechanism's world model. Consequently, information is that knowledge — or conceptual context — which has to be perceived and/or produced by the system. Information must become part of the processing system's KS to solve ambiguities or problems. Otherwise, the actual problem cannot be solved in its entirety. Thus, the system — man, for instance — may try to find the required information, either by obtaining it from outside itself, i.e. perceiving knowledge from other systems, and/or by 'thinking', i.e. modifying its KS (Ingwersen, 1984b).

If information is supplementary to a processing system's own KS, then that which is stored in information systems and in the mind of users and intermediaries is not information but 'potential information' which becomes data when transmitted (by speech, reading or electronic transmission, etc.). Data then becomes information when perceived. If it is not perceived by the KS, then it is as if it has never existed. This perception depends on the state of the actual KS, for example when a user looks up a book, searches an online system or negotiates with an intermediary.

Similar conditions apply to the IR systems and the intermediary. As a result, we are able to understand why librarian–user or librarian–database communication can encounter difficulties, such as: (1) communicated or entered concepts do not correspond to the concepts forming part of the actual KS in the receiving processing system (brain or IR mechanism), or (2) they are not linked properly to recognize/recalled concepts.

Conversation between humans is prey to misunderstandings and non-recognition of concepts. But a clarifying dialogue is often sufficient to ensure the conversation's continuation. Learning processes and interpersonal rules and habits are involved. Hutcheson and Laver (1972) have made a useful distinction between three kinds of information which may be transferred during a negotiation:

(1) 'cooperative' information organizing the dialogue;
(2) behavioural information;
(3) information on the factual meaning of the dialogue.

The human–human interaction is a social situation. Both the messages and the source itself are evaluated by the receiver with respect to knowledge, authority, reliability and status.

Similar evaluations occur when the source is a machine. However, today's computer systems are rarely able to take part in a dialogue which includes meaningful factual information transfer. Their means of clarifying non-recognized concepts are both very simple and insufficient. AI research in human–machine dialogue may provide certain clues, some of which are outlined and elaborated on by Vickery (1984).

The rather poor dialogue facilities of present online IR systems as opposed to the more complex abilities of human intermediaries are illustrated below. For both the computer system and the human mediator, the communicated terms are unknown or ambiguous:

The user: '. . .something to do with 'ABC' in form of patents'.
The information specialist: 'I see, no, I can't recall it, but what you say reminds me of 'XYZ'; has your problem something to do with 'XYZ? — besides, our catalogue/database here (pointing) has no index on document types!'

This answer contains both conceptual data — 'XYZ' — and IR data — 'index on document types', as well as cooperative information ('I see'— 'has your problem . .'), and behavioural information ('here').

The host system today: '0 (zero) hits'

The searcher does not know if the zero hits are a result of the entered conceptual data — the search term 'ABC' — or the erroneous use of searchable fields in that particular database. Error messages are very uniformative in commercial online vendor systems, whereas microcomputer packages seem to have taken these cognitive problems into account.

At the very least, the system, in form of a human-like interface device, should have answered:

either: '0 hits — no document type field (DT=) available'
or: '0 hits — 'ABC' not recognized; perhaps wrong spelling? — Please reenter'
and (assuming correct spelling): '0 hits — I don't know 'ABC' — please enter another word or a context incl. 'ABC''

A human-like intermediary or interface ought therefore to be designed with cognitive structures that are recognizable to both a human enquirier and the source system. Furthermore, it should be able to undersand new concepts, e.g. 'ABC' related to 'XYZ' or some other context, i.e. a learning ability is required.

2.2 Personal cognitive structures

How do we envision cognitive knowledge structures at the present time?

Current trends in cognitive psychology and psycho-linguistics may contribute to an understanding of the information processing involved. The pivotal theories about functions of the human brain are outlined by Lindsay and Norman (1977) and Johnson-Laird and Wason (1977) among others. Besides presenting information-processing models as a whole, both works cover the psycholinguistic aspects, problem-solving, decision-making and experimental techniques. The central model consists of a sensory organ, followed by a filter which sorts out, from the extensive amount of potential information or data received by the senses, that which is allowed to pass to processing in short-term memory (STM) and long-term memory (LTM). The filtering action is thought to be controlled by information stored in LTM and recalled at the time of the processing event — see Fig. 2.

The cognitive view explains why certain stimuli may activate a particular 'map' or part of KS in LTM, on which the individual operates in the actual thought process. The process can be illustrated in the form of a very simple kind of thought experiment — see Fig. 3.

A person operating a videotex terminal wishes to 'hire a car'. LTM 'pulls down' the appropriate map (map 3), 'telling' the filter to draw attention to words and phrases containing the required concepts and other relevant details. After some attempts, by which different maps have been pulled down (and up again), triggered by computer output on the screen, the person sees the words:

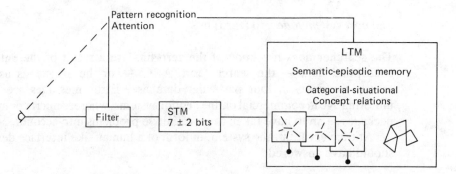

Fig. 2 — Model of information perception and processing.

*** Rent a CAR — HONDA — $20 a day — tel: 759 362 954 ***

Depending on his experiences, previous knowledge, etc. and his degree of attention, he may reason (thinking) that 'renting a car' is identical to 'hiring a car'. (We assume in this case that in LTM a relation is established between the '20 $ a day' concept and at least one map elsewhere containing the knowledge that 'xx $ a day means hire something'.) Alternatively, he recognizes the word 'rent' on sight, pulling down a new map containing the relation 'Rent=Hire'. This process is memory recall. Unfortunately for our friend, no printer or pencil is available. He must thus try to memorize the price and telephone number he just ascertained.

The STM can easily store the '$ a day' concept for a time since it consists of only 4 bits of data; 7 bits±2 seems to be the average. The telephone number is more difficult. He may remember them if he is able to relate the figures to some known items in his memory, adding the number on to the relevant maps in LTM.

Several concepts are connected to this interpretation of memory: 'schemata' by Bartlett (1932), 'images' by Boulding (1971) and 'knowledge structures' by Brookes (1977). Weizenbaum (1984) calls the entire affair 'something', since we cannot see the maps or structures and because our experimental techniques may be obtrusive, resulting in wrong interpretations. Weizenbaum touches upon the same kind of reality interpretation problems as have been seen in connection with complementarity and interpretations of experiments in quantum mechanics. These objections are valid, especially with respect to our present understanding of LTM. When designing 'intelligent systems' we may therefore apply models that function, but that do not mirror the workings of the human brain, although they fit our experimental results.

The theories also distinguish between two kinds of knowledge structures: episodic and semantic memory. The first is formed by the individual's personal experiences, e.g. renting cars. Semantic memory is a formal

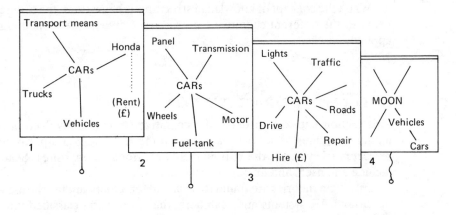

Fig. 3 — A map visualization of some knowledge structures concerned witht he concept 'cars'.

knowledge, also shared by others, for example, the knowledge acquired through education. In information science we may distinguish between IR knowledge structures and conceptual knowledge structures. Both are encompassed by the episodic/semantic memory according to the experience of the individual. These two kinds of KS are discussed in detail below.

The representation or classification of knowledge in the development of cognitive processes has been studied by, for instance, Luria, Brunner, Vygotsky and Piaget. Luria (1976) isolates two kinds of human approaches to the classification of objects:

(1) categorical classification, i.e. a person sorts out an abstract concept and choses the objects which can be included under this concept, e.g. 'transports means↔cars+trucks', see map 1, Fig. 3.
(2) situational classification, i.e. a person tries to involve the objects in different concrete situations, thereby grouping objects which belong together. For example, 'driving↔cars+roads' — map 3.

This approach to conceptualization is important for the design of intermediary mechanisms because it has been demonstrated that children as well as adults often attempt to apply situational categories at the beginning of an intense learning situation. Often, episodic memory is also involved. Not until learned are more categorial relations applied. Luria's approach seems to be in harmony with Vygotsky's (1962) dichotomizing of concepts into scientific and common concepts, and it is similar to the frame concept of Minsky (1975) and the script concept of Schank and Abelson (1977). The script model — like the situational categorization — is concerned with personal memories of patterns of events. There are strong indications that other memory structures, concerned with plans, goals and themes (social patterns) are involved, as also suggested by Schank and Abelson.

When the concept of knowledge structures is being used, the distinctions between the different cognitive patterns and elements mentioned must be applied.

3.   COGNITIVE STRUCTURES IN IR

This section explores in detail the cognitive structures involved in information searching. The focus is partly on the IR system and partly on the searchers of systems, the two elements regarded as opposites. Searchers include end users and human intermediaries.

Paradigm theories are found to be useful for understanding the matching of authors, IR systems and searchers, the latter being classified into four different types according to the kind of KS they possess.

3.1   Knowledge structures in IR systems

The kinds of KS that are involved in IR, their origin and relations are demonstrated in Fig. 4 (Ingwersen & Pejtersen 1986).

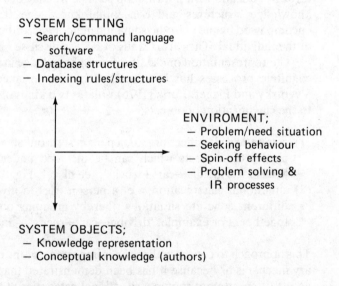

SYSTEM SETTING
— Search/command language
   software
— Database structures
— Indexing rules/structures

ENVIROMENT;
— Problem/need situation
— Seeking behaviour
— Spin-off effects
— Problem solving &
  IR processes

SYSTEM OBJECTS;
— Knowledge representation
— Conceptual knowledge (authors)

Fig. 4 — KS forming part of an information system.

To the left in the figure we find two different kinds of knowledge structures:

(1) structures concerned with the system setting, i.e. KS established or 'fixed' prior to or at the design event;
(2) structures regarding the objects of the system, i.e. KS that are constantly added to the system. 'Knowledge representation's' KS mirror

the 'database structures' and 'indexing rules'. When added, all KS become 'fixed'.

To the right we observe the KS adhering to the environment of the system, i.e. to users and intermediaries. They consist of KS which constantly change. The IR system can process potential information, but is not (yet) geared to transforming it in relation to a request, only to reacting according to the expectations (e.g. of user behaviour and entered search terms) previously laid down by systems designers, indexers' etc.

Furthermore, users and intermediaries must adapt their models or structures to those of the system via interaction, thought and learning. Hence, the system becomes dominant. This is a consequence of the design approaches applied thus far. They are, in general, system-driven, i.e. they rely on the nature of setting and object structures. Indeed, online catalogues are perfect examples of object-dependent systems, not even utilizing the possibilities inherent in the modern setting.

In other words, systems design ought to consider all three main components outlined in Fig. 4. The design should rely far more on empirical analysis and characteristics of searchers. Repetitive analysis resulting in follow-up modifications ought to be practised more often than is done at the present, for example file reloads, whereby changed search behaviours (spin-off of current system) can be accounted for in a new version.

In recent years, such design models have been strongly recommended in research conducted in the field of General Systems Theory (Samuelson *et al.* 1977). Although often rejected by computer practitioners, this empirical design approach may prove valuable (also economically) in the long run. The next logical step is to make it possible for the system to adjust itself to changes in the environment, and to create models of, or adapted to, the actual searcher requiring information.

Thus, the crucial task of IR is to bring individual cognitive structures of the following dissimilar individuals into accord:

Generators:	Searchers:
— Authors	— Users
— Indexing system designers	— Intermediaries
— Systems designers	
— Database/tool producers	
— Indexers/maintenance staff	

The prerequisites for effective retrieval now become apparent.

Collective cognitive structures, often described in paradigm theories of behavioural science, most explicitly by Kuhn (1970), may influence both the structure of classification and indexing systems and the conceptual patterns of authors and searchers. Hence, they have implications for the relations of topics and concepts treated in the body of literature and information requirements. Similarly, paradigmatic structures may influence design, implementation and maintenance of information systems. Paradigmatic structures are formed by the semantic memory.

Both the Dewey and the UDC classification schemes are still used in public and university libraries throughout the world. These schemes undoubtedly mirror the categorization of the scientific knowledge, fields and viewpoints generally accepted by scholars — including classification systems designers and librarians — in the latter part of the nineteenth century America.

The paradigm approach makes it probable that IR is more likely to be effective when a majority of the involved persons within a subject field share common knowledge structures. Scientific views, terminological pattern and vocabulary can thus be kept under control. The 'match of concepts' may then have a chance for a time, for example, within very limited and specialized subject fields. Another example taken from the infancy of online IR some decades ago was within certain scientific/technological fields: people with engineering or medical backgrounds as end users, generators and intermediaries. However, such permanent conditions rarely exist in developing fields, whether in differentiating or in interdisciplinary fields, such as social sciences, humanities and several of the current technological domains.

Finally, it may have come to one's attention that our educational systems attempt to dictate certain common KS. The dynamic nature of our societies, however, hinders homogeneity and produces a wide range of educational and learning levels. Hence, expert systems work under similar conditions — today and in future.

Furthermore, the scope of the information concept is not limited to scientific knowledge alone, but covers all types of knowledge, including affective and 'common' issues. Indeed the cognitive approach often illustrates why children and adults meet obstacles — or succeed — when performing that kind of retrieval (Wanting 1984, Ingwersen 1982).

3.2   Searchers' knowledge structures
The intermediary may seem a Janus figure, and his task becomes more and more complicated. He is surrounded by a corpus of increasing complexity, consisting of traditional bibliographic tools, new IT applications, complicated search languages, a diversity of distributed information services and databases, each displaying different structures, and a growing body of more or less experienced users or clients.

Basically, two kinds of cognitive structures are involved in the IR processes (compare with Fig. 4):

IR knowledge, consisting of knowledge about:
— system setting
— IR processes, search interviewing, tactics and logics
conceptual knowledge, consisting of knowledge about:
— topic areas, including conepts, relations, terms, etc.
— imaginative areas, goals, ideas, intentions, expectations.

Both types of knowledge are transferred and used during retrieval in the form of data which may (or may not) become information in the receiver's mind. The outcome of a search is determined by the quality of the types of knowledge and the ability to combine them. An information system contains per definition both types, although until now in fixed form. Let us briefly investigate the **searcher groups** which interrogate IR systems, and observe which kind of KS they possess (Ingwersen, 1984b):

(1) the **elite**, possing both IR and highly specialized conceptual knowledge;
(2) the **intermediary**, with IR knowledge but limited specialized conceptual knowledge;
(3) the **end user**, possessing highly specialized knowledge but scarce or no IR knowledge;
(4) the **layman**, having neither specialized nor IR knowledge in general.

The elite group is small — approximately 15 percent — and consists mainly of information specialists who may act as intermediaries or end users within their specialized field. A large proportion of searches (and search time payed for) can be attributed to this group — perhaps up to 40 percent, as pointed out by Deunette (1983).

Group 2 may be regarded as the typical intermediary group today. It consists of librarians, information specialists and others who have obtained IR skills via formal education and/or experience. A vast majority of searches are carried out by intermediaries.

The typical end user belongs to group 3, which together with some of the intermediaries and a major part of group 4 constitute the shallow category of 'casual users'.

The 'elite' searchers are the most fortunate ones. They are experts and possess a maximum of both kinds of KS. According to Howard (1982), highly experienced searchers knowledgeable in a field have the lowest preparation and connect time and greatest use of commands, terms searched and sets viewed, and they achieve the best results. This would indicate that this group can effectively adapt to (=learn) the setting and process the conceptual KS embedded in the system, in relation to their requirements.

Casual searchers perform individual searches far too infrequently to keep abreast of changes in the setting structure, such as new search commands or newly added database structures of potential value to their field. The characteristics of the 'layman' are not covered as yet with regard to online systems, but will sooner appear in both Scandinavian and Anglo-American contexts (Library Association). However, this category constitutes the potential future user of the online market: the ordinary person.

As we can observe, the intermediary is a person who may belong to either the 'elite' or to the second group consisting of 'generalist information specialists'. In fact, he/she may act as intermediary although forming part of the third group of searchers! Klasen's (1982) investigation of Swedish online searchers shows, that 55 percent of the persons characterized as 'end users' in the sense of possessing little or no IR knowledge, perform intermediary work.

However, instead of focusing on searcher groups, one can regard the search situation cognitively, in other words from an individual point of view. Looked at that way, an individual may be forced to shift between all four different main roles or levels in the course of the day or during each IR system search. This would indicate that the system or an intermediary mechanism would be perceived as more user-oriented and efficient if it could explore and adapt to the appropriate level.

4. THE INTERMEDIARY IN IR SITUATIONS

An elaborated model is presented, based on the cognitive point of view and the analysis of the cognitive nature of information retrieval systems and searchers, emphasizing the interactive communication in IR. The types of intermediary mechanism required, human as well as computerized, — are discussed in the light of empirical research results and different kinds of user requests.

4.1 Fundamental problems in IR systems

Library and information science's view of an intermediary's role is largely dependent upon information scientists' interpretation of the nature of information needs and requests. Until the mid-seventies the focus was not generally on the information processes inherent in a request to a system. It was assumed that the request formulation — the 'need statement' or query — was identical to the actual, unarticulated information problem. Until ten years ago, most information search models exhibited an ignorance of the fact that users often have difficulties expressing their requirements.

Investigations of IR often followed a similar pattern. The reasons seem to be several. Studies were made in laboratory environments with subjects selected from 'elite' or 'end user' groups with information needs defined by the researchers. The core of productive research issues was concerned with the efficiency of the 'system' rather than with the 'environment'. Thus, the intermediary, if a participating element at all, was regarded as part of the system. Its role was to guide the user by applying its knowledge of the systems' setting and topic areas which were taken for granted.

The framework of this understanding of IR is called the 'best match principle' or 'best match paradigm'. Almost all of today's online services operate within this rather traditional scope. The 'best match principle' is based on two fundamental assumptions:

(a) that the individual user is able to specify the required information;
(b) that the information need expressions are functionally equivalent to document texts, i.e. equivalent to information or knowledge.

Both assumptions are basically erroneous, as stated by Belkin *et al.* (1982a,b). Assumption (a) may be correct if an intermediary participates.

The keyword is interviewing to obtain knowledge about the problem behind the initial request. Assumption (b) is correct in form of expression–text (term–term) equivalence. However, texts (or text representation) are not necessarily equal to information/knowledge in regard to the actual, individual requirement — as discussed in section 2.1. Assumption (b) is closely related to two other fundamental problems regarding IR systems:

(c) accessibility, in terms of physical, bibliographical or intellectual access;
(d) concept interpretation and feedback in terms of contextualization.

Recently, Lancaster and Wormell have questioned whether document retrieval systems provide improved intellectual or bibliographical access to potential information compared with IR systems several decades ago. Although improvements have been made by advances in IT, Lancaster (1986) is convinced that the quantitative and qualitative complexity of potential information has counter balanced those efforts. Wormell (1985) argues that intellectual accessibility can be improved to a certain degree by applying natural language indexing methods rather than controlled vocabularies when representing document texts. One may, for example, utilize the inherent chapter headings of monographic texts, and by relying less, or not at all, on descriptors, the indexer's conceptual structures will not influence the retrieval process. A double concept interpretation is thus avoided, and the searcher is brought closer to the author's conceptual meanings and intentions.

As for language translation and pattern recognition, concept interpretation in IR is a question of how much context is needed to disambiguate a message. In IR systems based on 'best match', it is not only homographs and ambiguous words and phrases that pose problems. Entire free-text search strategies applied to large, multidisciplinary databases, such as PASCAL or NASA, may indicate quite different subject areas. For instance, skilfully elaborated strategies containing several relevant search concepts related to 'information retrieval' and 'microcomputer(s)' still point to such different disciplines as: information science, computer science, aerospace technology, and — to the author's cognitive surprise — the biological sciences with a relatively high hit-score.

Assuming that need statements in all situations really are identical to information needs, an intermediary is still required to support the user in finding the relevant context in IR systems. Conversely, the mediator can serve the system by defining the right context by filtering the problem formulations of a user. In general, both intermediary and searcher are poorly supported by the system outputs in the form of abstract, keyword, thesaurus and full-text formats resulting in inefficient and time-consuming relevance judgement processes. However separately, the concept interpretation problem — point (d) — may be solved in part since automatic conceptual mapping of texts is now possible. Furthermore, experiments are under way on searching via natural language and probability or mapping (Robertson *et al.* 1982).

Feedback mechanisms in very simple forms are currently in commercial operation, for example the term frequency analysis facility Zoom on ESA-IRS which displays ranked lists of terms applied to selected records (Ingwersen 1984b). Other feedback features are the Focusing Devices on 3-RIP and BRS-SEARCH, allowing for display of search terms in context.

Salton and MacGill's (1983) relevance feedback approach, in which the inquirer's reaction to initial retrieved data is used to modify the query until the optimal formulation is found, is a more subtle solution and may improve the IR situation, but does not change it dramatically. These approaches tend to accept the dominant role of the system and the principle of equivalence between information need expressions and document texts (point (b)) but attempt to avoid the pitfalls of 'best match' retrieval by indicating context (point (d)). See also the discussion on system dominance in section 3.1.

These rather contextual ways of treating entered search concepts do not solve the principle problem of 'best match'-assumption (a), which lies in the relationships between need formulations and 'real' information needs or problems.

4.2   A cognitive model of IR interactivity — the label effect
In 1960 Mackay posed a fundamental question: What makes the question? His definition of the information need is very cognitive: '...a certain incompleteness in his picture of the world, an inadequacy in what we might call his 'state of readiness' to interact purposefully with the world around him' (Mackay, 1960).

Eight years later the psychologist and librarian R. S. Taylor (1968) pointed out the need for investigating the nature of the development of information needs in the mind of the user, from the problem situation to the formulation(s) for the system. He defined four stages in this development:

(1) the actual, but unexpressed need;
(2) the conscious need;
(3) the formalized need;
(4) the compromised need, i.e. the question as presented to librarian or IR system.

Stages (1) to (3) are considered internal representations in the mind of the user and are difficult to investigate. However, it was important to identify the relationship betweeen stages (3) and (4), since it determines the following retrieval processes, including the roles and functions of the intermediary. The basic problem for the intermediary — according to Taylor's hypotheses — is interviewing the user backward throuh stage (3), preferably reaching stage (2). Taylor stresses not only that certain communicative and cognitive skills are necessary for intermediaries, but that users do not always ask straightforward, unambiguous questions.

Since the appearance of his often-quoted paper, a great number of research projects have been devoted to the study and analysis of possible consequences of his ideas for intermediary behaviour, reference work, education of information specialists and IR systems design. The model presented in Fig. 5 outlines the cognitive, interactive processes in IR placing the intermediary as a key figure, separate from the system itself.

In the model, 'image' refers to the discussion in section 2.1 of concepts related to knowledge structures. All KS incorporated in an IR system, i.e. all KS of participating generators, are grouped on the *left* — elaborated outline of cognitive structures in IR systems.

The model outlines the IR system as it is known today, containing fixed structures of potential information transformed into texts (terms) or other symbols and representations (indexing terms). If we view it as a system of the future, the 'potential information' contains the knowledge base and the 'representation' has a form of knowledge representation. In the case of the latter, reverse arrows signifying dynamic interactive processes must be introduced between 'representation', 'potential information' and 'conceptual and setting knowledge'.

The intermediary mechanism, e.g. an information specialist, is placed in the *centre*. It contains three main elements, operating together dynamically:

— conceptual knowledge, i.e. knowledge of topics, terms, etc.;
— IR knowledge, i.e. knowledge of IR systems and processes, interviewing;
— a perception device allowing for modelling of user information needs/problems.

This triangular view of the intermediary follows the line of discussion in section 3 about interactive adaption of user behaviours and knowledge levels or searcher groups. Similarly, to the *right* in the model the user side takes the shape of a triangle: conceptual knowledge, with an anomalous state of knowledge (ASK); requests in the form of formulated problem statements; and a Model of the information provider, i.e. intermediary or/ and IR system. This model may be more or less filled out with IR knowledge as discussed particularly in section 3.2.

When the user's conceptual KS are considered incomplete or inadequate in a specific area of interest from a user point of view (termed as 'anomalous' by Belkin (1982a)), they are transformed into an 'ASK' — equal to stages 1–2 in Taylor's model.

In the transformation from ASK to a query presented to the intermediary one must bear Taylor's remaining steps in mind. Investigations in the UK as well as in Denmark indicate that the fourth stage — the 'compromised' need as an initial statement — really exists for certain reasons in the form of a **label**. This label consists of one or several subject concepts more generic than or out of context of the need, formalized within the mind of the user (=stage 3 of Taylor). In the Danish studies, the so-called 'thinking aloud' technique was applied to obtain information about the client's own preliminary searching during which 'formalized need' statements were recorded. The recordings showed that even when users have specified statements clearly in mind, this label effect appears when the

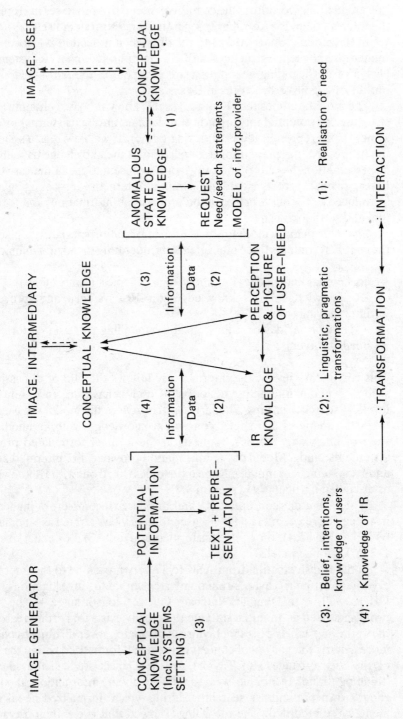

Fig. 5 — A cognitive communication system for IR (from Belkin (1982a) and Ingwersen (1984b)).

intermediary–client negotiation is initiated (Ingwersen 1982). One reason seems to be the expectations and beliefs underlying the user model of system and mediator, in relation to what they may offer that particular user. This is possibly due to the user's socio-psychological environment at the moment of negotiation, which does not always favour a high degree of problem specification to an information provider. Clearly, we are dealing with interpersonal communicative factors, such as confidence and degree of familarity between user and provider, as well as quality of IR knowledge possessed by the client. Another reason appears to be the difficulties involved in expressing many interrelated concepts concisely, preferably in a single sentence. Consequently, this labelling effect often misrepresents the subject area requirements to the intermediary. The limited number of concepts that often constitute the label normally refer to several different subject areas or aspects. The 'concept interpretation' problem described in section 4.1 in relation to IR system output also faces the intermediary with respect to user output.

Basically, three different kinds of information requirements may exist, depending on the cognitive conditions of the user in the actual problem-solving or ASK situation:

(1) Verificative or locational information problems, i.e. the user wants to verify or locate items — e.g. some specific articles. Characteristic bibliographic data — e.g. source, pages, author or title — are in this case known to the user. In other words, the conceptual KS contain the hard data necessary to express the required piece of potential information, i.e. the user is in Taylor's stage 3.

(2) Conscious topical information problems, i.e. the user wants to clarify, review or pursue aspects of known subject matter. The KS contain the concepts and terms necessary to express the required potential information, as in Taylor's stage 3.

(3) Muddled topical information problems, i.e. the user wants to explore some new concepts or concept relations outside known subject matter. For instance, a scientist wants to trace analogous theories and possible solutions applied in other disciplines and he/she has no real idea of how to express the problem. The conceptual KS are weak (or muddled) or non-existent with respect to the required potential information. The user is in Taylor's stage 1/2.

In theory, the label effect may appear in type 3, rarely in type 2 and never in type 1. In practice however, the effect is common in the case of both types 2 and 3 — as demonstrated by Brooks et al. (1984) among others.

The following typical example from a dialogue protocol's initial phase demonstrates both a specific communicative behaviour (an interruption), certain expectations of the system ('I have now been.'), and the difficulty of expressing a problem. The sample is from the Danish investigations (Ingwersen, 1982). The 'real' information problem is:

Literature concerning *identities of Boolean alebra* in *a form suitable* for *application* to *design* and *repair* of *circuits* in *computers.*

Emphasized terms are important concepts defining the problem.
The user's initial request formulation:

(*At the desk*) 'Yes, I am looking for err.... *Boolean algebra...and. or logic algebra* and uhmmm I have now been in [???]...*Philosophy'*
[*???*]=*Insertion by information specialist:* 'Would you please repeat that?'

In practice, even type 1 problems may take the form of a label. This depends again on the actual expectations. Some of these barrier-creating factors may carry less weight when the intermediary (or system) is familiar to the inquirer, for instance when end users and the same information specialist work together daily in connection with a project.

In general, however, each intermediary, whether human or computerized, as well as IR system(s) faces information requirements which, to an unpredictable degree, are formulated in the form of 'labels'. Consequently, the tasks of the intermediary are:

(i) to determine the type of information requirement being dealt with, and
(ii) to interview the user back to the original problem on the basis of the correct type.

Obviously, the intermediary must use different interviewing techniques with respect to the two tasks. In task (i), one may propose the interview pertaining to types 2 and 3 (the topical requirement types) per default, but including questions or hints that may lead to the first (verificative) type. This may possibly be pursued more easily by means of a computer interview (menu-driven?) than by human negotiation, owing to the dominant role of computerized systems, to which we already are accustomed. Inquisitorial questions by human mediators often create severe communicative barriers. The second form of interview (ii) is discussed in more detail in section 4.3.

4.3 Investigations of the intermediary role
In cases where no intermediary exists between system and inquirer, the determining factor in IR success is the quality and structure of the knowledge in the model of the IR system. Thus, in Fig. 5 the centre would be replaced by the user side. Because contemporary systems rely on prompts that must be activated by the client throughout the retrieval processes, 'muddled' information requirements can be solved only by 'intermediary'-like individuals. They at least know how to search. Typical 'end users', casual users and 'laymen' will meet obstacles and may not be able to perform a qualitatively successful retrieval (section 3.2). The crucial problems or limitations of the intermediary in IR are to:

(a) Understand the user's ASK, forming a picture of it by means of interviewing and learning, i.e.
— to define the type of information requirement
— to grasp the formalized or conscious need
— to form a picture of it using conceptual KS
(b) Analyse the current IR situation and the setting of the IR system(s), i.e.
— to define the most effective kinds of setting structures to apply strategically, by use of IR knowledge (experience):
— to select the IR system(s) and databases that suit the planned strategy;
— to modify or change the strategy in accordance with initial feedback from systems, applying cognitive IR structures to learn about the involved system(s) and files.
(c) create representations of conceptual structures of large-scale systems in relation to the required subject area, to form part of its own conceptual KS, i.e.
— tactically to apply search concepts — identical to or modifications of concepts embedded in the picture of the need — using both IR and conceptual knowledge;
— to modify or change search tactics, as suggested by Bates (1979), by learning about the conceptual structures embedded in searched database(s) using both IR and conceptual KS.
(d) link interactively via dialogue the picture (eventually modified by the client during previous steps) and the representation, presenting potential information to the user, i.e.
— to assure consistency — not necessarily a perfect match — between the conceptual structures in the picture of the ASK, the search outcome in form of representations and potential information, as well as the client's formulated ASK;
— to check WHY, if certain structures in outcome are out of context in relation to the 'formalized need', i.e. ascertain reasons for failing to grasp the formalized need (or the problem situation).

This sequence of performance steps worked through by the intermediary mechanism may be formally distinct. However, real retrieval situations involve mingling, subtleties and loops during steps (a) to (d).

In addition to the label effect described above, several recent investigations of the intermediary functions have produced findings highly relevant to both training programmes and design. The main concerns have been the study of human interview or dialogue characteristics, mental processes and information search procedures. Belkin (1982a,b) and other UK teams (Brooks et al. 1984) have concentrated on the pre-search online negotiation, i.e. stage (a) above. Several Danish teams have investigated both the pre-search stage and the search procedures, focusing on stages (a) to (d); for example, childrens' ASK models and searching (Wanting 1984) and adults factual search and ASK patterns in traditional library settings (Ingwersen

1982). Online fiction retrieval is currently being studied by Pejtersen (1984) in real life contexts. Although the above mentioned studies deal with fairly different information environments, user groups and information requirements, the results demonstrate a very high degree of consistency. The research methods used range from computer recordings of search patterns, to observations and interviews as well as tape recordings and 'thinking aloud' techniques. The consistency of the results suggests that the application of these empirical methods is valid. For a discussion of the different methods, see Ingwersen and Pejtersen (1986).

Belkin uses university students as subjects and information specialists as intermediaries; Ingwersen and Pejtersen study public library clients and librarians. In all projects, the users belong to the typical 'end user' or 'laymen' groups which present their own requirements. These are 'conscious' and 'muddled' types with emphasis on the former.

The Belkin/Ingwersen objectives are of supplementary nature. The first attemps to find possible structural dialogue patterns or junctions concerned with the users' and intermediaries' problem situation, subject knowledge, goals and beliefs, as well as reasons for requiring information. The second investigates the interview situation explicitly concerned with the conceptual part of the subject requirement through the entire search process. The results are interesting from a cognitive point of view and may be applied in further investigations dealing with natural language man–machine dialogues, design of IR expert systems and knowledge transfer.

4.3.1 Interviewing and searching
The following resumé of findings may be useful with respect to interviewing situations concerned with definition of ASKs.

A major problem in establishing a fruitful dialogue is whether the intermediary believes or does not believe he understands the information requirement expressed in the initial user statements (the label). A strong conviction that he understands the need may make it difficult for the user to correct the intermediary by communicative regulatory behaviour such as filled pauses and insertions. The impact of a misleading label is devastating for the IR outcome. The questions (Q) asked by the intermediary depend on the conceptual KS. Open Q are rarely posed to clients, although they might reveal data useful to the intermediary. Closed and leading closed Q are used instead. When the intermediary really possesses conceptual KS in relation to a need, closed Q are used to confirm and delimit the intial picture of the information problem. Here, one might suggest applying open questions, since new items within the user's answers probably may match some KS in the intermediary conceptual structures. The open questions may follow a pattern similar to that suggested by Kearsley (1976), operating on the 'wh' words, i.e. 'why', 'what for', 'where', etc.

Questions leading to the assessment of the kind of problem-solving lying behind information needs may reveal very relevant data on clients' goals and subject knowledge. From the Danish studies one may observe that user answers frequently take the form of situational classification of concepts, including highly relevant relations to processes or working situations, often containing common concepts linked to more special/scientific terms.

However, the human intermediary should use closed Q, e.g. 'Is it (the label) something like this (a concept)?', when the first user statements make it apparent that he does not possess sufficient conceptual knowledge. This serves to make the user contextualize, whereby closed Q have nearly similar effects as open Q.

Leading Q, e.g. 'So, this is perhaps applied mathematics', should be posed to make the user affirm or disprove. One problem seems to be the rather broad conceptual level on which the dialogue take place, inhibiting specification of concepts. A contributing factor is the fact that human intermediaries tend to make use of not well understood, but valid and specific, concepts (the problem of perception and loss of data, section 2.1). The suggestion is to make the intermediary store such unknown concepts deliberately, for instance on paper or in a computer, for later use in the search process (this is rarely done!). Computers have the well-known advantage over humans in that they do not forget and they can recall 'unknown', but automatically stored, words or relations instantaneously.

The overall problem regarding open questions, with respect to all types of intermediaries, is the tendency toward overload of exchanged potential information, often resulting in a loss of valid and recognized concepts. This situation may explain the use of double questions, e.g. an open question immediately followed by a leading closed one. Although a client may display confusion as to which question to answer, this manner of questioning has a reverse positive effect: the closed Q exemplifies explicitly the mode of answer, warning the client against delivering too much context, or telling him to maintain a certain categorization level.

Several modes of searching seem to exist, from which the so-called 'open search' displays the best results. This mode is characterized by an heuristic IR process in which the intermediary is concerned with extending his conceptual KS from the beginning. The intermediary is open to new information from the environment, i.e. systems and client. The open mode is determined by factors such as working environment, IR knowledge and experience (previous searches), motives and expectations regarding IR systems. It is interesting to observe that search strategies and interviewing are applied differently, according to the intermediary's aim in the IR process: interviewing is, to a certain degree, used to define the information need. Simultaneously, searching is used to obtain knowledge in order to understand a requirement beyond conceptual range from the start. Often, this understanding or perception of a need is achieved via concepts or relations which act as clues. Later in the process, the interview and search routines change in order to retrieve the required information.

Intermediaries adhering to the open mode draw upon both their own conceptual KS and external KS to a greater extent than when using other search modes. This is also true in the use of search concepts. In online IR situations one may observe the impact of the existing simple IR feedback mechanisms, for instance Zoom mentioned previously in section 4.1.

Firstly, they may be used to help the searcher define his problem; secondly (often simultaneously) they may be used to specify or modify search strategy or tactics. Associative models geared to information specialists or implemented in inanimate intermediaries may serve as a means of structuralizing need formulations deriving from conscious types of information problems. Such models have been applied to IR training programmes in Denmark (Ingwersen *et al.* 1980). They are in principle based on situational case grammar, adhering to indexing systems and linguistic approaches suggested by Coates (1983) and Fillmore (1968).

However, such models were designed and applied only for search purposes. Similar models might be built-in in future intermediaries, the advantage being that a few terms (e.g. the label) can in all probability be placed in specific roles whereby related terms are traceable via structured conversations and/or associations. The models function like puzzles and incorporate both situational and categorial relations. Roles are action, agent, instrument, preliminary object (part of whole), principal object with properties, secondary object (reason), and location including time. The more roles associated with grasped terms, the greater the chance for valid contextualization and conceptual disambiguation. For example, 'cars' may be principal object in both 'production of cars' and 'car driving', but agents, actions, locatons, etc. are different. By defining the proper roles, one may have an idea about to which area the information need belongs and where to search: in information systems on 'manufacture' or 'transportation', two quite different areas to search.

The browsing approach, suggested very recently by Bates, (1986) may point in another direction and serve, especially, the 'muddled' type of information requirement. It is worth noting, that the common pattern in search and negotiation in IR involves continuous search interviewing and parallel searching processes. One ought therefore to advise information researchers to abandon the concept of 'pre-search' interview and concentrate on the 'search interview', in which the former plays only a small part. The pre-search concept tends to split up the intermediary's simultaneous searcher and interviewer roles solely for reasons of online access costs.

Despite the problems surrounding pre-search, very interested research has been produced, especially by Atherton (1981). An extensive review of projects and results has recently been published by Auster (1983), including ones dealing with the importance of non-verbal behaviour and research methods.

4.4 TYPES OF INTERMEDIARY MECHANISMS

We can observe that active learning processes as well as communication in natural language, concept interpretations and modifications play key roles throughout the IR stages (a) to (d), section 4.3.

In the case of computerized intermediaries introduced between client and IR systems' structures — whether forming part of a system mainframe or a microcomputer placed at a user's disposal — the principal performance issues are similar to those of humans. Fig. 6 outlines the kind of computerized intermediaries — or human intermediary skills — one might recommend for design or training in concordance with two basic groups of factors:

(1) type of information requirement, as discussed in section 4.2;
(2) level of client's knowledge structures when requiring information, i.e. the actual level of IR and conceptual KS at the event of approaching an IR system as outlined in section 3.2.

KNOWLEDGE LEVEL – SEARCHER:	TYPE OF INFORMATION REQUIREMENT		
	Type 1 VERIFICATIVE CKS exists	Type 2 CONSCIOUS CKS exists	Type 3 MUDDLED No CKS
"ELITE" +IR +CKS	1. NONE	2. NONE (SUPPORT A¹)	3. ------------ ------> 6.
"INTERMD" +IR –CKS	4. NONE	5. ------------ ----> 2.	6. SUPPORT A
"END–USER" –IR +CKS	7. SUPPORT B	8. SUPPORT B	9. ------------ ------> 12.
"LAYMAN" –IR –CKS	10. ------------ ----> 7.	11. ------------ ----> 8.	12. SUPPORT C

Explanation:		
CKS	:	Conceptual Knowledge Structures.
NONE	:	No intermediary needed.
------> 6.:		Logically, the case doesn't exist, see the case number referred to.
(SUPPORT)	:	May assist, but not necessary.
SUPPORT A	:	DIALOGUE and CONCEPTUAL SUPPORTER
SUPPORT B	:	DIALOGUE and IR SUPPORTER
SUPPORT C	:	COMPLETE IR CUSTOMER SUPPORTER (CIRCUS)

Fig. 6 — Types of intermediary mechanisms or skills.

The figure demonstrates three quite different intermediary types including one variation needed for searcher support according to his/her state of knowledge and information requirement. We assume that the intermediary mechanism, in all relevant cases, has filtered out the type of information requirement before trying to cope with the actual contents of the need behind a label. In certain boxes in the table no intermediary is needed, as the searcher possesses sufficient KS. For instance, an 'elite' or 'intermediary-like' searcher does not need an intermediary concerned with problems of the verificative type: boxes 1 and 4. In box 2, the retrieval may be improved or speeded up by introducing a mechanism, a variation of the Conceptual Supporter described below. However, the supporting role is not mandatory. In several cases, or boxes, the searcher type with the indicated type of requirement cannot exist. For example, when pursuing a muddled need, an 'elite' searcher becomes an 'intermediary' type. Conversely, a 'layman' becomes a typical 'end-user' when posing a conscious information problem to an intermediary, since he possess sufficient conceptual KS.

Regardless of the type of mechanism used, its main components consist of the different knowledge structures and user–model facilities outlined in Fig. 5. Preferably it should function on parallel processing. Since the mechanism is mandatory only in some, but not in all, cases and because the two advanced searcher groups may find it awkward being forced to use it in relatively easy search situations, it may be advisable to introduce an interruption possibility in the mechanism. Socio-psychological experience recommends this alternative. However, for the sake of less experienced searcher groups and in the case of more complex requirements, the mechanism ought to function per default.

The Conceptual Supporter — Supporter A (and A^1) — is aimed at searchers with IR knowledge. Its goal is to grasp and clarify the information problem deriving for example from a label, and to support the searcher in the conceptual translation/conversion of the defined problem into IR systems' prefered vocabulary and concept relations. See also points (a) and (c), section 4.3, and Fig. 7 below. Its means are primarily its own conceptual knowledge (knowledge base), supplied with potential information acquired from external sources (e.g. remote databases or knowledge bases). Its IR knowledge structures act as a hidden sub-supporter in order to make the supplementary knowledge available by selection and searching of relevant sources .

The difference between Conceptual Supporter A and A^1 lies in two circumstances:

(1) the dialogue/interview form;
(2) the use of conceptual models.

Supporter A must actively help the searcher in defining his information problem via open questions, in the first place by clarifying the goals, intentions and reasons for the searcher's requirement, and secondly by aiming at the subject. The mechanism must learn about the problem and produce conceptual alternatives from which the searcher may chose terms and need formulations: for instance, by applying browsing facilities (perhaps resulting in fruitful serendipity effects), followed by types of conceptual mapping and/or structured models to be filled out by the searcher. See, for example, the Association model and question models as suggested by Saracevic (1978). Since one may expect combinations of every-day language, scientific concepts and more or less broad categories as well as situational relations to appear, the supporting mechanism should remember and employ terms and term relations previously used by other searchers.

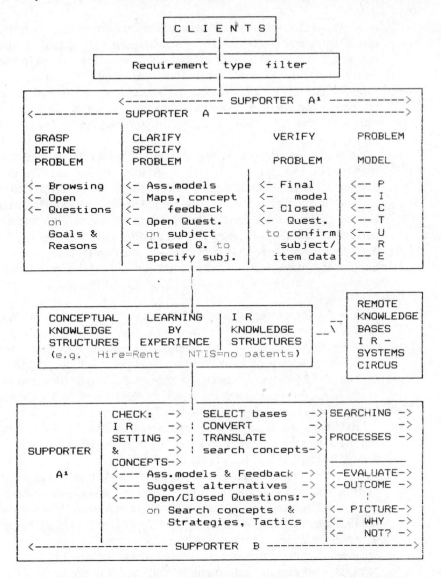

Fig. 7 — Model of the Complete IR Customer Supporter. Supporter C=CIRCUS, including a Conceptual and an IR Supporter, Supporter A & B. Explanation: ←=questions/feedback to client →=questions/feedback to systems.

With this continuous 'learning by experience' mechanism, it may link rarely used, new or non-preferred terms, e.g. synonyms, to concepts preferred by systems. See, for instance, the 'ABC'–'XYZ' example in section 2.1, in which the link between 'ABC' and 'XYZ' becomes established for future use.

Supporter A^1 limits its interview to specific questions, open Q to obtain and closed Q to confirm subject contents of a requirement. Alternative conceptual relations answered back may help to disambiguate terms, as may the 'learning by experience' device mentioned in supporter A. In short, one can say that the A^1 supporter uses the second part of supporter A in interviewing and concept verification. A^1 is aimed at persons with a 'conscious' type of information requirement, boxes 2 and 8. Through interviews the client is guided back to the consicious need (see Taylor's stages, section 4.2), while A in addition must support query creation. See Fig. 7.

It is not the purpose of the Conceptual Supporter to perform actual search. For this purpose Supporter A may suggest the use of the IR Supporter, or the advanced client may perform the search himself.

The IR Supporter or supervisor is needed in boxes 7 and 8, owing to the lack of IR know-how among the searchers involved. The objective is to perform retrieval by analysing the IR situation and settings of IR systems as well as converting search concepts and modifying tactics. In addition, Supporter B may select and search databases and check consistency between its conception of the problem and the search outcome. See also points (b) to (d), section 4.3.

The IR Supporter is capable of acquiring information in the case of verificative or conscious types of information problem. Consequently, it may use the Conceptual Supporter A^1 as sub-supporter, or routine, to establish knowledge of the real requirement possibly hidden behind a label. In box 8 Supporter A^1 must be activated entirely, whereas only the verificative and some specifying interview elements of A^1 are applied to the rather simple retrieval problem in box 7.

By means of a dialogue or interview with the client and interaction with remote systems, with IR Supporter attempts to elicit the most relevant search concepts. It attempts to translate search structures into source structures in relevant IR systems. In doing so, it may utilize some of the interview features mentioned in Supporter A^1, namely those dealing with concept interpretation, e.g. the 'learning by experience' device. In addition, the IR Supporter must inform the client about search strategies, application of useful databases or knowledge bases. Strategical and tactical alternatives are presented to the inquirer. In parallel, it searches systems that are judged relevant, and presents intermediate/final output in the form of traditional contextual data (records, pictures, pieces of full text, etc.) and/or in the form of representative, contextual and conceptual structures. For example, it may apply models, maps or frequency ranking (e.g. like Zoom) to present (alternative) concept relations and interpretations to be applied in further searching (in contrast to Supporter A in which such models are used to define and clarify a problem), as well as probabilistic parameters and threshold manipulation. The IR Supporter must avoid the temptation known to human intermediaries and traditional IR systems of altering the 'real need' or requirement issue when first established, in order to satisfy the systems!

Finally it should store knowledge about the consistency and validity of the intermediate/final search outcome. The evaluative results have interest for future use as a kind of 'meta-search-knowledge'. (For instance: 'NTIS database: do not use for patent searching' — 'Hire=Rent' — 'Retrieval→also Biology aspects'.)

The Complete IR Customer Supporter — CIRCUS — Supporter C in box 12, contains the entire A and B supporting systems — see point (a) through (d), section 4.3, and Fig. 7.

As such, the IR Supporter may be regarded as an 'IR Expert System', while the CIRCUS system is similar to a 'system for experts' as described by Walker (1981), i.e. a system designed for persons searching for 'new ideas and new answers'. Thus, none of the supporters described can be considered ideal expert systems, embodying digested potential information.

It is important to note that the supporting systems in this section are, in the long run, to be designed as systems of a collective, universal nature, placed physically in networks of distributed, linked configurations, drawing upon each other's cognitive structures, and connected to remote IR source systems. The user will not sense the network when accessing the CIRCUS. Hence, the configurations function in the same way as information specialists linked, for example, by phone. They are not intended to serve as dedicated stand-alone front-ends to particular systems, since the quality of a single supporter's own 'image' or 'world knowledge' never may be satisfactory. If a dedicated stand-alone solution is chosen without interlinking intermediary mechanisms, we will again be confronted with a typical retrieval problem: Which dedicated Supporter to access when? However, the filter component Fig. 7, for instance, can be placed on microcomputer software, incorporating communication programs adapted for the CIRCUS operations.

One may note that users of expert systems might eventually face problems similar to those encountered by users of bibliographic databases. At present expert systems are restricted to narrow domains and are not very accessible either. When (supposedly in future) they cover wider, less clearly defined areas and are more numerous and publicly accessible, then people will have the problem of deciding which expert system to use. Therefore, the lessons of cognitive studies of IR may have relevance for those who hope to see a very wide-spread use of expert systems.

5. CONCLUDING REMARKS

A fair amount of experimental contributions have already been made to design retrieval supervisor systems containing parts of the CIRCUS mechanism outlined above. The IIDA system by Meadow *et al.* (1982) is geared toward novice searchers, 'end users' or 'laymen' in the present context, it instructs them in search techniques, and is also able to assist in searching. The IIDA system works with command language translation and database structures, i.e. assisting clients in accessing heterogeneous System Settings, as does the CONIT system by Marcus and Rentjes (1981). Other very interesting and promising search supporters are currently under development, for instance the Cancer Therapy IR Expert System by Pollit (1986) which aims to assist an 'end-user' type client in retrieving information within a limited subject area. It presupposes a 'conscious' type of information problem-solving. The HYPERCat experiments by LibLab in Sweden may also conribute valuable design information relating to problem-solving of the more verificative type of IR tasks (Hjerppe, 1986).

As stated by Smith (1986), the general short-term trends seem to be the design of alternative interfaces for existing, traditional 'best match' systems, making them more powerful tools for trained searchers as well as supporting at least some level of querying by end users. One may view the IR Supporter — Supporter B — as a model outlined in this light. The Conceptual Supporter and the CIRCUS mechanism as described here may be seen as long-term challenges. If information specialists and librarians are able to ask themselves AI-type questions about how they use their knowledge, and how they can model the knowledge in their field in the form of an understanding system (Schank & Childers, 1984) they may achieve improvements on the IR front. This chapter is a contribution to the attainment of this goal.

REFERENCES

Atherton, P. A. Cochrane (1981) *Tasks performed by online searchers in presearch interviews: A report of the Presearch Interview Project.* Syracuse, N.Y., School of Information Studies.

Auster, E. (1983) User satisfaction with online negotiation interview: Contemporary concern in traditional perspective. *Ref.Q.* **Fall** 47–59.

Bartlett, F. C. (1932) *Remembering.* Cambridge, Cambridge University Press.

Bates, M. J. (1979) Idea tactics, *JASIS,* **30,** 280–289.

Bates, M. J. (1986) An exploratory paradigm for online information retrieval. In: Brookes, B. C. (ed), *Intelligent information systems for the information society. Proceedings from the IRFIS 6 Conference, Frascati, 16–18 September, 1985.* To be published by North-Holland.

Belkin, N. (1977) *Linguistic and cognitive models of information and state of knowledge.* London, British Library (BLRDD Report, 5381).

Belkin, N. (1978) Information concepts for information science. *J. of Doc.,* **34,** 55–85.

Belkin, N. *et al.* (1982a) ASK for information retrieval, part I. *J. of Doc.,* **38,** 61–71.

Belkin, N. *et al.* (1982b) ASK for information retrieval, part II. *J. of Doc.,* **38,** 145–164.

Boulding, K. E. (1971) *The image.* Michigan, University of Michigan Press.

Brookes, B. C. (1977) The developing cognitive viewpoint in information science. In: De Mey, M. (ed), *International Workshop on the Cognitive Viewpoint.* Ghent, University of Ghent, pp. 195–203.

Brooks, H. M., Daniels, P. J. & Belkin, N. (1984) Using problem structures for driving human–computer dialogues. Private communication.

Coates, E. J. (1983) *BSO referral test.* FID/BSO Panel. Final Report. FID.

De Mey, M. (1980) The relevance of the cognitive paradigm for information science. In: Harbo, O. & Kajberg, L. (eds) *Theory and application of information research. Proceedings of the SIRE Conference, Copenhagen, 1977*. London, Mansell, pp. 48–61.

Deunette, J. (1983) *Survey of UK online users: A report on current online usage*. London, The Online Information Centre, ASLIB.

Fillmore, C. J. (1968) Case for case. In: Bach, E. & Harns, L. G. (eds) *Universals in linguistic theory*. New York, Holt, pp. 1–88.

Hjerppe, R. (1986) The HYPERCAT system: a new development in cataloging. In: Brookes, B. C. (ed) *Intelligent information systems for the information soceity. Proceedings from the IRFIS 6 Conference, Frascati, 16–18 September, 1985*. To be published by North-Holland.

Howard, H. (1982) Measures that discriminate among online searchers with different training and experience. *Onl. Rev.* **6** (4) 315–327.

Hutcheson, S. & Laver, J. (1972) *Communication in fact to face interaction: selected readings*. Harmondsworth, Penguin.

Ingwersen, P. *et al.* (1980) *Informationsprocesser*. Copenhagen, Royal School of Librarianship. (In Danish, English title: Information processes.)

Ingwersen, P. (1982) Search procedures in the library analysed from the cognitive point of view. *J. of Doc.* **38** (3) 165–191.

Ingwersen, P. (1984a) Psychological aspects of information retrieval. *Soc. Sc. Inf. Stud.* **4** 83–95.

Ingwersen, P. (1984b) A cognitive view of three selected online search facilities. *Onl. Rev.* **8** (5) 465–492.

Ingwersen, P. & Pejtersen, A. M. (1986) User requirements: Empirical research and information systems design. In: Ingwersen, P. *et al.* (eds) *Information technology and information use. Proceedings of NORDINFDO Conference on Information Technology as a Tool for Information Use, Copenhagen, May, 8–10, 1985*. To be published by Taylor-Graham, London.

Johnson-Laird, P. N. & Wason, P. C. (1977) *Thinking: Readings in cognitive science: an introduction to the scientific study of thinking*. Cambridge, Cambridge University Press.

Kearsley, G. P. (1976) Questions and question-asking in verbal discourse: a cross-disciplinary view. *J. of Psyc. Ling Res.* **4** (5) 355–375.

Klasén, L. (1982) *Online använding. DFI Rapport*. Stockholm, DFI, ISSN 0349–9324, pp. 80–128. (English title: Online use.)

Kuhn, T. S. (1970) *The structure of scientific revolutions*, 2nd edn. Chicago, University of Chicago Press.

Lancaster, F. W. (1986) The impact of technology on the use of information sources. In: Ingwersen, P. (ed) *Information technology and information use. proceedings from NORDINFO Conference on Information Technology as a Tool for Information Use, May, 8–10, 1985*. To be published by Taylor-Graham, London.

Library Association. Current research in libary and information science. Database no. 61 on 'Dialog Inf. Syst. London, LA.

Lindsay, P. H. & Norman, D. A. (1977) *Human information processing: an introduction to psychology.* New York, Academic press.

Luria, A. R. (1976) *Cognitive development: its cultural and social foundations.* London: Harvard University Press.

Mackay, D. M. (1960) What makes the question? *The Listener,* **63,** 789–790.

Marcus, R. S. & Rentjes, J. F. (1981) A translating computer interface for end-user operation of heterogeneous retrieval systems. *JASIS* **32** (4) 287–317.

Meadow, C. T. *et al.* (1982) A computer intermediary for interactive database searching. *JASIS* **33** 325–332 (Part I), 357–364 (Part II).

Minsky, M. (1975) A framework for representing knowledge. In: Winstow, P. (ed) *The psychology of computer vision.* New York, MacGraw-Hill, pp. 211–277.

Pejtersen, A. M. (1984) Design of a computer-aided user-system dialogue based on an analysis of users' search behaviour. *Soc. Sc. Inf. Stud.,* no. 4, 167–183.

Pollit, A. S. (1986) AI and information retrieval: tackling some of the problems of naive end-user search specification and formulation. In: Brookes, B. C. (ed) *Intelligent information systems for the information society. Proceedings from IRFIS 6 Conference, Frascati, 16–18 September, 1985.* To be published by North-Holland.

Robertson, S. E., Maron, M. E. & Cooper, W. S. (1982) Probability of relevance: a unification of two competing models of document retrieval. *Info. Tech. Res. Dev.* **1** 1–21.

Salton, G. & McGill, J. M. (1983) *Introduction to modern information retrieval.* New York, McGraw-Hill.

Samuelson, K., Borko, H. & Amay, G. (1977) *Information systems and networks.* Amsterdam, North-Holland.

Saracevic, T. (1978) Problems of question analysis in information retrieval. *Proc. ASIS 41th. An. Meet. 15,* pp. 281–283.

Schank, R. C. & Abelson, R. P. (1977) *Scripts, plans goals and understanding: an inquiring into human knowledge structures.* Hillsdale, N. Y., Erlbaum.

Schank, R. C. & Childers, P. G. (1984) *The cognitive computer: on language, learning, and Artificial Intelligence.* Reading, MA, Addison-Wesley.

Smith, Linda C. (1980) Artificial intelligence applications in information. *An. Rev. Info. Sc. & Tech.* **15** 67–105.

Smith, Linda C. (1986) Knowledge-based systems — artificial intelligence and human factors. In: Ingwersen, P. (ed) *Information technology and information use. Proceedings from NORDINFO Conference on Information Technology as a Tool for Information Use, May, 8–10, 1985.* To be published by Taylor-Graham.

Taylor, R. S. (1968) Question-negotiation and information seeking in libraries. *Coll. & Res. Lib.* **29** 178–194.

Vickery, A. (1984) An intelligent interface for online interaction. *J. of Inf. Sc.* **97**–18.

Vygotsky, L. S. (1962) *Thought and language.* Boston: MIT Press.

Walker, D. E. (1981) The organisation and use of information. *JASIS* **32** (5) 347–363.

Wanting, B. (1984) How do children ask questions in children's libraries?- : concepts of visual and auditory perception and language expression. *Soc. Sc. Inf. Stud.,* no. 4, 217–234.

Weizenbaum, J. (1984) *Computer power and human reason: from judgement to calculation,* new edn. Harmondsworth, Penguin.

Wormell, I. (1985) Subject access project: SAP: improved subject retrieval for monographic publications. Doctoral thesis, Lund University.

9

A cognitive model for intelligent information systems

Mildred L. G. Shaw and **Brian R. Gaines**, Department of Computer Science, Calgary University, Calgary Alberta, Canada T2N 1N4

1. INTRODUCTION

We are in era of rapid change in information systems technology. The information processing systems of yesterday are becoming the knowledge processing systems of today. Software and hardware developments are proceeding at such a pace that it has become impossible to keep up-to-date with the basic technology. In addition, human–computer interface (HCI) and knowledge-based system (KBS) developments are also occurring so rapidly that the relevant literature is exploding. The specifiers and designers of intelligent information systems, the libraries of the future, have to contend with this world of change and make reasonable projections about technologies and user expectations over the next decade. This chapter provides one framework for such projections, a cognitive science model of the user community and the role of information technology within it.

Fifth generation knowledge-based systems

Knowledge has always been significant to our civilization. However, in the past fifty years this significance has grown to a level where it is coming to dominate other socio-economic factors (Marschak 1968). Machlup (1962) drew attention to the major and growing role of information services in the US economy and estimated that in 1958 knowledge production accounted for 29 percent of the US GNP. Porat (1977) made a detailed analysis of the 1967 US national-income-and-accounts and estimated that the information sector accounted for 46 percent of GNP. Drucker (1968) took this up as a major issue in his book, *The Age of Discontinuity*, and estimated that by 1975 the knowledge sector would account for 50 percent of US GNP.

More dramatic presentations of the socio-economic consequences have been made by Toffler (1980) in his book, *The third Wave*, by Dizard (1982) in this book, *The Information Age*, and by many other information scientists and social commentators. Bell (1973) has given a thoughtful economic analysis on his book, *The Coming of Post-Industrial Society*, and Wojciechowski (1983) has analysed the increasing significance of the knowledge construct to human society and emphasized the importance of understanding and managing the knowledge ecology. These global models of a changing human civilisation emphasize the increasing dependence of the human race on the effective dissemination, use and extension of the store of knowledge. Our over-crowded planet with its diminishing resources can support the still-increasing human population only because we have the knowledge to make efficient use of the resources available.

From the perspective of a shift to a knowledge ecomomy, the explosive growth of computer technology from the 1940s may be seen not as a cause of the information society but rather as providing a necessary infrastructure through which to support it. Computer technology has advanced at a rate that is extremely high and has been sustained over such a period that it can be seen as a series of revolutions rather than as technology evolution. Between 1959 and 1980 the number of active devices on a circuit chip increased from one to one million; by 1990 it will reach one thousand million (Robinson 1984). Over the same period information storage costs have declined to the level where it is now possible to store the *Encyclopaedia Britannica* on an optical disk costing a few dollars in a drive that is coupled to a personal computer and costs a few hundred dollars (Gaines & Shaw 1984b). Every eight years computer technology has advanced in performance parameters by the order of one hundred times (Gaines & Shaw 1985b). Five such periods of advance may be distinguished historically, and we are now in the sixth, termed the **fifth generation**. For comparison the aircraft industry has seen only one such comparable advance in its 75-year history.

The technological culmination of the socio-economic pressure to generate technologies adequate to support a knowledge-based civilization may be upon us now in fifth generation computing systems (FGCS). The Japanese initiative in 1981 of scheduling a development program for FGCS (Motooka 1982, ICOT 1983) triggered off a wave of similar activities around the world (HMSO 1982, Steier 1983). The work at ICOT in Tokyo is projected to integrate advances in very large scale integration, database management systems, artificial intelligence, and the human computer interface into a new range of computers that are closer to people in thier communication and knowledge processing capabilities (Fuchi 1984, Gaines 1984a,b). The major change expected in this generation will be a shift from information technology to knowledge technology with FGCS providing knowledge bases that are readily accessed by people with no specialist computer skill and are integrated into all aspects of the operation of society.

The impact of early FGCS is already apparent in the rapid growth in the past five years of an expert systems industry concerned with encoding the high-level knowledge and decision-making skills of key professionals and making them widely available through computer systems (Gevarter 1983). Initially these systems were expensive and primarily of interest to the petrochemical mineral exploration and pharmaceutical industries where expert knowledge in explorative research is essential to risk-reduction in high-cost ventures. Declining computer costs have made expert systems significant for more routine knowledge and skill dissemination, for example in industries where the retirement of skilled employees is a major problem (Hayes–Roth 1984).

Sixth generation knowledge science

Understanding the nature of knowledge is a topic for several branches of philosophy (Gaines & Shaw 1983). In the context of applications it is part of the philosophy of science, of technology, of the professions and of practical reasoning. The practical tools are those of logic, of which only the logic underlying mathematics is very well developed. Computer scientists, particularly those working on FGCS are aware of the important role of logic in knowledge -based systems and are becoming increasingly aware of the philosphical problems involved. Philosophers also are becoming increasingly interested in the role of computing as an operational domain for the expression and exploration of philosophical problems.

Understanding the role of knowledge in an application is a topic for the scientific discipline and profession associated with that application. Every discipline and every profession will become increasingly involved with the knowledge-based technology of FGCS. This universality presents major problems in the social-economic management of knowledge technology. There is no natural forum for information collection and dissemination. There is no single discipline that can serve as a focus for most, let alone all, activities. Computer science is only now becoming well-established and is primarily concerned with the development of the technological infrastructure, the scaffolding. Each of the professional disciplines has its own contribution to make to the encoding of the knowledge that underlies it for dissemination through computing systems. Each of the scientific disciplines has the possibility of a new impetus to its own development through the use of knowledge technology. The social sciences and the humanities have dual roles to play in that they can make major use of knowledge technology in thier own development and are also important to the understanding of its impact on our society and civilization.

This need for cross-disciplinary interchange has been recognized in the sixth generation computing system (SGCS) development proposal put forward in the report, 'Promotion of R&D on Electronics and Information Systems that may Complement or Substitute for Human Intelligence', from the Subcommittee on Artifical Intelligence of The Council on Aerospace and Electronics Technology in Tokyo (STA 1985). The Council was asked by the Ministry of Science and Technology in January 1983 to report on AI in these terms. It formed a sub-committee that met twelve times in preparing this report, used the term *knowledge science* for its subject matter, and reported in March 1985. The English translation comprises some 18,000 words. It is reported that MITI has agreed to fund at least part of the SGCS proposal with $32 million over 10 years commencing mid-1986 as an extension of ICOT's activities (Chapman 1985).

Four objectives are specified for promoting knowledge science:

innovations in frontier high technologies; economic and cultural advancements; contributions to the explosion of human potential; and establishing a foundation for creative science. The proposed research program moves outside the boundaries of computing technology and requires inter-disciplinary interaction between computing science and physiology, psychology, linguistics and logic. The report analyses the state of the art in these four relevant sciences and proposes the development of eight technologies based on them for application in four major areas (Fig. 1). The application areas do not differ from those of the FGCS program but the path specified to them is far more foundational.

"Innovations In Frontier High Technologies"
"Societal, Economic And Cultural Advancements"
"Expansion Of Human Potential"
"Foundation For Creative Science"

SCIENCE	TECHNOLOGY	APPLICATIONS
Physiology *Brain Models Cognition Implementation*	Pattern Recognition / Cognition	**Expert Systems**
Psychology *Understanding Intelligence Man-machine interface*	Learning / Problem Solving	**Machine Translation Systems**
Linguistics *Speech Syntax Semantics Psycholinguistics*	Natural Language / Image Processing	**Intelligent CAD/CAM Systems**
Logic *New systems Complex facts Induction*	Speech Recognition / Man-Machine Interface	**Intelligent Robot Systems**

Fig. 1 — The Japanese Sixth Generation Computer System development proposal — knowledge science, technology and applications.

This path through the brain and human sciences to future generation computing was previewed in an interview with Fuchi, the Director of ICOT, when in reply to the question: 'Are you saying that the design of the fifth-generation may be modeled by learning more about the human thinking process?', he answered:

> Yes, we should have more research on human thinking processes, but we already have some basic structures. For more than 2000 years man has tried to find the basic operation of thinking and has established logic. The result is not necessarily sufficient; it's just the one that mankind found. At present we have only one solution — a system like predicate calculus. It is rather similar to the way man thinks. But we need more research. What, really, is going on in our brain? It's a rather difficult problem. (Fuchi *et al.* 1984)

The FGCS program has been targeted on the development of very high-speed deductive reasoning machines using predicate calculus as a knowledge-representation language. However, standard logic bears only a remote resemblance to human reasoning processes (Wason & Johnson-Laird 1972). Modern formal logic was developed as a foundation for mathematics just because mathematical rigor is so foreign to everyday human activity (Mohanty 1982). Causal models may be incapable of encompassing the process of biological systems, and currently we have no formalism in which to express the anticipatory dynamics of living systems (Rosen 1985). What is going on in our brain is certainly a difficult problem, but the development of intelligent information systems demands that we resolve it. The SGCS proposal sets out to do this and makes no detours to avoid using words such as 'intuition, analogy and creativity' in its description of human reasoning capabilities.

Information technology has reached a stage in its development where it is necessary to cross disciplinary boundaries: within information science to integrate technology into knowledge-based systems; and outside information science to achieve an understanding of knowledge processing adequate to apply these systems. The fifth generation computing system development program is aimed at the system integration, and the sixth generation computing system development program is aimed at knowledge science. The remainder of this chapter provides a cognitive science framework for knowledge-based systems which encompasses the social and psychological processes of people as well as similar processes in knowledge-based systems.

2.   SOCIAL FOUNDATIONS OF COGNITIVE SCIENCE

Sociologists and social psychologists have long held that human behaviour, and that of human society, can only be understood in the context of the total social milieu. The individual must be seen as embedded in the life-world consituted by the social processes of other individuals and made explicit through cultural pressures, social norms, language, literature and the total knowledge base accreted by society and stored in variety of media (Schutz and Luckman 1973). In recent years this concept has been extended to the knowledge acquisition itself, and it has been noted that the processes of science can be best understood as social cognitive dynamics (Rubinstein, Laughlin & McManus 1984).

This examination of human cognitive behaviour, the processes of science and the dynamics of knowledge acquisition have led to increasingly formal and operational theories. The sociologist, Luhmann (1979), has used systems theory to formalize the operation of trust and power in organizations, commencing with the survival drive and noting the peculiar problems presented to one individual by the cognitive processes of another. The philosopher, Popper (1968), has noted that knowledge itself forms a world with an ontological status equivalent to that of the physical world, which he terms World 3. Another philosopher, Wojciechowski (1983), has documented the exponential rate of increase of human knowledge, noting that most human problems are now created by that knowledge as well as soluble by it, and proposed a set of laws underlying an ecology of knowledge. The American economist, Machlup (1980, 1982, 1984), has carried our statistical studies of the increasing role of knowledge-based industries in the US economy and highlighted their dominant role from the 1970s onwards.

Whereas the deductive logical inference that underlies the operation of conventional computers is well-understood and well-founded, the inductive inference that underlies human learning is not. Deduction guarantees to take us from valid data to valid inferences, but the inferences are thereby part of the data — no new knowledge is generated. Induction takes us from valid data to models of that data that go beyond it — by predicting data we have not yet observed, and by giving explanations of the data in terms of concepts that are unobservable. Induction generates new knowledge but, as Hume (1739) pointed out over 200 years ago, the process is not deductively valid, and it is a circular argument to claim that it is inductively valid.

Philosophers have continued to debate Hume's arguments and search for justification of the inductive process. Goodman (1973) proposed that we accept the circularity but note that it involves a dynamic equilibrium between data and inference rules: 'A rule is amended if it yields an inference we are unwilling to accept; an inference is rejected if it violates a rule we are unwilling to amend.' Rawls (1971) in his theory of justice terms this a reflective equilibrium. Recently Stich and Nisbett (1984) noted flaws in Goodman's argument and repaired them by proposing that the equilibrium is social not individual: 'a rule of inference is justified if it captures the reflective practice not of the person using it but of the appropriate experts in our society.'

This social formulation of inductive inference is a significant development for intelligent information systems because:

(1) It suggests that the basic cognitive system that should be considered is a social organization, rather than an individual;
(2) It gives an operational model of the notion of expertise and the role it plays in our society, and hence provides formal foundations for expert systems (ESs);

(3) It emphasizes the social nature of expertise and suggests that we should be considering groups of experts rather than individual experts in developing ESs;

(4) It provides an operational model for the growth of knowledge in a society involving the differentiation into 'disciplines' corresponding to the reflective equilibria of different areas of expertise — and hence supports knowledge encompassing the complete process and necessarily crossing disciplinary boundaries;

(5) It provides a model for the role of media in communicating and storing knowledge with a continuity from classical media to present computer-based systems;

(6) The computational models of inductive inference already developed can be applied directly to the social model;

(7) There are links between these models and neurological processes in the brain which begin to give meaning to the role of brain physiology studies in the proposed SGCS program.

The remainder of this chapter sketches the key features of cognitive science based on a social reflective equilibrium, showing how these results arise and give substance to the sixth generation objectives.

3. THE COMMUNAL SCIENTIST

Fig. 2 shows the basic system under consideration, a knowledge-acquiring social organisation which experiences the world and acts upon it. Kelly (1955) proposed a cognitive model of the individual as an anticipatory system making distinctions about the world, which he called 'personal constructs', and recursively building up distinctions about distinctions which are predictive models of the world. His model has been termed that of the individual as a *personal scientist* (PS), (Shaw 1980) and we have extended the terminology to social organizations as *communal scientists* (CSs). The term 'scientist' should be read as meaning 'knowledge acquirer', with no connotations of postive physical science — Kelly's model applies to all the psychological processes of the individual.

The key concept behind Fig. 2 is that the primary goal of living organizations is survival, and this manifests itself in a drive to anticipate the future by modelling the world. Action is accounted for as active anticipation which acts upon the world to change it to make it more predictable and project survival further into the future. In system-theoretic terms the CS is a system using prediction and control to maximise the probability of its continued existence. General models of the structure necessary to such systems have been developed, and the interior of the CS in Fig. 2 shows Klir's (1976) epistomological hierarchy of modeling systems. The system makes distinctions which produce data about experience which it models in such a way as to regenerate the data. At the higher levels this sequence is

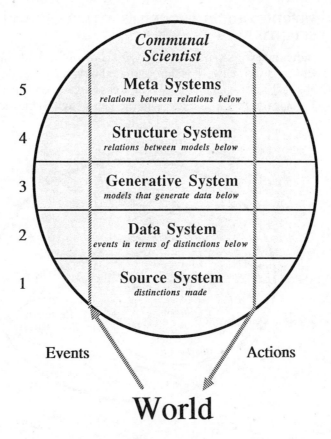

Fig. 2 — Systematic structure of communal scientist as a modeling system, experiencing the world and acting upon it.

applied recursively to the internal models to enable change between model classes and the transfer of models from one class of experience to another.

Gaines (1977) gave a general account of the algorithms for implementing such modelling systems and demonstrated their efficacy with problems of inferring probabilistic models from behavioral data. One side-effect of this account is to introduce two very general control signals: *surprise* flowing up the hierarchy as lower levels cannot account for data; and *preference* flowing down the hierarchy as higher levels attempt to influence the anticipated future. This modelling schema has been shown formally to solve the problem of inductive inference for worlds that conform to certain classes of widely used models, deterministic, linear, probablistic, fuzzy, and so on.

There is physiological and behavioral evidence of the existence within the brain of the two channels of communication shown in Fig. 2 (Tucker & Williamson 1984). The *arousal* system passes surprise upwards to the cortex from the limbic region when unexpected event occur. The *activation* system passes preferences down from the cortex to the motor regions.

4. PSYCHOLOGICAL PROCESSES WITHIN A COMMUNAL SCIENTIST

The individual within society is a cross-section of the modelling hierarchy of Fig. 2. Fig. 3 shows two PSs differentiated within the CS, and also replaces the abstract vocabulary of Fig. 2 in a cognitive science context by giving psychological terms to the levels in the hierarchy (Gaines & Shaw 1981a).

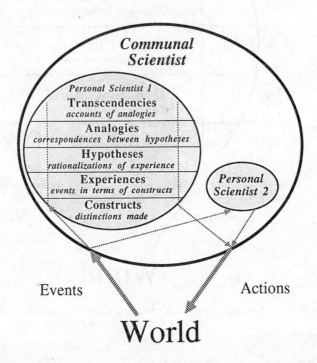

Fig. 3 — Psychological structure of personal scientists within a communal scientist.

An individual is defined in cognitive terms as a psychological process. The brain carrying out this process may be seen as a psychological processor (Pask 1980).

More complex psychological and social structures may also be shown in terms of such concepts by taking into account the possibilities of timesharing, process switching and distributed processing with psychological processors. For example, one person may assume many psychological roles (process switching), whereas a group of people working together may act as a single goal-seeking entity and hence behave as one process (distributed processing). Fig. 4 shows two people, each with two roles, forming a group. The original CS, CS1, and PS1 through PS4, are all psychological processes. Person A and Person B as physical entities are psychological processors.

Symbolic communication is important in co-ordinating psychological processess. In Fig. 4, PS1 and PS2 are shown as having internal communication. PS3 and PS4 are shown not to have such communication and can only coordinate by monitoring one another's actions as events in the world. PS2 and PS3 have external communication corresponding to the use of language.

These concepts are exemplified in more concrete terms in Fig. 5 showing people in a number of roles and groups (Shaw 1985). John has roles as a husband, a sales Vice-President of his company, a backpacker and a fisherman. John uses different constructs when he is in the role of husband from when he is in the role of fisherman, but some of the constructs he uses in the role of fisherman are also used in the role of backpacker and this is shown as overlapping PSs. Anne is John's wife, a mathematician and a golfer. Larry is the technical Vice-President in John's company, and Sue is the production Vice-President. Sometimes John is acting with his wife or colleagues to form group processes that have some constructs that are shared between participants and others that arise from only one of them. For example, John and Anne (and their children) form a nuclear family. This is distributed process which has legal rights, specific behaviour, concepts and language which go beyond those of its sub-processes. The product executive of the company is another distributed process which has authority, responsibility, and behaviour which is unique to the entity and not that of any one of its participants.

5. EXPERTISE AND MEDIA WITHIN A COMMUNAL SCIENTIST

The roles of media are readily modeled within a CS (Shaw & Gaines 1984). Fig. 6 shows Person A interacting with the world through a representational medium such as radio or television. The interaction contrasts with that of Person A interacting directly with the world in that it is only one-way rather than two-way (Gaines & Shaw 1984a). Person A can preceive the world through the medium but not influence it. Representational storage media, such as film or videotape being used by Person C, give similar access that transcends time allowing past events to be experienced but are still one-way. The simulation media based on computer graphics being used by Person D allows two-way access to a simulated world, and as they become more realistic can increasingly replace direct experience (Gaines & Shaw 1985a). Note how Persons C and D have no necessary interaction with the real world. Computer graphic media in intelligent information systems can give access to experience in worlds of simulated reality that may, or may not, model real world events.

The role of an expert may also be modeled within a CS. Person C in Fig. 7 is carrying out a task with help from an expert advisor, Person B who has no other interaction with the task. The role of symbolic media is also shown in that Person A is carrying out the task with broadcast advice from Person B. However, as with representational media, the mediated communication is one-way whereas the direct communication is two-way (Gaines & Shaw 1984a). Some of the problems of knowledge engineering, of transferring knowledge from experts to expert systems, are also apparent in Fig. 7.

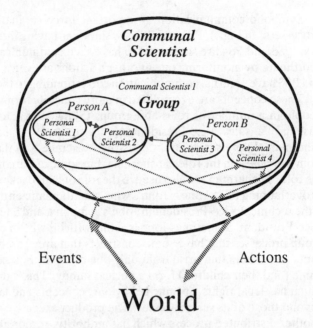

Fig. 4 — Roles and groups as different forms of psychological process within a communal scientist.

PS4 is the processor with the required skill in Person B and has to communicate through PS3, an external language processor, but sometimes this link may be unavailable (Bainbridge 1979). Similarly PS5 requires the skill in Person C and has to be able to communicate internally with a language processor PS6 which itself has to be able to communicate externally with PS3; lack of effective communication on either link will prevent knowledge transfer.

6. PLANET: A CONVERSATIONAL SUPPORT SYSTEM

The CS and PS models apply to the expert system in Fig. 8 as much as they apply to the person, and the structure of the ES can be represented in the inductive system hierarchy of Fig. 2. Fig. 9 shows the feedback processes at different levels of this hierarchy to provide a model for knowledge acquisition in both people and ESs. The levels have been labeled in terms of Hall's (1959) forms of cultural transmission, and the right hand side indicates the way in which knowledge is transferred at each level. Without cultural transmission the only way a task can be learnt is by primitive inductive acquisition based on attempted performance, a slow and uncertain process. The first level of cultural transmision is the *informal* where knowledge is acquired by mimicry; the second is *formal* where knowledge is acquired by

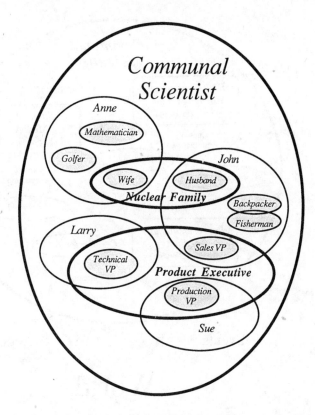

Fig. 5 — People in a number of roles and groups within a communal scientist.

the reinforcement of reward and punishment; the third level is *technical* where knowledge is acquired from its overt expression largely in symbolic media; the fourth is *comparative* where knowledge is acquired by analogies between cultures; and the fifth is *transcendental* where knowledge is acquired by deriving the principle underlying it.

Knowledge transfer to ESs now takes place at the technical level, although experiments are taking place on its transmission at all the other levels. In particular, successful systems have been based on mimicry at the informal level (Michalski & Chilausky 1980), and on interview techniques based on personal construct psychology at the formal level (Shaw & Gaines 1983b, Shaw 1984, Gaines & Shaw 1986, Boose 1985). Fig. 10 shows the conversational support system, PLANET, that we have developed using repertory grid elicitation to capture personal models of the world and make them available through an expert system (Gaines & Shaw 1981b, Shaw 1982, Shaw & Gaines 1981a,b, 1983a). Kelly (1955) developed the repertory grid as a means of accessing the personal construct systems of individuals. We have operationalized it through a suite of interactive computer programs that have been widely used in educational, clinical management and indus-trial applications (Shaw 1980, 1981, Pope & Keen 1981, Shepherd & Watson

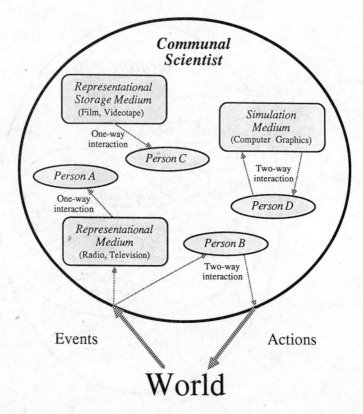

Fig. 6 — Various forms of representational media within a communal scientist.

1982).   PLANET, expert systems, communications networks and advanced simulation may be seen as precursors to intelligent information systems that support the knowledge processes of large-scale communities through interactive computer knowledge bases. The library of the future will add such capabilities to the symbolic and representational storage media of current library systems. Fifth and sixth generation computer technologies should be thought of as extending and integrating current media rather than replacing them. Fig. 11 shows how Popper's World 3 and Wojciejowski's knowledge construct are becoming manifest through the integration of past and present knowledge using computer and communications media. The conversational and experiential access that we have with other people and the existing world is being extended to conversational and experiential access to people and events of the past, and to knowledge and experience that correspond to possible worlds rather than reality. As the steam engine provided power that gave control over the physical world and triggered off the industrial revolution so is computing providing power to control the knowledge construct, enabling us to construct vehicles to traverse World 3 (Gaines 1978), and trigger off an information revolution.

The social perspective of Fig. 11 is complemented by the personal

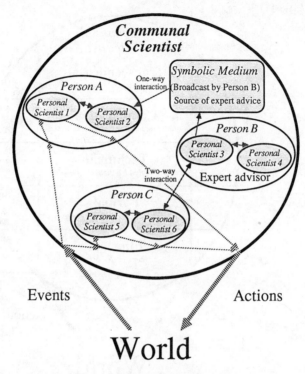

Fig. 7 — The representation of expert advisors and symbolic media within a communal scientist.

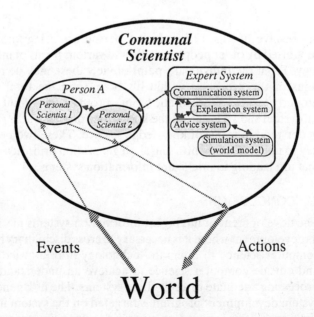

Fig. 8 — Structure of an expert system as a two-way symbolic medium within a communal scientist.

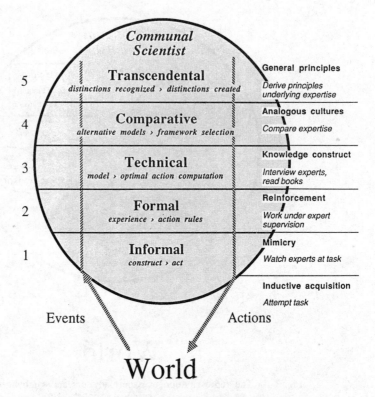

Fig. 9 — Feedback processes at different levels of a modeling system representation
knowledge acquisition in both people and expert systems.

perspective of Fig. 12 in which a person acquiring knowledge is seen as
supported by other people, media and various forms of information technology. From the individual's point of view these may be regarded as extensions of the processes within his brain, and the total structure may be
properly termed a 'prosthetic brain'. From a social point of view the entire
subsystem shown is part of the knowledge process of the society and may be
understood in terms of knowledge science. These two perspectives are the
key to understanding fifth and sixth generation priorities and developments
that are leading to intelligent information systems.

7. CONCLUSIONS

The development of intelligent information systems has reached a stage in
its development where it is necessary to cross disciplinary boundaries: within
computer science to integrate technology into knowledge-based systems;
and outside computer science to achieve an understanding of knowledge
processing adequate to apply these systems. The fifth generation computing
system development program is targeted on the system integration and the
sixth generation computing system development program is targeted on
knowledge science.

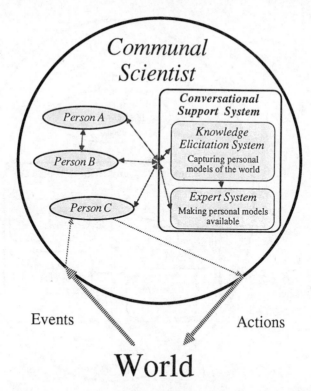

Fig. 10 — Conversational support system eliciting individual knowledge and making it available to a community.

This chapter has provided a cognitive science framework for intelligent information systems which encompasses the social and psychological processes of people as well as similar processes in computer-based systems. The foundations are based on a systemic model of inductive knowledge acquisition and the overall model accounts for the role of culture, media, experts and expert systems in the human knowledge process. Physiological systems are known in the brain that appear to carry out the basic functions of arousal and activation required by the model. Language plays the role of co-ordinating the multiple processors which are individual brains within a knowledge-acquiring society.

ACKNOWLEDGEMENTS

Financial assistance for this work has been made available by the National Sciences and Engineering Research Council of Canada.

REFERENCES

Bainbridge, L. (1979) Verbal reports as evidence of the process operator's knowledge. *International Journal of Man–Machine Studies* **11**(4) 411–436.

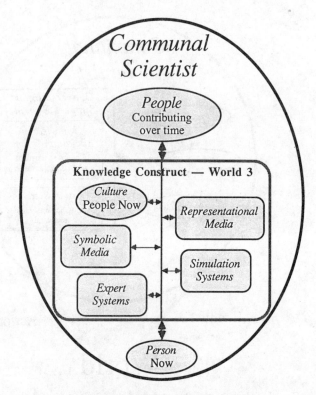

Fig. 11 — Intelligent information systems supporting the knowledge construct —
computing as a vehicle to traverse World 3.

Bell, D. (1973) *The coming of post-industrial society*. New York, Basic
    Books.
Boose, J. H. (1985) A knowledge acquisition program for expert systems
    based on personal construct psychology. *International Journal of Man-
    –Machine Studies* **23** (5) 495–526.
Chapman, R. E. (1985) *Background paper on biologically-related comput-
    ing (Japan's 'sixth' generation)*. Falls Church, Virginia: Technicom
    International Corporation.
Dizard, W. P. (1982) *The coming information age: an overview of techno-
    logy, economics and politics*. New York, Longman.
Drucker, P. F. (1968). *The age of discontinuity*. New York, Harper & Row.
Fuchi, K. (1984) Significance of fifth generation computer systems research
    and development. *ICOT Journal* (3), 8–14.
Fuchi, K., Sato, S. & Miller, E. (1984) Japanese approaches to high-
    technology R&D. *Computer* **17** (3) 14–18.
Gaines, B. R. (1977) System identification, approximation and complexity.
    International Journal of Genreal Systems **3** 145–174.
Gaines, B. R. (1978). Computers in world three. *Proceedings of the*

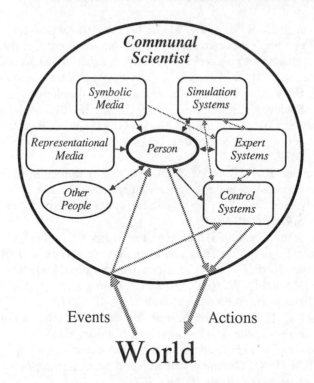

Fig. 12 — The knowledge support system of an individual — the prosthetic brain.

International Conference on Cybernetics and Society, 78CH-1306-0-SMC III, (November) Tokyo, Japan, 1515–1521.

Gaines, B. R. (1984a) A framework for the fifth generation. *Proceedings of National Computer Conference, 53.* Arlington, Virginia, AFIPS Press, pp. 453–459.

Gaines, B. R. (1984b) Perspectives on fifth generation computing. *Oxford surveys in information technology* **1** 1–53.

Gaines, B. R. & Shaw, M. L. G. (1981a) A programme for the development of a systems methodology of knowledge and action. In: Reckmeyer, W. J. (ed), *General systems research and design: precursors and futures.* Society for General Systems Research, pp. 255–264.

Gaines, B. R. & Shaw, M. L. G. (1981b) New directions in the analysis and interactive elicitation of personal construct systems. In: Shaw, M. L. G. (ed), *Recent advances in personal construct technology.* London, Academic Press, pp. 147–182.

Gaines, B. R. & Shaw, M. L. G. (1983) Is there a knowledge environment?. In: Lasker, G. (ed), *The relationship between major world problems and systems learning.* Society for General Systems Research, pp. 27–34.

Gaines, B. R. & Shaw, M. L. G. (1984a) *The art of computer conversation: a new medium for communication.* New Jersey, Prentice-Hall.

Gaines, B. R. & Shaw, M. L. G. (1984b) Logical foundations of expert systems. *Proceedings of IEEE International Conference on Systems, Man and Cybernetics (October), Halifax, Nova Scotia*, pp. 238–247.

Gaines, B. R. & Shaw, M. L. G. (1985a) Expert systems and simulation. In: Birtwistle, G. (ed), *AI, graphics and simulation*. La Jolla, California: Society for Simulation Research, pp. 95–101.

Gaines, B. R. & Shaw, M. L. G. (1985b) The infrastructure of fifth generation computing. *Compint'85 (September), Montreal*, pp. 747–751.

Gaines, B. R. & Shaw, M. L. G. (1986) Induction of inference rules for expert systems. *Fuzzy sets and systems*, to appear.

Gevarter, W. B. (1983) Expert systems: limited but powerful. *IEEE Spectrum* **18** 39–45.

Goodman, N. (1973) *fact, fiction and forecast*. Indianapolis, Bobbs-Merrill.

Hall, E. T. (1959) *The silent language*. New York, Doubleday.

Hayes-Roth, F. (1984) The industrialization of knowledge engineering. In: Reitman, W. (ed), *Artificial intelligence applications for business*. Norwood, New Jersey, Ablex, pp. 159–177.

HMSO (1982) *A programme for advanced information technology: the report of the Alvey Committee*. London, HMSO.

Hume, D. (1739) A treatise of human nature. London.

ICOT (1983) *Outline of research and development plans for fifth generation computer systems*. Tokyo, ICOT.

Kelly, G. A. (1955) *The psychology of personal constructs*. New York, Norton.

Klir, G. J. (1976) Identification of generative structures in empirical data. *International Journal of General Systems* **3** 89–104.

Luhmann, N. (1979) *Trust and power*. Chichester, John Wiley.

Machlup, F. (1962) *The production and distribution of knowledge in the United States*. Princeton University Press.

Machlup, F. (1980). *Knowledge and knowledge production*. Princeton University Press.

Machlup. F. (1982). *The branches of learning*. Princeton University Press.

Machlup, F. (1984). *The economics of information and human capital*. Princeton University Press.

Marschak, J. (1968) Economics of inquiring, communicating and deciding. *American Economic Review* **58** 1. May 1–18.

Michalski, R. S. & Chilausky, R. L. (1980) Knowledge acquisition by encoding expert rules versus computer induction from examples — a case study involving soyabean pathology. *International Journal of Man–Machine Studies* **12** 63–87.

Mohanty, J. N. (1982) *Husserl and Frege*. Bloomington, University of Indiana Press.

Moto-oka, T. (ed) (1982) *Fifth generation computer systems*. Amsterdam, North-Holland.

Pask, G. (1980) Developments in conversation theory — Part I. *International Journal of Man–Machine Studies* **13** (4) 357–411.

Pope, M. L. & Keen, T. R. (1981) *Personal construct psychology and education*. London, Academic Press.

Popper, K. R. (1968) Epistemology without a knowing subject. In: Van Rootselaar, B. (ed.) *Logic, methodology and philosophy of science III*. Amsterdam, North-Holland Publishing Co., pp. 333–373.

Porat, M. U. (1977) *The information economy*. Washington, US Department of Commerce.

Rawls, J. (1971) A theory of justice. Cambridge, Massachusetts, Harvard University Press.

Robinson, A. L. (1984) One billion transistors on a chip? *Science* **223** 267–268.

Rosen, R. (1985) *Anticipatory systems*. Oxford, Pergamon Press.

Rubinstein, R. A., Laughlin, C. D. & McManus, J. (1984) *Science as a cognitive process*. Philadelphia, University of Pennsylvania Press.

Schutz, A. & Luckmann, T. (1973) *The structures of the life-world*. London, Heinemann.

Shaw, M. L. G. (1980) *On becoming a personal scientist*. London, Academic Press.

Shaw, M. L. G. (ed) (1981) *Recent advances in personal construct technology*. London, Academic Press.

Shaw, M. L. G. (1982) PLANET: some experience in creating an integrated system for repertory grid applications on a microcomputer. *International Journal of Man–Machine Studies* **17** (3) 345–360.

Shaw, M. L. G. (1984) Interactive knowledge elicitation. *Proceedings of CIPS SESSION 84*. Calgary: Canadian Information Processing Society.

Shaw, M. L. G. (1985) Communities of knowledge. In: Epting, F. & Landfield, A. W. (eds), *Anticipating personal construct psychology*. Lincoln, University of Nebraska Press, pp. 25–35.

Shaw, M. L. G. & Gaines, B. R. (1981a) The personal scientist in the community of science. In: Reckmeyer, W. J. (ed), *General systems research and design: precursors and futures*. Society for General Systems Research, pp. 59–68.

Shaw, M. L. G. & Gaines, B. R. (1981b) Exploring personal semantic space. In: Rieger, B. (ed), *Empirical Semantics II*. Bochum, West Germany, Studienverlag Brockmeyer, pp. 712–791.

Shaw, M. L. G. & Gaines, B. R. (1983a) Eliciting the real problem. In: Wedde, H. (ed), *International working conference on model realism*. Oxford, Pergamon Press, pp. 100–111.

Shaw, M. L. G. & Gaines, B. R. (1983b) A computer aid to knowledge engineering. *Proceedings of Expert Systems 83*. London, British Computer Soceity, pp. 263–271.

Shaw, M. L. G & Gaines, B. R. (1984) Fifth generation computers as the next stage of a new medium. *Proceedings of National Computer Conference, 53*. Arlington, Virginia, AFIPS Press, pp. 445–451.

Shepherd, E. & Watson, J. P. (eds) (1982) *Personal meanings*. Chichester, John Wiley.

STA (1985) *Promotion of R&D on electronics and information systems that may complement or substitute for human intelligence.* Tokyo, Science and Technology Agency.

Steier, R. (1983) Cooperation is the key: An interview with B. R. Inman. *Communications of the ACM* **26** (9) 642–645.

Stich, S. P. & Nisbett, R. E. (1984) Expertise, justification and the psychology of inductive reasoning. In: Haskell, T. L. (ed), *The authority of experts.* Bloomington, Indiana, Indiana University Press, pp. 226–241.

Toffler, A. (1980) *The third wave.* New York, Bantam.

Tucker, D. M. & Williamson, P. A. (1984) Asymmetric neural control systems in human self-regulation. *Psychological Review* **91** (2) 185–215.

Wason, P. C. & Johnson-Laird, P. N. (1972) *Psychology of reasoning.* London, Batsford.

Wojciechowski, J. (1983) The impact of knowledge on man: the ecology of knowledge. *Hommage à Francois Mayer.* Marseille, Laffite, pp. 161–175.

Part V

Lessons of history

In the previous chapter, Shaw and Gaines ventured to describe what may lie beyond our immediate intellectual horizons, but an understanding of where we are going may be improved by a knowledge of where we have already been. In re-tracing a line of thought, especially if it is broken in places, it is necessary to steer a course between the Scylla and Charybdis depicted by Blaug (1978, p. 1) in his survey of the history of economic theory:

> The danger of arrogance toward the writers of the past is certainly a real one — but so is ancestor worship. Indeed, there are always two sorts of dangers in evaluating the work of earlier writers: on the one hand, to see only their mistakes and defects without appreciating the limitations both of the analysis they inherited and of the historical circumstances in which they wrote; and, on the other hand, to expand their merits in the eagerness to discover an idea in advance of their own times, and frequently their own intentions. To put it somewhat differently: there is the anthropomorphic sin of judging older writers by the canons of modern theory, but there is also what Samuelson once called 'the sophisticated — anthropomorphic sin of not recognising the equivalent content in older writers; because they do not use the terminology and symbols of the present'.

'Anachronistic' would be a more suitable term than 'anthropomorphic' in this context. Nevertheless, of the two sins dicussed by Blaug, that of neglect seems the more likely in connection with the antecedents of artificial intelligence. Indeed the pace of change is such as to leave little time for scholarly reflection. Admittedly, it has been claimed that 'as intellectual forebears of AI, few philosophers have failed to be named by one or another observer ...' (Moyne 1985, p. 238); but, though that may be true of mainstream, rigorous philosphers, it is far less true of social philosophers such as Condorcet, nor is it true of other thinkers, not normally regarded as philosophers, who have been bold enough to venture form the safe and narrow paths of orthodoxy. Wilkins, Smee, Jevons, Reuleaux, Geddes and Zwicky could all be regarded as forebears of artificial intelligence, but their claims, like that of Condorcet, are rarely if ever considered.

The need to organize knowledge in a way that facilitates its extension has been recognized since the time of the Ancient Greeks, while combinatorial procedures for generating new knowledge have been investigated on various occasions over the past seven centuries. Leibniz, Condorcet and Jevons each considered the combinatorial explosion and ways around the difficulties it causes. Mechanical models of cognitive processes were created by Smee and by Jevons. Later, a real problem in the domain of urban planning involving 49 million cominations was solved by using heuristics at a time when nearly all AI researchers were still studying toy problems. Librarians too, though they often preach the importance of information retrieval in avoiding needless duplication of effort, have nevertheless sometimes shown a tendency to try and re-invent the wheel.

Of course this does not necessarily mean that the progress of AI would have been faster if the researchers had spent more time studying history and less in writing computer programs. The reverse might have been true. Retrieving information when you cannot even define the problem is a trickly business as Ingwersen made clear in his chapter, and the arguments presented by Shaw and Gaines in the same section imply that assimilation of retrieved information is problematic if the user's mind does not contain the appropriate constructs. If a proper appreciation of earlier work requires an equivalent level of knowledge, then there are obvious limitations to the usefulness of information retrieval in accelerating the acquisition of that knowledge. Herbart, whose theory of apperception was discussed briefly in the introduction to Part IV, was a leading exponent of the culture-epoch approach to education according to which each individual should learn by progressing step-by-step through the stages that mankind as a whole has passed through. It seems that researchers as well as children often find that the easiest way to learn from history is to re-live it.

Nevertheless one positive conclusion may be drawn from the historical account in this section. The dream of discovering procedures for extending or augmenting mankind's mental abilities is ancient and deep rooted, rather like the dream of flight. Indeed two of the individuals dicussed in the chapter, Bishop John Wilkins (1640) and Fritz Zwicky (1969) also seriously considered the possibility of voyaging to the Moon. A delight in undertaking tasks that have no strictly utilitarian motive, e.g. building pyramids, climbing Everest, going to the Moon, is one of the marks of a vigorous civilization. We need challenges, and the study of natural and artificial intelligence offers plently.

REFERENCES

Blaug, M. (1978) *Economic theory in retrospect*, 3rd edn. Cambridge, CUP.

Moyne, J. A. (1985) *Understanding language: man or machine*. New York, Plenum Press.

Wilkins, J. (1640) Discourse concerning the possibility of a passage to the world in the moon. Reprinted in: Wilkins, J. (1970), *The mathematical and philosophical works*, 2nd edn. London, Frank Cass.

Zwicky, F. (1969) *Discovery, invention, research through the mophological approach*. New York, Macmillan.

10

Classification and ratiocination: a perennial quest

Roy Davies, The University Library, Exeter

1. INTRODUCTION

Both librarianship and artificial intelligence are concerned with knowledge. The invention of writing extended human memory and libraries exist primarily for the purpose of imposing some sort of organization on this external memory, thereby providing access to the public knowledge which is the heritage of all mankind. The emulation or augmentation of our reasoning faculties is, however, a vastly more ambitious goal than the extension of our memories, and consequently the development of artificial intelligence (in the 1980s) is still greatly restricted by severe limitations in the breadth of the knowledge that can be utilized.

Although there is a huge disparity between the treatment and role of knowledge in libraries and 'intelligent' systems, the gap should not in principle be unbridgeable. The organization of knowledge, whether for access or to support the reasoning process, has historically involved similar techniques.

2. ORIGINS

2.1 The legacy of the ancient Greeks

There is an obvious link between memory and learning. Without learning, our memories would not contain anything other than a chaotic jumble of impressions; without our memories, we could not be said to have learnt anything. Plato in the *Meno* went further and maintained that all learning was remembering of inate knowledge. In support of this view he recounted how an untutored youth was able to solve a problem in geometry after being asked a series of questions by Socrates. We would hardly be likely to draw a similar conclusion from a demonstration of a sophisticated form of programmed learning. Bifurcate or dichotomous classification, a technique we owe to the Greeks, provides a more acceptable example of a link between reasoning and the organization of knowledge.

Socrates himself gave a demonstration of the technique, in the *Sophist,* when he defined an angler as 'a technician who practises an art of the acquisitive, coercive sort through the hunting of living things that swim in the water by striking at them during the day with a hook.' By adding all the steps on the right hand side of the diagram in Fig. 1 the definition is obtained.

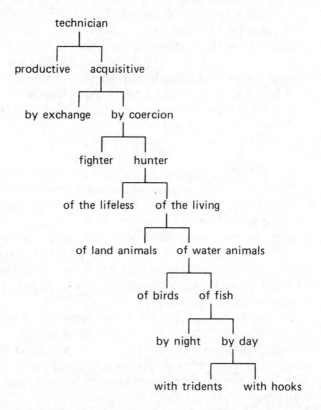

Fig. 1 — Definition by successive dichotomies.

Jevons (1879) argued that this procedure of cutting off the negative part of a genus when we discover by observation that an object possesses a particular feature is identical with the art of diagnosis. The method of repeated division is also used in most of the well-established bibliographic classification schemes, but normally these divisions are not dichotomous. In the Dewey scheme they are of a decimal nature. There is, though an alternative method of classification, also discovered by the Ancient Greeks, that has been used in libraries.

Aristotle studied no fewer than 158 different constitutions before writing the *Nicomachean Ethics*. Yet he realized that the existing types did not exhaust all possibilities and in his *Politics* he used the following argument by analogy:

> if we are going to speak of the different species of animal, we should first of all determine the organs that are indispensable to every animal, as for example, some organs of sense and the instruments of receiving and digesting food, such as the mouth and the stomach, besides organs of locomotion. Assuming now that there are only so many kinds of organ, but that there may be differences in them — I mean between different kinds of mouth, and stomach, and perceptive and locomotive organ — the possible combinations of these differences will necessarily furnish many varieties of animal. (For animals cannot be the same which have different kinds of mouth or ear). And when all the combinations are exhausted there will be as many sorts of animals as there are combinations of the necessary organs. The same, then, is true of the forms of government that have been described.

Not until the twentieth century was the combinatorial method used as the basis of a bibliographic classification scheme. Instead of repeatedly dividing classes, basic terms or concepts may be grouped into sets, each set reflecting some 'facet' of a subject. By combining appropriate terms from different facets in a prescribed order, any book may be classified (Ranganthan 1967). It is now widely recognized that 'analytico-synthetic' or 'faceted' schemes are superior to the traditional enumerative, hierarchical kinds as it is easier to classify books on interdisciplinary topics and to accommodate newly developed subjects.

It could be argued that novel combinations of concepts may represent new knowledge. In the words of Ranganathan (1951) who pioneered the faceted approach in librarianship, 'classification can illumine the field of knowledge. It can even be prophetic.' Combinatorial classifications, and other enumerative procedures have been used quite successfully since World War II in technological forecasting (Wills 1972) and planning and design theory (Bloch 1979), but the idea that knowledge could be generated in this way goes back to the thirteenth century (Gregory 1969, McCorduck 1979).

2.2 Ramon Lull (1232–1315)

In about the year 1272 on Mount Randa in Majorca, Ramon Lull, a Catalan poet, had a revelation of the attributes of God infusing the whole of creation. This experience inspired him to create an art of reasoning, the Ars Magna, which he thought would be universally applicable and with which he hoped he would be able to convert the Muslims, a task to which he had dedicated himself following his own conversion after leading a dissolute existence as a troubadour and courtier (Gardner 1983).

For the purpose of expounding his art, Lull frequently made use of diagrams, particularly concentric circles. The influence of his experience on Mount Randa is seen in Fig. 2, where the divine attributes, goodness,

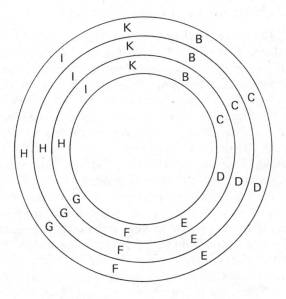

Fig. 2 — Lullian circles for combining symbols.

greatness, eternity, power, wisdom, will, virtue, truth and glory, represented by the letters B–K exluding J, are inscribed around the circumference of three circles. By imagining the circles revolving with respect to each other, pairs and triads of attributes could be enumerated with ease. Similar diagrams based on the attributes of the soul, lists of virtues and sins, the four elements (earth, air, fire and water), the signs of the zodiac, physical properties, etc. were produced. Different circles could contain symbols representing the same or different sets of concepts and there was no fixed limit to the number of concentric circles that could be employed. Lull believed that any subject could be explored by studying or meditating on the interactions between the small number of fundamental concepts on which that subject is based (Gardner 1983).

Numerous books were written by Lull in which he applied his art to subjects ranging from finding topics for sermons to comprehensive surveys of sciences of his day. The diagrams had mnemonic qualities and, furthermore, there is no need to memorize the combinations relevant to a topic as they can be generated from first principles. For these reasons the method was regarded as an art of memory as well as discovery (Yates 1966).

Lull is believed to have died a martyr's death in North Africa in 1315. His missions to the Moors were failures, but his art lived on in Europe despite the ridicule that it sometimes attracted. Francis Bacon in his *Advancement of Learning* condemned it was worthless. Nevertheless Lull's work had some influence on attempts in the seventeenth century to create a universal language and also inspired Leibniz's early work on logic.

3.   COMMUNICATION AND REASONING

3.1   The dream of a universal language

The Renaissance, the Reformation and the invention of printing were accompanied by an increase in the use of vernacular languages in writing, at the expense of Latin. While these languages made scientific, philosophical and above all, religuous ideas more accessible within national boundaries, they constituted a barrier to international communication. The confused linguistic situation in Europe was often contrasted with that in China where speakers of different langugages share a common written one. Strictly speaking, Chinese characters represent neither sounds nor concepts but morphemes or minimal grammatical units. Nevertheless, Europeans assumed that like Arabic numerals the ideograms were 'real characters', or symbols which represent concepts directly and do not merely stand for the names of those concepts in a particular langugage (Large 1985).

Francis Bacon had pointed out that language can be responsible for the clarity or the obscurity of our ideas (*Philosphical Works,* aphorisms 59 & 269), and subsequently this notion was expounded by John Locke in his *Essay Concering Human Understanding.* As the intention of many of the advocates of a universal language was not just to make communication easier but also to make misunderstanding far more difficult, a direct means of representing concepts had considerable appeal. However, in Chinese the number of different characters to be learned is vast, and it can be difficult to determine what they represent, as although they may have originated as pictograms they have come to stand for things by convention. A lanuage of systematically designed characters arranged in logical groups would be much simpler to learn (Knight 1981).

3.2   John Wilkins (1614–1672)

The best known of all the schemes of this kind was developed by Bishop John Wilkins with the assistance of colleagues in the Royal Society, of which he was a founder. Among his collatorators was the naval administrator and diarist Samuel Pepys, who helped in connection with nautical terminology. Wilkins's scheme, set forth in his *Essay towards a Real Character and a Philosophical Language* (1668), consisted of a classification with 40 principal groups. As in the case of bibliographical schemes the symbols chosen to represent a concept depended on that concept's position in the classification. Within the classes the arrangement was hierarchical. However, concepts not enumerated in the schedules could be represented by combining the most relevant term or 'radical' from an appropriate class with another from a table of 'transcendental particles' used to modify the meanings of other terms, e.g. 'library' would be indicated by the symbols for the radical 'book' and the particle 'room' (Vickery 1953).

Convinced of the great benefits that would accrue to mankind if the scheme were adopted widely, Wilkins's supporters sought ways of popularizing it. Suggestions included a game making the system pleasurable for children to learn; a series of 'maps' for identifying plants, animals, rocks, metals etc.; and a method for learning and memorizing whatever one reads or observes (Knowlson 1975). The specimens in the Royal Society's natural history collection were arranged by Robert Hooke in accordance with the classification and he also published a description of a pocket watch using Wilkins's real character which he thought was an ideal medium of communication (Slaughter 1982).

It has been claimed that 'as a study of semantics, the analysis of concepts into their basic elements of meaning and the systematic ordering of those elements, the Essay is a work of genius' (Vickery 1953). Nevertheless, as a language Wilkins's scheme was a complete failure. To assist in reasoning, a classification should be natural not arbitrary, but in many instances philosophical considerations had been sacrificed in favour of mnemonic ones. Furthermore, the scheme reflected the state of knowledge at the time it was drawn up. As science progressed changes in previously held views and the lack of provision for the inclusion of new classificatory critera made the defects of the scheme more apparent.

To overcome such problems Seth Ward, Bishop of Salisbury, suggested the creation of a new universal language based on about one hundred fundamental concepts which could be combined to express more complex ones, an idea he justified by reference to Ramon Lull's writings. By dispensing with any pre-conceived structure of ideas and instead basing the scheme on indivisible semantic units, the adaptability of the scheme would be guaranteed. Three centuries later, prompted by problems with his own Colon classification, Ranganthan (1952b, 1967) suggested the construction of a 'self-perpetuating' scheme reminiscent of Ward's in some respects, including the fact that it did not materialize. However, views similar to those of Ward were also expressed at about the same time by Leibniz who, like Ward, was more concerned with strict reasoning than everyday discourse.

3.3 Leibniz (1646–1716)

While still in his teens Leibniz had been greatly impressed by Lull's theories which inspired his early attempts to create a logic of discovery. However, Leibniz realised that Lull had overlooked two factors which were vital if the method were to be really useful: first, the basic set of concepts should be complete; and second, it was necessary to have a procedure for ensuring that all possible combinations were considered. Satisfaction of the latter criterion would be bedevilled by the 'combinatorial explosion' as Leibniz realized about three hundred years before the Lighthill (1972) report on artificial intelligence coined the term:

Fine truths are often reached by 'synthesis', going from the simple to the composite, but when it is a matter of finding, exactly the right way of doing what is required, synthesis is not usually sufficient — to try to make all the necessary combinations would often be like drinking the ocean. However the 'method of exclusions' can often help with this by eliminating a good proportion of the useless combinations, and often nature permits no other method. (Leibniz 1765)

The plan for a calculus of reasoning was just on of Leibniz's proposals for systematically extending and disseminating human knowledge, which include the establishment of scientific societies, the compilation of a very detailed encyclopaedia and the production of a journal to review all publications (Ornstein 1963). The importance of a comprehensive library to support German scientific research was also stressed, as might be expected of a man who for most of his life was a librarian. Although Leibniz failed to achieve his objectives, his vision excelled in scope and coherence the recent policies of governments which have regarded information technology simply as a means of rejuvenating stagnant economies.

After Leibniz, work on logic and on an international language continued to diverge. It is true that Guiseppe Peano (1858–1932), one of the great figures in the history of logic and mathematics also created Interlingua which, in comparative study of artificial languages undertaken by Sylvia Pankhurst (1927) a daughter of the Suffragette leader, was awarded the palm. Nevertheless there was no direct connection betwen Peano's work on the axiomization of arithmetic and the development of Interlingua.

3.4 Biological taxonomy

Despite the failures of the attempts to create a language which would also function as a calculus of reasoning, they did leave some useful legacies. Roget (1852) got the idea of a thesaurus from Wilkins's classification, and later, more specialized thesauri became common tools of information retrieval. The scheme's notation may also have influenced the development of shorthand since Isaac Pitman possessed a copy of the *Essay* (Vickery 1953). Far more importantly the work of Wilkins's collaborators gave an immense boost to the study of biological taxonomy culminating in the work of Linnaeus.

One recent writer has seen Linnaeus as a pioneer of information retrieval (Knight 1981) while another has described his work, along with Euclid's *Elements,* as an outstanding example of knowledge engineering (Wegner 1983). The resemblance to the techniques used in the creation of expert systems is more obvious in the case of biological keys, i.e. special classifications for the identification of plants or animals. The first true key was produced by Lamarck in 1778 (Voss 1952). Most commonly they consist of successive dichotomies in the form of descriptive couplets based on readily observable characteristics. Often they are constructed so that they can also be used backwards for ease of tracing mistakes or for disproving or confirming suspected identities (Metcalf 1954).

Besides the conventional printed kinds, versions using edge-notched or body-punched cards have been developed. These are known as multiple access keys or polyclaves and have the advantage that the characteristics of the organisms may be considered in any order, which is particularly valuable in attempts to identify incomplete or fragmentary material (Morse 1975). In the late 1960s online versions of polyclaves were first developed (Pankhurst 1978). These could be regarded as intermediate in nature between information retrieval and expert systems. In this context it is interesting to note that some recent work on medical systems has emphasized the superiority of a taxonomic approach to one based purely on production rules (Gomez & Chandrasekaran 1984).

If a classification is a natural one then the observation of a single characteristic may allow us to make a whole series of inferences. Cuvier (1834) pointed out that if we come across a print of a cleft hoof we may deduce that it was made by a ruminant and this deduction gives us information about the animal's teeth and jaws, the form of its vertebrae and the bones of the legs, shoulders and pelvis. However, Linnaeus had based his system on a mixture of natural and arbitrary distinctions as compromises were necessary if the scheme were to be employable without excessive labour. This meant that many important characteristics were ignored for the sake of expediency.

3.5   Condorcet (1734–1794)

The French biologist Michel Adanson, who is now regarded as a fore-runner of the numerical taxonomists, argued in contradistinction to Linnaeus that all significant features should be taken into account. His compatriot Condorcet, a mathematician and social philosopher, advocated that the same approach should be taken in the organization of observations in astronomy, meteorology, physical geography and the social sciences as well as natural history (Baker 1975). This would allow objects or phenomena to be compared on the basis of any feature whereas enumerative classification permits certain comparisons but precludes others.

Condorcet's classification used a numerical notation and therefore has been compared to Dewey's (Baker 1962), but it was of a faceted kind (Whitrow 1982, 1983). He claimed that the scheme, when perfected, would allow one to set out in a small chart 'what could possibly not be expressed so well in a whole book' (Condorcet 1795). In his unpublished writing he envisaged the uses listed below, of which the last three were regarded as the most important:

(1) as a key for identifying plants or animals if all the relevant characteristics were known;

(2) to indicate what to look for if only certain characteristics had been observed;
(3) for ascertaining whether any object was new or was already known;
(4) to reveal gaps in knowledge and make possible the formation of hypotheses which would act as a spur to discoveries in these areas;
(5) by allowing data to be arranged in every conceivable way the framing and testing of hypotheses based on statistics would be facilitated, e.g. mortality tables constructed in this way could be used for investigating links with age, occupation, sex, marital status, climate etc.;
(6) for the production of subject indexes to documents and as a personal filing system which would enable writers to avoid repetitions and contradictions in long works.

These uses presuppose a detailed analysis of the topic under consideration. Condorcet gave a lot of thought as to how this was to be achieved and his explanation has a remarkably modern ring to it in view of the amount of attention devoted to chess by artificial intelligence researchers.

If one asks the nature of this analytical method, we shall say that it is precisely the same by which one plays a game of chess, except that in chess the number of combinations is finite.... What happens, in fact, in a game of chess? One does not analyze all the possible combinations for each move, but one seeks those that can produce a certain outcome in two or three moves (depending on the range of one's mind) ... If by the complete analysis of an idea one understands ... all the possible combinations involved, this would doubtless lead infallibly to the truth sought. But a complete analysis in this sense is impossible ... Yet this is to give the term 'analysis', in the sense of decomposition of ideas, a more extensive sense than it should have, since it would result from such a definition that no one has ever made or could ever make an analysis of any idea. (quoted in Baker 1975, p. 117)

Condorcet's intimation of the way in which technology could facilitate the operations for which his classification was designed was equally prescient:

I shall not speak here of the mechanical means which could be employed; it is easy to envisage them, but this mechanism would appear ridiculous until the time when experience has shown the utility of these tables for the discovery of relations and general laws between natural substances, observed facts and variations of a phenomenon which without this method would have long escaped our research. (quoted in Baker 1962)

In view of his remarkable foresight it is unfortunate that Condorcet never had the opportunity to develop his ideas fully. His democratic ideals were as noteworthy as his scientific attitudes. Following the French Revolution he was elected to the National Assembly where his draft for a new, decidedly liberal constitution was rejected in favour of the repressive one introduced in 1793. Forced to go into hiding from the Jacobins, Condorcet used the seclusion to write the posthumously published book on which his reputation mainly rests today — *The Sketch for a Historical Picture of the Progress of the Human Mind* (Condorcet 1795) — which was meant to be simply an introduction to a far more detailed work he had long intended to produce. In March 1794, Condorcet was arrested at a country inn where, it is said, the famished fugitive aroused suspicion by demanding an enormous omelette requiring a dozen eggs (Bouissounouse 1962). The day after his imprisonment he was found dead in his cell (Baker 1975). Thus Condorcet's study of classification, which had received somewhat cursory treatment in his published work, languished in obscurity together with his speculative comment on mechanization until the text of a hitherto neglected manuscript of his was published in a paper by Baker (1962).

4.   THE AGE OF MACHINES

4.1   Charles Stanhope (1753–1816) and Charles Babbage (1792–1871)

Although Condorcet had contemplated the possibility of using machinery for logical operations, the honour of being the first person to construct a device capable of solving simple problems of that nature belongs to Charles Stanhope, third Earl Stanhope, a prolific inventor. A steam carriage, the first steamship, and a very successful printing press were just some of the products of his ingenuity (Newman 1969). According to one of his descendants (Stanhope 1914), he was close friend of Condorcet. Nevertheless, it is uncertain whether the Frenchman influenced the Earl's work on logic. Compared with what Condorcet seemed to have had in mind, the capabilities of Stanhope's device were very limited. The instrument, which looked like a squat, almost square-shaped slide rule, was known as the 'Stanhope Demonstrator' since it demonstrated symbolically the inferences which follow from the propositions of syllogisms, in a manner similar to Venn diagrams which the Earl's invention anticipated in certain respects (Gardner 1983). It could also solve simple problems of probability. No description of the instrument was published until 63 years after Stanhope's death (Harley 1879); but another of his inventions, an improved calculator, may have had more influence, as two of the machines came into the possession of Charles Babbage (Stanhope 1914, Newman 1969).

The Stanhope Demonstrator, like the calculator, pales into insignificance compared with Babbage's Difference and Analytical Engines, which are too well-known to require description here. It is worth noting though, that Babbage envisaged the Analytical Engine being used not just for mathematical calculations but also for other information processing tasks; e.g. he suggested the construction of a machine, capable of learning from experience, for playing games of skill (Babbage 1864).

Furthermore, Babbage concluded his autobiography by reiterating an assertion he had made earlier in the same volume, ascribing whatever success he may have had to an early perception of the immense power of signs in aiding the reasoning faculty and, above all, to the conviction that 'the highest object a reasonable being could pursue was to discover those laws of mind by which man's intellect passes from the known to the discovery of the unknown' (Babbage 1864). Surprisingly, these claims seem to have received little attention from writers on semiotics and cognitive science. However, in the Victorian age Babbage's convictions were not unique. Smee, Boole and Jevons shared a similar motivation.

4.2   Alfred Smee (1818–1877)

Alfred Smee, a doctor and chemist, held a position specially created for him of surgeon to the Bank of England, which afforded him the opportunity to combine the practice of medicine with the pursuit of research in the field of electrochemistry. An improved method of printing banknotes was one of the innovations for which he was responsible. According to his daughter, though, Smee's main interest was in the workings of the human mind (Odling 1878). Believing that different thoughts were associated with electrochemical activity in different combinations of nerve fibres in the brain, Smee developed an elaborate theory of 'electro-biology' (Smee 1849, 1875). Although somewhat fanciful, the theory did lead him to construct simple devices which he believed modelled certain cognitive processes.

Smee assumed that the number of nerve fibres that could possibly be stimulated by concepts of a given class, e.g. 'mortal beings', would be greater than that affected by any single subset of that class, e.g. 'men', which in turn would be larger than that associated with any member of that subset, e.g. 'Socrates'. Therefore, by drawing a tree diagram and tracing the appropriate path, the conclusion 'Socrates is mortal' could be drawn. Unlike syllogisms these diagrams could be extended to include any number of premises, e.g. the brances 'not Greek' and 'Greek' could be inserted immediately below 'men' in Fig. 3(a). In the terminology of artifical intelligence the lower concepts inherit the properties of the higher.

Of course, simple concepts may interact to produce a complex but more specific concept as shown in Fig. 3(b). The adjectives serve to limit membership of the set of all men. Smee studied the interrelationships of all the different parts of speech, not just nouns and adjectives, and tried to show that the meaning of any sentence could be resolved using one or more dichotomous diagrams. He suggested that acts of parliament and other legal documents could be drafted in this way to avoid ambiguity (Smee 1851).

From this analysis of language Smee concluded that thought is governed by fixed principles and that 'by taking advantage of a knowledge of these principles ... mechanical contrivances might be formed which obey similar laws, and give those results which some may have considered only attainable by the operation of the mind itself' (Smee 1851). Several prototypes were constructed of a 'relational machine' which comprised a series of hinged joints for modelling the formation of successive dichotomies in the mind. The opening of a particular sequence of joints corresponded to the tracing of a particular path in a tree diagram. According to Smee, the relational machine could have been adapted to perform arithmetical operations using

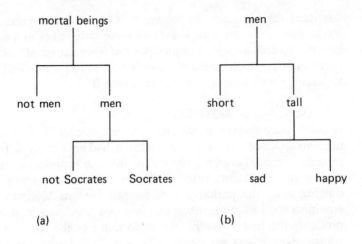

Fig. 3 — (a) Analysis of a syllogism. (b) Analysis of a phrase.

logarithmic scales (and presumably also linear ones), but he stressed that its primary purpose was the manipulation of symbols.

Smee also attempted to compare ideas, theories, doctrines etc. by means of a 'differential machine' consisting of a box containing two parallel rows of appendages, like piano keys but of uneven length, each representing a particular concept or fact. In the case of the first theory or doctrine, any concept which formed part of it would be represented by an appendage of unit length, while a concept on which the doctrinal stand-point is unknown or uncertain would be represented by one that is twice as long. Where the second doctrine is in agreement with the first, the corresponding appendages in the parallel row would also have unit length. In cases of uncertainty and disagreement, the respective lengths would be two and four units. Therefore when the rows were brought together their combined width would be 2, 3, 4 or 5 units representing complete, probable or possible agreement, or complete disagreement respectively. The positions of any gaps would also indicate the points of possible or actual disagreement.

One suggestion made by Smee was that the differential machine might be used to reach verdicts in trials, the role of the jury being to decide what the lengths of the appendages should be. However he did realise that a practical version of his other device, the relational machine, would have to be comprehensive, like a dictionary, in its inclusion of concepts, and he concluded that 'it would cover an area exceeding probably all London, and the very attempt to move its respective parts upon each other would inevitably cause its own destruction' Smee (1851).

The real value of both machines was, Smee believed, in modelling the processes of thought. Whether present-day models will appear equally naive a century hence is open to question. In fact, our knowledge of how the brain represents symbols is in some respects hardly more advanced than it was in Smee's day. Hofstadter (1979), who seems unaware of Smee's work, has discussed the question 'do the symbols in the brain represent classes or instances? ... Or can a single symbol serve duty either as a class symbol or instance symbol depending which parts of it are activated?' he describes the latter theory, which would seem to have been held implicitly by Smee, as appealing, but on further reflection rejects it.

4.3   W. S. Jevons (1835–1882)

A much more successful machine was designed by W. S. Jevons, who was unaware of Smee's creations until after he had built his own. Today Jevons is probably remembered mainly for his work in economics, where he was a pioneer of marginal utility theory, but he wrote extensively on other subjects ranging from the philosophy of science (Jevons 1879) to the role and administration of public libraries (Jevons 1904). As a logician Jevons was probably the first to realize the importance of the work of Boole (1854) whose algebra was intended to be a formal description of the laws of thought.

The approach which characterized Jevon's own work on logic and the philosophy of science was to generate all possible combinations of a set of terms and then eliminate those incompatible with the facts of the case under investigation (Jevons 1879). To represent assertions and negations he used capital and lower case letters respectively. Therefore the complete set of combinations of the three terms A, B and C would be ABC, ABc, AbC, aBC, aBc, abC and abc. Now consider the propositions 'all A is B' and 'no B is C'. The first eliminates all combinations of A and b while the second rules out those of B and C. Of the valid combinations, ABc, aBc, abC and abc, none contain both A and C so we conclude 'no A is C'. Furthermore, as the only set containing A includes c and the only one with C contains a, we may infer that 'some A is not C' and that 'some not A is C'. According to Gardner (1983) this method is better suited to problems involving propositions, but Jevons confined his attention almost exclusively to class logic.

A considerable part of Jevons's *Principles of Science* (1879) is devoted to classification and with the aid of a simple zoological example he showed that if the presence and absence of particular characteristics were indicated by the symbols for assertion and negation, a dichotomous classification could be converted quite simply into a faceted one.

Jevons simplified the application of his method in various ways. First he produced a 'logical slate' upon which were engraved the combinations of a certain number of terms. As the invalid combinations were simply chalked out, the slate could be used any number of times. He also produced rubber stamps for use, with an ink pad, in printing sets of terms (Jevons 1870). For classroom demonstrations he developed a kind of abacus with light movable pieces of wood representing the combinations. Finally, in 1869 he produced his 'logical piano', so-called because of its appearance. Unlike his other innovations which simply saved the user the trouble of generating the complete list of combinations, this machine also mechanically eliminated those incompatible with any propositions fed into it (Jevons 1879).

Jevons's 'piano' was the first machine to enable logical problems to be solved faster than they could be solved without mechanical aids (Gardner 1983). However its primary purpose was educational. The fact that a machine could solve logical problems constituted proof of the existence of certain immutable laws of thought. Jevons realized that the number of combinations involved in problems of a practical nature would often far exceed the capabilities of his machine and he became probably the first person to make a serious attempt to quantify the combinatorial explosion. This attempt grew out of his study of the nature of scientific laws.

According to Jevons, the process of forming a class is identical to induction, and classification results in the production of generalizations such as scientific definitions and laws. Consider the definition of a metal as a good conductor which is ductile. This involves 3 terms and there are 8 possible combinations of these. Using Jevons's method we could identify those compatible with the propositions implicit in the definition. However certain selections of combinations could be eliminated in advance as they are inherently contradictory, e.g. the groups of assertions ABC and their negations abc cannot both belong to the valid set of combinations. The set of combinations compatible with a scientific law or fact will be one of the self-consistent sets that can be generated from those combinations.

If we had 4 terms, we would have 2^4 or 16 combinations and would need to consider 2^{16} or 65,536 combinations of these combinations to determine which might possibly be valid. With 6 terms there would be 64 combinations and in excess of 1.8×10^{19} selections to be considered. Jevons estimated that only 5 terms would suffice to fill a library of over 65,000 volumes and remarked 'surely there is scope enough here for 'euristic' [sic] processes' (Jevons 1908, p. xi). This is probably the first use of the term 'heuristic' in connection with the combinatorial explosion.

4.4   Franz Reuleaux (1829–1905)

In view of the foregoing arguments the search for a logical method of discovery or invention might seem as chimerical as the dream of perpetual motion. Nevertheless, a contemporary of Jevons, the German engineer Franz Reuleaux endeavoured, with some success, to devise a systematic procedure for inventing machines. Leibniz (1675) had looked forward to an era, which he believed was imminent, 'when the invention of machines will be no more difficult than the construction of geometric problems'; but later researchers concentrated on the analysis of existing machines and the explication of the principles upon which they were based. The deeper problem of explaining the creative process was avoided 'by considering Invention either avowedly or tacitly as a kind of revelation, as the consequence of some higher inspiration' (Reuleaux 1876).

Reuleaux's aim was to change the process of invention from an art into a science. On the basis of his kinematic theories he developed a classification of mechanisms and their parts. By combining mechanisms of the appropriate type, machines for a given task could be designed. While indubitably a landmark in the history of theoretical kinematics, as a system of invention

Reuleaux's work was only partly successful. Felix Wankel, whose very name is synonymous with the rotary internal combustion engine, criticized Reuleaux's classification as being too artificial and developed a much more comprehensive classification of possible types of rotary piston engines in the course of investigations spanning three decades (Wankel 1965).

Today, research in kinematics has assumed a fresh importance because of the upsurge of interest in robotics (Rooney 1984). The trend from mechanization to automation had been discerned at an early stage by Reuleaux (1876), who thought it inevitable that 'as each machine develops into more perfect forms both its director and its regulator are made automatic'. He also expressed the hope that future technological developments would make small-scale, decentralized production economically viable, thereby helping to reverse some of the deletrious changes in society caused by the industrial revolution.

5. INTELLECTUAL SYNTHESIS

5.1 Patrick Geddes (1854–1932)

The application of a systematic approach for discovering solutions to social problems would appear vastly more difficult than the task confronting engineers. Yet, for the Scottish polymath Patrick Geddes that was to become a life-long task. The idea of a combinatorial method came to Geddes, as to Ramon Lull, in a flash of inspiration, but whereas Lull's ideas were conceived in a vision, Geddes' were born of blindness. In 1879, while searching for fossils in Mexico, Geddes temporarily lost his sight as a result of chronic eye strain and was forced to spend 10 weeks in a darkened room. One day, while feeling his way about the room, his hands alighted on the window with its small panes separated by a criss-cross of frames and he suddenly realised that if the panes represented different concepts then by vertical, horizontal and diagonal movements he could trace their interrelationships (Boardman 1978, Mairet 1957).

In order to escape from the limitation of a fixed number of panes, Geddes next applied his powers of visualization to the creases of sheets of paper folded into the required number of panels. These he termed his 'thinking machines'. When his sight returned he continued to use the method but with symbols or terms written on the squares of paper so that the end result would be a table in the form of a grid. By that time the diagrams had become a lasting obsession and Geddes used them routinely for organizing his thoughts and to synthesize a mass of facts and ideas in his work in biology, sociology, town planning, and the administration of museums (Defries 1927).

The biologist J. Arthur Thomson believed that the 'thinking machines' were responsible for Geddes' extraordinary versatility, but another colleague the American social scientist Lewis Mumford (1966) was repelled by the infatuation, even though he believed that Geddes might come to be remembered as a systematic thinker comparable to Leibniz, Aristotle or Pythagoras (Defries 1927). Nevertheless, whatever the merits of his work Geddes' methods had few imitators. A crucial drawback was that the concepts he used were so broad that the interpretations to be placed on their combinations were not objective and self-evident but subjective and the product of deep thought. Little about the 'thinking machines' was mechanical.

5.2   Paul Otlet (1868–1944)

If Geddes had applied the combinatorial method to quite specific topics his approach might have seemed less idiosyncratic and more practical like that of Reuleaux. It is surprising that in his published examples he did not do so since his interest in classification was deep and not confined to biology. Melvil Dewey was one of his acquaintances and Geddes was also a friend and keen supporter of Paul Otlet and Henri La Fontaine who, on the basis of Dewey's scheme, developed the very comprehensive Universal Decimal Classification for arranging the bibliography which was intended to cover the entire stock of the world's recorded knowledge (Boardman 1978, Rayward 1975).

For La Fontaine, a Belgian senator, the universal bibliography was just one aspect of the work to further international cooperation, for which he was awarded the Nobel Peace Prize in 1913. Otlet's interests were also extensive, but he concentrated mainly on the organization and exploitation of knowledge. Geddes was a powerful ally and tried to persuade the League of Nations to support Otlet's plans , though with limited success.

The technology of the card catalogue proved hopelessly inadequate for the grand conception of the two Belgian bibliographers. However, Otlet realized the significance of advances in information storage, processing and transmission as represented by microfilm, Hollerith punched card systems and the early experiments with television, respectively (Otlet 1934). Writing in 1935 Otlet foresaw an era when technology would allow the realization of his and La Fontaine's dream of universal access to information. 'All the things of the Universe, and all those of man, would be registered from afar as they were produced ... Any one from afar would be able to read the passage, expanded or limited to the desired subject, projected on his individual screen. Thus, in his armchair any one would be able to contemplate the whole of creation or certain of its parts' (quoted in Rayward 1975).

Originally Otlet had become interested in classification because, like Condorcet, he thought it could give to the social sciences the coherence and consistency characteristic of the natural sciences. He was convinced of the importance of classification as a tool of intellectual synthesis and was influenced by Geddes' diagrammatic techniques but failed to explore the possibilities inherent in the combinatorial approach. However, by the time of his death, a method more practical than that of Geddes and more widely applicable than Reuleaux's was developed independently in the United States.

6. ANALYSIS AND SYNTHESIS OF KNOWLEDGE

6.1 The morphological approach

Fritz Zwicky (1898–1974), a Swiss astrophysicist working in California, was the originator of a method of problem-solving generally known as 'morphological analysis' (Zwicky 1969). He himself sometimes used the term 'morphological approach' instead, which is more appropriate since synthesis is also involved. There are five stages in the application of the method:

(1) description of the aims of the investigation;
(2) identification of all relevant factors;
(3) enumeration of all possible means of achieving the aims;
(4) evaluation of all the means enumerated;
(5) selection and application of the most suitable solutions.

Although Zwicky (1962) described morphological analysis as a new form of classification, solutions are enumerated by a combinatorial method. The really novel aspect was the success he achieved, largely through the care with which he tackled problem selection and definition.

One of the earliest and best known examples of morphological analysis is Zwicky's (1962) study of propulsive power plants. Eleven key parameters were identified, e.g. the source of chemical energy, the physical state of the propellant etc. Each of these parameters and the various values they may take are shown in Table 1.

The number of conceivable types of propulsive power plants using chemical energy is given by the product of the number of alternatives in each of the 11 categories, i.e. 36,864. Some combinations are inherently contradictory, e.g. a vehicle moving through the vacuum of space cannot be powered by a fuel requiring air for its oxidation. When such constraints are taken into account the number of feasible engines is reduced to 25,344, most of which are novel.

A simpler version of this analysis with fewer parameters was performed during World War II and resulted in the tabulation of 576 types of engine. One new type, regarded by Zwicky as being especially promising, was greeted with scepticism but, unknown to the Allies, it was already under development in Germany for the purpose of powering the V-1 flying bomb (Zwicky 1962). This dramatic demonstration of technological forecasting helped to gain acceptance for morphological analysis in that role (Wills 1972, Jantsch 1967).

Owing to the large number of alternatives generated, application of the complete morphological procedure can be rather laborious, but Zwicky devloped a simpler version of the technique, which he referred to as the method of negation and construction. It consists of listing the characteristics of whatever is being studied and then investigating the implications of negating those characteristics one at a time. Thus the method anticipated the artificial intelligence technique of genetic learning which is used for acquir-

Table 1 — Morphological analysis of chemical propulsive power plants

	i	ii	iii	iv
1 source of chemical energy	intrinsic	extrinsic		
2 thrust generation	internal	external		
3 thrust augmentation (1)	intrinsic	extrinsic	zero	
4 thrust augmentation (2)	internal	external		
5 jet	positive	negative		
6 energy conversion process	a	b	c	d
7 surrounding medium	vacuum	air	water	earth
8 motion	translatory	rotary	oscillatory	none
9 propellant (1)	gas	liquid	solid	
10 operation	continuous	intermittent		
11 propellant (2)	self-igniting	not self-igniting		

a=oxidant contained in propellant.
b=fuel reacts with oxygen in the air.
c=fuel reacts with water.
d=fuel reacts with earth.

ing knowledge automatically by introducing small changes or mutations in the structures used to represent complex concepts (e.g. Boolean expressions) and preserving only those which turn out to be improvements (Forsyth 1986).

In 1946, at Zwicky's suggestion, an attempt was made to blast metal slugs into space from a captured German V-2 rocket carrying shaped charges as used in weapons for firing armour-piercing projectiles. By comparing the molten slugs with meteors it was hoped to calibrate the luminous efficiency of the latter. Unfortunately the attempt failed. Hopes of repeating the experiment received a setback when critics claimed the slugs would be difficult to track with available telescopic equipment.

In answer to these objections Zwicky, using the method of negation and construction, conceived the idea of a class of substances he called 'coruscatives', which may be detonated like explosives producing great heat and light but without flying apart since their products are not gaseous. By examining various mixtures similar to thermite, which is used in welding, a suitable substance was found.

Eleven years were to pass before the new plan received approval. Then in October 1957 a tiny coruscative pellet was fired into interplanetary space, thus becoming the first man-made object to go into orbit around the sun (Zwicky 1962). However, the achievement was completely overshadowed by the launching of the world's first artificial satellite, Sputnik 1, just 12 days earlier. Similarly, the method of negation and construction has been overshadowed by the full morphological approach.

Zwicky believed that his method could be used to find solutions to problems 'not only in the sciences and technology but also in the arts, history, politics, language, teaching, ethics and the practice of religions' (Zwicky 1969, p. 254). In this he was unwittingly echoing the conviction expressed more than two centuries earlier by the mathematician Jacob Bernoulli (1713), who claimed that by means of the art of enumerating combinations 'the sagacity of the natural philosopher, the exactness of the historian, the skill and judgement of the physician, and the prudence and foresight of the politician may be assisted'.

Such expectations have proved over-sanguine so far. Nevertheless, applications have been found in management and planning as well as technological forecasting. Zwicky (1969) himself was responsible for a very successful programme of aid to scientific and technical libraries in Europe and Asia that had suffered damage to their holdings during the War. Another notable example is provided by the field of urban planning. The firm Doxiadis Associates drew up a plan with recommendations for the location of industrial sites, airports, educational institutions and other facilities in the greater Detroit region. Morphological analysis generated a set of 49 million alternatives. Obviously an exhaustive study would have been impossible even after all the inconsistent combinations had been eliminated. However, by applying a series of restrictive criteria the total was whittled down to just seven (Tyrwhitt 1968, Christakis 1972).

In coping with the combinatorial explosion by applying restrictions, this version of morphological analysis resembles the method of 'generate and test' as used in the expert system DENDRAL for identifying certain types of organic compounds from their mass spectra. However, whereas DEN-DRAL's generating algorithm has been proved correct, there is normally no certainty that morphoogical analysis will generate all possible combinations that are free of inherent contradiction, and no others. A probable exception to this generalization is Zwicky's (1962) study of energy transformations. According to the known laws of physics there are just 100 possible types.

This exception shows that the morphological approach is most reliable when guided by soundly based theories. Such a situation exists in architecture, where the generation of plans is governed by a theory of rectangular dissections (Steadman 1983). In production engineering Alting (1978, 1982) has endeavoured to establish a theoretical framework for the application of morphological analysis, just as Reuleaux's work on kinematics provided a basis for combinatorial procedures in mechanical engineering.

Where no suitable theory exists, the classifications used are generally of an ad hoc nature. This widens the applicability of the method but is a source of weakness for the reason mentioned earlier. To some extent this weakness might be counterated by using an existing classification scheme, if any cover the field, thus saving time and minimizing the chances of overlooking relevant factors. The Detroit area study employed a classification scheme for ekistics, the science of human settlements, devised by C. A. Doxiadis (1913–1975), a Greek planner with a breadth of outlook similar to that of Geddes. To cope with the myriad interrelationships of an immensely complex subject, the ekistic classification contains 500 million categories at the most specific level (Doxiadis 1977). Its purpose was to delineate a model which Doxiadis (1972, 1974) hoped would provide a framework not only for thinking and discussion, but also for operational research and the preparation of algorithms.

Unfortunately, very few classification schemes are designed with such wide-ranging possibilites in mind. In a report to the Organisation for Economic Co-operation and Development, Jantsch (1967) identified the absence of future-oriented categories in existing schemes as the basic obstacle to a better use of information for technological forecasting. Although information scientists and librarians have made limited use of morphological analysis on rare occasions (Anderla 1973, Cronin 1982), they too have used ad hoc classifications. However, a system devised by the late J. L. Jolley partly for the purpose of discovering gaps in knowledge did arouse some interest in library circles (*Aslib Proceedings* 1978).

6.2   Fundamental units of knowledge
6.2.1.   The holotheme
Jolley(1973) described his classification as the fruit of a 15-year search to find out how people think and to answer the questions 'what sort of ideas exist, how can we classify them, and how can we be sure that none have been overlooked?' He took as his starting point the theory of integrative levels which postulates the existence of a natural hierarchy of classes to which entities may be assigned in accordance with their complexity. Integration, unlike mere aggregation of entities, results in a new, more complex entity belonging to the next level up. The properties of a chemical compound, for example, are quite different from those of its constituent elements. Atoms, living creatures and nations would obviously belong to widely separated levels.

Next, Jolley considered the ways in which objects belonging to the same level differ. He concluded that only a limited number of types of distinction could be made and they were all repeated at each level. This supposedly natural pattern was called the 'holotheme' by Jolley. He believed it could be used to make manifest the relationships between concepts just as the periodic table reveals those between the chemical elements. Yet, despite praise from the mathematician C. W. Kilmister who wrote the foreword to Jolley's book on the subject, most librarians remained sceptical, remembering the failures of other attempts to fit all human knowledge into a neat and simple framework (*Aslib Proceedings* 1978). Bishop Wilkins's real character is the classic example, but similar failures had occured much more recently.

6.2.2 Classification and translation

During World War II, machines had been used to crack codes with great success. This led Warren Weaver, vice-president of the Rockefeller Foundation, to consider the possibility of translation by computer. It is a curious coincidence that Wilkins (1641) had written a book on cryptography long before staring work on his real charcter and philosophical language. Anyway, in an influential memorandum on machine translation, Weaver (1949) suggested using a universal intermediary language. This would have the advantage of reducing the number of pairs of languages for which programs would be required.

A year earlier an American speaker at an Indian library conference had suggested that the Colon scheme of the leading authority on bibliographic classification, S. R. Ranganthan, might serve as the basis of a universal language (Ranganthan 1952a). In pursuance of this possibility Ranganthan visited the United States in 1950 at the invitation of the Rockefeller Foundation. He concluded that classification might be relevant in the communication of purely factual information provided the problem of keeping the scheme up-to-date without re-working the existing structure could be solved. Even so, it would be inadequate for conveying the subtle nuances of poetry and other artistic forms of expression (Ranganathan 1952a, 1967).

6.2.3 Semantic factors in information retrieval

In the realm of information retrieval, too, the lessons of Wilkins's failure had to be re-learned. During the 1950s at the Case Western Reserve University in the United States, a major effort was made to identify the semantic factors which make up all other concepts. A list of 214 such factors supplemented by a much smaller list of role indicators was drawn up. These were used in much the same way as the radicals and transcendental particles of Wilkins's scheme. The semantic factors and role indicators making up a concept constituted its definition: e.g. a clock would be represented as a device for measuring time. Use of definitions rather than names for indexing appeared to offer a way round the problems of synonyms and homographs. It also grouped related concepts together. Where two concepts shared the same factors, e.g. 'clock' and 'watch', information about the second would be filed immediately after that concerning the first.

However the system had two major flaws (Foskett 1982). First, there was no obvious answer to the question of how far the factoring process should be taken. Should a factor like 'temperature' be analysed into 'kinetic energy of molecules'? Second, a definition of an object may not include attributes which could be of interest from certain viewpoints. Many thermometers and barometers contain mercury, but that fact is not essential for their definition, and anyone looking for information on instruments containing mercury would fail to find it. Of course the class of barometers and that of thermometers could be sub-divided before factoring, but that again would entail a decision about how far to carry the process of analysis.

After disappointing results in retrieval tests, the WRU semantic factor-based indexing system was abandoned by its principal supporter, the American Society for Metals. Nevertheless, the search for fundamental concepts has continued in other fields.

6.2.4 Linguistics and artificial intelligence

Linguistics is a field in which the dream still lives of identifying a set of universal semantic primitives which are impossible to define satisfactorily but in terms of which all other expressions may be defined. Wierzbicka (1972) has suggested that there may be as few as 10 to 20 such concepts, her principal candidates being 'want', 'don't want', 'feel', 'think of', 'imagine', 'say', 'become', 'be a part of', 'someone', 'I', 'you', 'would' and 'this'.

From the standpoint of semiotics Guiraud has considered the significance of Zipf's law which describes a statistical relationship between rank and frequency observed in many areas of human activity, including some in linguistics. The frequency of words depends on the number of phonemes they contain, but it is the sense of words that determines their use. Consequently Guiraud (1971) reasoned that concepts are the product of the combinations of a system of semic elements analogous to the phonemic system, so that 'Zipf's distribution would be PRODUCED by the structure of the signified [i.e. concepts] but would be REFLECTED in that of the signifier [i.e. vocabulary]'. The possibility that Zipf's law might have implications for knowledge engineering has been suggested by Brookes (1984a, 1984b) and also by Addis (1982), though the latter considered its application to activities rather than vocabulary.

Activities are also the subject of Schank's theory of conceptual dependency, which has been used in natural language processing (Harris 1985) and in modelling human memory (Kolodner 1984). Of Schank's eleven basic acts, six have names which are self-explanatory: PROPEL, INGEST, EXPEL, SPEAK, GRASP and MOVE. The others are ATRANS — transfer of ownership, possession or control, PTRANS — physical transfer of an object, MTRANS — transfer of information from one mental location to another, MBUILD — creation of new information from old concepts, and ATTEND — to focus a sensory organ on a stimulus (Schank 1975). Like the other theories and techniques of artificial intelligence, the theory of conceptual dependency has been applied in narrow domains only. Whether this limitation can be overcome remains to be seen.

7. CONCLUSION

No difficult problem would ever be solved if too much attention were paid to discouraging precedents. The use of automatic or semi-automatic procedures for augmenting our knowledge has often attracted ridicule. Swift (1727) probably had in mind Lull and those influenced by him when in *Gulliver's Travels* he described the Professors of Laputa and their invention whereby 'the most ignorant Person ... may write Books in Philosophy,

Poetry, Politicks, Law, Mathematicks, and Theology, without the least Assistance from Genius or Study'.

It is easy to dismiss Ramon Lull as a mystical dreamer, and some of the fanciful statements of other advocates of combinatorial procedures invite similar attitudes. Geddes identified a corner of nine squares in one of his diagrams with Parnassus, the home of the gods in Greek mythology (Boardman 1978) and some of his 'thinking machines' have been compared to the Hindu Mandala (Kitchen 1975) and the medieval Jewish Kabbala (Defries 1927).

An equally apt comparison might be with the *I Ching* or *Book of Changes,* a system of divination based on a set of 64 concepts represented by combinations of binary symbols which led Leibniz to believe mistakenly that the Chinese had anticipated his discovery of binary arithmetic (Needham 1952). The *I Ching* functions, in Needham's (1952) words, as 'a repository of concepts to which every concrete fact of nature could be referred and from which a pseudo-explanation could be found for any event'. Even before Turing had proposed his famous test, whereby the inability to distinguish between written responses from a human being and machine would be taken as the criterion for ascribing intelligence to the latter, the psychologist Jung (1951) was of the opinion that the answers he received to questions by means of the *I Ching* would have seemed quite sane had they come from a person. Whether that is more of a reflection on the Turing test than on Jung's gullibility is debatable. Needham (1956) in his great survey of the history of Chinese science dismissed claims that various inventions had been made while contemplating the *I Ching* and referred disparagingly to its use as 'a search for peace of mind through classification'.

In fact, analogies with pseudo-science have been drawn by some of the pioneers of combinatorial classification themselves. Geddes and Zwicky compared their 'thinking machines' and morphological analysis respectively, with the philosopher's stone of the alchemists (Boardman 1978, p. 143, Zwicky 1962, p. 199). Artificial intelligence has also been compared to alchemy but not by way of commendation (Dreyfus 1979). Zwicky's (1962) extravagant attitude also manifested itself in a scorn for specialists and a claim that his method would lead to a re-emergence of the universal or Renaissance man. One of his books written in German was entitled *Jeder ein Genie* (Everyone a genius) (Zwicky 1971).

In comparison with such claims, the so-called 'hype' that often surrounds artificial intelligence seems modest indeed. Nevertheless, the inflated claims should not be allowed to disguise the very real achievements of the morphological approach. It has the advantage of being a tool of divergent thinking, thereby facilitating the discovery of alternative solutions to a given problem. For this reason Lawson (1984) has contrasted morphological analysis favourably with artificial intelligence which he regards as inherently convergent (searching for the 'correct' solution) in its approach.

If that criticism is valid, then automating the application of morphological analysis in all its stages, not just the trivial task of generating the combinations, would change the situation. Given a precise specification of the problem to be solved it might be possible to search existing classification schemes and thesauri and automatically identify relevant factors. However, if it were necessary to eliminate large numbers of combinations by introducing heuristic constraints, the selection of these constraints would presumably be a human task. Alternatively, it has been suggested that Brouwerian algebra, a more restrictive version of Boolean algebra, could be used in generating the combinations so that the production of self-contradictory solutions could be avoided (March 1983) though whether that will prove to be practical proposition remains to be seen.

Even if all this should eventually prove feasible, the task of identifying and defining problems, which can be difficult, would still remain, barring a massive breakthrough in artificial intelligence. Therefore, a more practical approach might be to rely on machine-aided human intelligence. With online access to different classification schemes and thesauri a user could identify relevant parameters. The system would then generate the combinations and search databases of journals, patents etc. to determine which solutions were novel or little-studied.

For centuries from the time of Ramon Lull onwards, classification, especially the combinatorial approach, was regarded as the key to automating the operations of the mind. Ironically, the greatest successes were achieved at a time when this old tradition was being eclipsed by a more machine-oriented approach resulting from the development of the computer. It is indisputable that the combinatorial approach can be useful as a means of developing human creativity, but whether it has anything to offer in making computers creative is much less certain. Nevertheless, the history of classification as an instrument of ratiocination testifies to the fact that the pursuit of artificial intelligence is not some twentieth century aberration but a natural step in the intellectual development of mankind. Irrespective of the attainability of the goal its pursuit is worthwhile, for, as Browning so aptly put it:

> Ah, but a man's reach should exceed his grasp,
> or what's a heaven for?
>
> (*Andrea del Sarto* by Robert Browning)

REFERENCES

Addis, T. R. (1982) Knowledge refining for a diagnostic aid. *International Journal of man-Machine Studies* **17** (2) 151–164.

Alting, L. (1978) A systematic theory of manufacturing. *Environment and Planning* **B5** (2) 131–156.

Alting, L. (1982) *Manufacturing engineering processes*. New York, Marcel Dekker.

Anderla, G. (1973) *Information in 1985*. Paris, OECD.

Aslib Proceedings (1978) Leo Jolley memorial seminar **30** (6).

Babbage, C. (1864) *Passages from the life of a philosopher*. London, Longman.

Baker, K. M. (1962) An unpublished eassay of Condorcet on technical methods of classification. Annals of Science **18** (2) 99–123.

Baker, K. M. (1975) *Condorcet: from natural philosophy to social mathematics*. Chicago, University of Chicago Press.

Bernoulli, J. (1713) *Ars conjectandi*. Quoted in Jevons (1879), p. 177.

Bloch, C. J. (1979) Catalogue of small rectangular plans. *Environment and Planning B***6** (2) 155–190.

Boardman, P. (1978) *The worlds of Patrick Geddes: biologist, town planner, re-educator, peace-warrior*. London, Routledge & Kegan Paul.

Boole, G. (1854) *An investigation of the laws of thought*. London, Macmillan. (Republished New York, Dover, 1953).

Bouissounouse, J. (1962) *Condorcet: le philosophe dans la Révolution*. Paris, Hachette.

Brookes, B. C. (1984a) The relevance of Laplace's 'rule of succession' to knowledge representation. In: Dietschmann, H. J. (ed), *Representation and exchange of knowledge as a basis of information processes*. Amsterdam, North-Holland.

Brookes, B. C. (1984b) Towards informetrics: Haitun, Laplace, Zipf, Bradford and the Alvey programme. *Journal of Documentation* **40** (2) 120–143.

Christakis, A. N. (1972) The limits of systems analysis in economic and social development planning. *Ekistics* **34** (200) 37–42.

Condorcet, A. N. (1795) *Sketch for a historical picture of the progress of the human mind*. (English translation: London, Weidenfeld & Nicolson, 1955).

Cronin, B. (1982) New technology and marketing — the challenge for librarians. *Aslib Proceedings* **34** (9) 377–393.

Cuvier, G. (1834) *Ossemens fossiles*, 4th edn (quoted in Jevons 1879).

Defries, A. (1927) *The interpreter Geddes*. London, Routledge & Sons.

Doxiadis, C. A. (1972) Order in our thinking *Ekistics* **34** (200) 43–46.

Doxiadis, C. A. (1974) Action for a better approach to the subject of human settlements: the Anthropocosmos approach. *Ekistics* **38** (229) 405–412.

Doxiadis, C. A. (1977) *Ecology and ekistics*. London, Elek.

Dreyfus, H. L. (1979) *What computers can't do: the limits of artificial intelligence*. rev. edn. New York, Harper & Row.

Forsyth, R. (1986) Machine learning. In: Yazdani, M. (ed), *Artificial intelligence: principles and applications*. London, Chapman & Hall, pp. 205–225.

Foskett, A. C. (1982) *The subject approach to information*, 4th edn. London, Bingley.

Gardner, M. (1983) *Logic machines and diagrams*, 2nd edn. Brighton, Harvester.

Gomez, F. & Chandrasekaran, B. (1984) Knowledge organisation and distribution for medical diagnosis. In: Clancey, W. J. & Shortliffe, E. H. (eds), *Readings in medical artificial intelligence.* Reading, Mass., Addison-Wesley, pp. 320–338.

Gregory, S. A. (1969) Morphological methods: antecedents and associates. In: *Proceedings of the Design and Innovation Group Symposium on Technological Forecasting, Aston* (mimeograph).

Guiraud, P. (1971) The semic matrices of meaning. In: Kristeva, J., Rey-Debove, J. & Umiker, D. J. (eds) *Essays in semiotics.* The Hague, Mouton, pp. 150–159.

Harley, R. (1879) The Stanhope Demonstrator. *Mind* **4** (14) 192–210.

Harris, M. D. (1985) *Introduction to natural language processing.* Reston, Reston Publishing Co.

Hofstadter, D. R. (1979) *Gödel, Escher, Bach: an eternal golden braid.* Hassocks, Harvester Press.

Jantsch, E. (1967) *Technological forecasting in perspective.* Paris, OECD.

Jevons, W. S. (1870) *Elementary lessons in logic.* London, Macmillan.

Jevons, W. S. (1879) *Principles of science* 2nd edn. London, Macmillan.

Jevons, W. S. (1904) The rationale of free public libraries. In: Jevons, W. S., *Methods of social reform and other papers* 2nd edn. London, Macmillan, pp. 28–51.

Jevons, W. S. (1908) *Studies in deductive logic,* 4th edn. London, Macmillan.

Jolley, J. L. (1973) *The fabric of knowledge.* London, Duckworth.

Jung, C. G. (1951) Foreword to the *I Ching,* or *Book of Changes:* the Richard Wilhelm translation rendered into English. London, Kegan Paul. (The foreword was written in 1949.)

Kitchen, P. (1975) *A most unsettling person: an introduction to the ideas and life of Patrick Geddes.* London, Gollancz.

Knight, D. (1981) *Ordering the world.* London, Burnett Books.

Knowlson, J. (1975) *Universal language schemes in England and France, 1600–1800.* Toronto, University of Toronto Press.

Kolodner, J. L. (1984) *Retrieval and organization strategies in conceptual memory.* London, Lawrence Erlbaum.

Large, A. (1985) *The artificial language movement.* Oxford, Blackwell.

Lawson, H. (1984) Computer architecture education. In: Tiberghien, J. (ed) *New computer architectures.* London, Academic Press.

Leibniz, G. W. (1765) *New essays on human understanding* (translated and edited by Remnant, P. & Burnett, G. Cambridge, CUP, 1981).

Leibniz, G. W. (1675) Letter to Henry Oldenburg. In: Leibniz, G. W. (1956), *Philosophical papers and letters* (editored by L. E. Loemker). Chicago, University of Chicago Press, pp. 256–258.

Lighthill, J. (1972) *Artificial intelligence.* London, Science Research Council.

Mairet, P. (1957) *Pioneer of Sociology: the life and letters of Patrick Geddes.* London, Lund Humphries.

March, L. (1983) Design in a universe of change. *Environment and Planning B* **10** (4) 471–484.

McCorduck, Pamela (1979) *Machines who think.* San Francisco, W. H. Freeman.

Metcalf, Z. P. (1954) The construction of keys. *Systematic Zoology* **3** (1) 38–45.

Morse, L. E. (1975) Recent advances in the theory and practice of biological specimen identification. In: Pankhurst, R. J. (ed), *Biological identification with computers.* London, Academic Press.

Mumford, L. (1966) The disciple's rebellion. *Encounter* **27** (3) 11–21.

Needham, J. (1956) *Science and civilisation in China,* Vol. 2, Cambridge, CUP.

Newman, A. (1969) *The Stanhopes of Chevening.* London, Macmillan.

Odling, E. M. (1878) *Memoir of the late Alfred Smee.* London, Bell.

Ornstein, M. (1963) *The role of scientific societies in the seventeenth century.* Hamden, Archon Books.

Otlet, P. (1934) *Traité de documentation.* Brussels, Editiones Mundaneum.

Pankhurst, E. S. (1927) *Delphos: the future of international language.* London, Kegan Paul, Trench, Trubner.

Pankhurst, R. J.)1978) *Biological identification.* London, Edward Arnold.

Ranganathan, S. R. (1951) *Classification and communication.* Delhi, University of Delhi.

Ranganathan, S. R. (1952a) Library classification: its added uses. *Libri* **2** (1/2) 31–36.

Ranganathan, S. R. (1952b) Library classification: relation between producer and consumer. *Libri* **2** (3) 226–232.

Ranganathan, S. R. (1967) *Prolegomena to library classification.* 3rd edn. London, Asia Publishing House.

Rayward, W. B. (1975) *The universe of information: the work of Paul Otlet for documentation and international organisation.* Moscow, F.I.D.

Reuleaux, F. (1876) *The kinematics of machinery.* London, Macmillan (republished New York, Dover, 1963).

Roget, P. M. (1852) *Thesaurus of English words and phrases.* London, Longman, Brown, Green & Longmans.

Rooney, J. (1984) Kinematic and geometric structure in robot systems. In: O'Shea, T. & Eisenstadt, M. (eds), *Artificial intelligence: tools, techniques and applications.* New York, Harper & Row, pp. 192–244.

Schank, R. C. (1975) *Conceptual information processing.* Amsterdam, North-Holland.

Slaughter, M. M. (1982) *Universal languages and scientific taxonomy in the seventeenth century.* Cambridge, CUP.

Smee, A. (1849) *Elements of electrobiology.* London, Longman, Brown, Green & Longmans.

Smee, A. (1851) *The process of throught adapted to words and language.* London, Longman, Brown, Green & Longmans.

Smee, A. (1875) *The mind of man.* London, G. Bell & Sons.

Stanhope, G. (1914) *The life of Charles, third Earl Stanhope.* London, Longmans, Green & Co.

Steadman, J. P. (1983) *Architectural morphology.* London, Pion.

Tyrwhitt, J. (1968) The IDEA method. *Ekistics* **26** (153) 185–195.

Vickery, B. C. (1953) The significance of John Wilkins in the history of bibliographic classification. *Libri* **2** (4) 326–343.

Voss, E. G. (1952) The history of keys and phylogenetic trees in systematic biology. *Journal of the Scientific Laboratories of Denison University* **43** (1/2) 1–25.

Wankel, F. (1965) *Rotary piston machines: classification of design principles for engines, pumps and compressors.* London, Iliffe.

Weaver, W. (1949) Translation. Reprinted in: Locke, W. N. & Booth, A. D. (eds) (1955), *Machine translation of languages.* Cambridge, Mass., MIT Press, pp. 15–23.

Wegner, P. (1983) Paradigms of information engineering. In: Machlup, F. & Mansfield, U. (eds) *The study of information.* New York, Wiley, pp. 163–175.

Whitrow, M. (1982) Condorcet: a pioneer in information retrieval. *Annals of Science* **39** (6) 585–592.

Whitrow, M. (1983) An eighteenth century faceted classification scheme. *Journal of Documentation* **39** (2) 88–94.

Wierzbicka, A. (1972) *Semantic primitives.* Frankfurt, Athenäum Verlag.

Wilkins, J. (1641) *Mercury: or the secret and swift messenger.* London, printed by I. Norton.

Wilkins, J. (1668) *Essay towards a real character and a philosophical language.* London, printed for S. Gellibrand.

Wilkins, J. (1970) *The mathematical works.* London, Frank Cass (includes both *Mercury* and a precis of the *Essay*).

Wills, G. (1972) *Technological forecasting.* Harmondsworth, Penguin.

Yates, Frances A. (1966) *The art of memory.* London, Routledge & Kegan Paul.

Zwicky, F. (1962) *Morphology of propulsive power.* Pasadena, Society for Morphological Research.

Zwicky, F. (1969) *Discovery, invention, research through the morphological approach.* New York, Macmillan.

Zwicky, F. (1971) *Jeder ein Genie.* Bern, Herbert Lang.

Notes on contributors

Helen Brooks is a lecturer in the Department of Information Science at the City University, London. Her research interest is in expert system development and applications in information retrieval. She graduated in neurobiology and has an M.Sc. in information science. Prior to her present appointment she worked for five years at the Central Information Service, University of London, undertaking research and software development for library and information environments. She is the chief investigator on the British Library project to develop, test and evaluate an expert system for referral.

Helder Coelho is a scientific research officer at the Laboratório Nacional de Engenharia Civil, Lisbon, where he is currently investigating the impact of information technology on organizations, and the application of knowledge-based systems in building management. After gaining diplomas at the Universidade Técnica de Lisboa and Philips International Institute, Eindhoven, he was awarded the degree of Expert in Computing Sciences by the Laboratório Nacional de Engenharia Civil and a Ph.D. in artificial intelligence by the University of Edinburgh. He is a former vice-president of the Associacão Portuguese de Informàtica and has also served on various committees of the International Federation of Information Processing.

Roy Davies is an assistant librarian and subject specialist for mathematics, computer science and operational research at the University of Exeter. He graduated in chemistry at the University of Strathclyde, where he also took a postgraduate diploma in librarianship. He started his career in the Ministry of Defence, Procurement Executive, before becoming science librarian at the Polytechnic of Wales, where he also gained a postgraduate diploma in computer science. His publications include papers on comparative librarianship, the implications for libraries of artificial intelligence, and the applications of Q-analysis, a recently developed taxonomic technique.

Brian R. Gaines is Killam Memorial Research Professor at the University of Calgary. He received his B.A., M.A. and Ph.D. from Trinity College at Cambridge University. He is a Fellow of the Institution of Electrical Engineers, the British Computer Society and the British Psychological Society. He is editor of the *International Journal of Man–Machine Studies*, the Computers and People book series and *Future Computing Systems*. He has authored over 150 papers and authored or edited 5 books on a wide variety of aspects of computer and human systems. His research interests include foundations of knowledge-based systems, knowledge transfer systems, and expert system applications in manufacturing, the sciences and humanities.

Peter Ingwersen is a senior lecturer at the Royal School of Librarianship, Copenhagen, where he graduated in 1973 and was then appointed lecturer in information storage and retrieval. From 1976 to 1980 he carried out experimental research on cognitive aspects of user–systems interaction. In 1982 he obtained two years' leave to join the ESA-IRS online serive in Frascati, Italy, as a European Space Agency Research Fellow undertaking R&D involving user–interface improvements, a new family of online support tools, and database management. Back in Copenhagen since 1984 he has worked in a new department dealing with information management and the design of specialized information services and systems for industry.

Michael Lebowitz (Ph.D., Yale, 1980; M.S., Yale, 1978; S.B., MIT, 1975) is an Associate Professor in the Department of Computer Science at Columbia University. Professor Lebowitz has a wide range of teaching and reasearch experience in artificial intelligence. He was named Henry M. Singer Assistant Professor for 1984–85. Dr Lebowitz's research interests lie primarily in the areas of natural language processing, machine learning and cognitive modelling. He is leading a research group at Colmbia that is designing intelligent information systems that read, remember and learn from natural language text.

Steven Pollitt is a Senior Lecturer in Computing and Information Systems in the Department of Computer Studies and Mathematics at Huddersfield Polytechnic. After graduating in Computer Science from Hatfield Polytechnic he worked at the Marconi Research Labs on experimental IR systems, and at the University of Leeds as co-ordinator of the British Library funded CANCERLINE Evaluation Project before joining Leeds Polytechnic as a Lecturer in Computing. He has recently completed a Ph.D. thesis entitled 'An Expert Systems Approach to Document Retrieval'. He was chairman of the Information Retrieval Specialist Group of the British Computer Society (BCS) from 1979 to 1984 and a member of Council of the BCS from 1981 to 1984.

Elaine Rich is a member of the technical staff of MCC (Microelectronics and Computer Technology Corporation), where she is leading a team working on natural language interfaces for knowledge-based systems. She received an A.B. in applied mathematics and linguistics from Brown University in 1972 and a Ph.D. in computer science from Carnegie-Mellon University in 1979. Prior to joining MCC Dr. Rich was on the faculty of the Department of Computer Sciences at the University of Texas at Austin. She is the author of *Artificial Intelligence* published by McGraw-Hill in 1983. Her primary research interests are in knowledge representation and natural language processing.

Mildred L. G. Shaw is Professor of Computer Science at the University of Calgary. She received her B.Sc. and M.Sc. from the University of London, and her Ph.D. from Brunel University. She is a Fellow of the Institute of Mathematics and its Applications and of the British Computer Society, and an Associate Fellow of the British Psychological Society. Dr Shaw is a member of the editorial board of the *International Journal of Man–Machine Studies* and a managing editor of *Future Computing Systems*. She has authored over 70 papers and authored or edited five books on a wide variety of aspects of computer and human systems.

Ian Sommerville is Professor of Computer Science at the University of Lancaster, England. From 1975 to 1978 he was a lecturer in Computer Science at Heriot-Watt University, Edinburgh, and from 1978 to 1986, a lecturer in Computer Science at Strathclyde University, Glasgow. His current research interests are in the general area of large-scale software engineering environments with particular emphasis on software reuse and the applications of IKBS techniques in software engineering.

Alina Vickery is Senior Information Systems Officer and Deputy Director of Central Library Services at the University of London. She has a B.Sc. in chemistry and an M.A. in linguistics. From 1957–1967 she was director of library and information services at the Atomic Energy Commission in Israel. Prior to her present appointment she designed a database in rock mechanics while at Imperial College. She has been responsible for many research projects conducted for the British Library, UNESCO and FID and is currently director of the British Library funded 'expert system for referral' project. Among her recent publications is a chapter in the book *Medical Librarianship in the Eighties and Beyond*, Mansell, 1986.

Brian Vickery is an emeritus professor of the University of London, where he was the director of the School of Library, Archive and Information Studies from 1973 to 1983. After graduating in chemistry from Oxford he worked for the Minstry of Supply, ICI, and the National Lending Library before becoming librarian of UMIST in 1964. From 1967 to 1973 he was head of research at Aslib. Since 1985 he has been chairman of LUCIS Information Systems Ltd. Professor Vickery is a fellow of both the Library Association and the Instute of Information Scientists and is the author of numerous papers and several books on information science.

Murray Wood graduated from Strathclyde University in 1983. His current research interests are in the area of software reuse and in particular the application of retrieval and representation methods to the development of a software component catalogue. He is currently a Research Assistant with the Software Technology Research Group at Strathclyde University.

Index